# LOVE FROM THE PINK PALACE

# Jill Nalder

**WILDFIRE**

First published in 2022 by
WILDFIRE
an imprint of HEADLINE PUBLISHING GROUP

First published in paperback in 2023 by
WILDFIRE
an imprint of HEADLINE PUBLISHING GROUP

2

Cataloguing in Publication Data is available from the British Library

ISBN 978 1 4722 8843 1

Foreword © Russell T. Davies
All photos courtesy of the author

Typeset in Aldine 401 by CC Book Production

Printed and bound in Great Britain by Clays Ltd, Elcograf S.p.A.

MIX
Paper | Supporting
responsible forestry
FSC® C104740

Headline's policy is to use papers that are natural, renewable and recyclable products
and made from wood grown in well-managed forests and other controlled sources.
The logging and manufacturing processes are expected to conform to
the environmental regulations of the country of origin.

HEADLINE PUBLISHING GROUP
An Hachette UK Company
Carmelite House
50 Victoria Embankment
London EC4Y 0DZ

www.headline.co.uk
www.hachette.co.uk

To Bob and Doreen Nalder, my wonderful parents,
for their unconditional love and support, and to all my family
for always being a joy to me.

To Colin Bell and Derek Chessor for their laughter
and inspiration.

To Juan Pablo Armitano and Dursley McLinden
for being irreplaceable.

Finally, to all the brave boys who died too soon.

*Love is the last light spoken.*

Dylan Thomas

# CONTENTS

# FOREWORD

We were kids. And we walked into a storm.

I met Jill Nalder in the late 1970s. I wonder when, exactly. No mobiles back then, no texts, no photos-every-second, those dates are impossible to pin down, all lost to the air. But we both belonged to the West Glamorgan Youth Theatre, a wonderful, life-changing workshop; a fierce combination of kids, drama, fun and hard work, forging friendships that have lasted my entire life. Nowadays, you'd call it a safe space, though that vocabulary didn't exist back then; safe to be ourselves, and if that meant being carefully, tentatively gay, then we'd found the one space in 1970s Britain where you wouldn't get punched in the face.

We put on plays, we partied, we roared with laughter, then we grew up and moved away. Jill went to London to become an actor, I went to Oxford to read English, but those two cities are only a short hop on the train. I'd pop to London at weekends. And that's where I discovered the Pink Palace. That's what Jill called her flat, an open door for one and all, rooms full of laughter and music and passion, all bristling with people simply discovering themselves. Maisie Trollette would be sitting in the kitchen, ladling out punchlines and wisdom. To hell with Oxford, *this* was my education!

And at the same time, the storm.

I sheltered from it. Jill faced it, head-on. The existence of HIV and AIDS began as a rumour ('How can a plague be gay?') and then something foreign ('It only affects Americans!') and then a conspiracy ('It was created to kill us!') but all the while getting closer and closer. Until people we knew started to die. And forgive my tunnel vision; I know HIV can affect men, women and children alike, but we saw events through the lens of our own lives, a lens focused very much upon gay men. And those men started to disappear.

As the 1980s marched on, Jill was working in the West End, and she'd tell me about men vanishing from the scene. From leading actors to chorus boys, front-of-house staff, costume and make-up; boys falling ill, going home, never heard of again. Some dying in hospital unvisited, some pretending they had cancer. The secrecy of it, the silence, the stigma and the shame. Well, not for Jill! The West End was one of the first to mobilise. To become activists. To protest, to fundraise, to hold the hands of the dying. And in rising, they found all the other voices crying out – the campaigners, the scientists, the allies, the families – and became a force to be reckoned with.

It must have been around 1990 when Jill first told me a story which had happened, and would keep happening all over the world. The true story of parents walking on to a hospital ward to discover that their son is gay, that he has AIDS, that he's dying, all in one moment. I thought about that for so long. The horror. The love. The consequences.

And I thought about it for thirty years. It took me that long, to understand what was happening, to grasp it, to see the size of it. I stare in awe at Larry Kramer's *The Normal Heart*, first performed off-Broadway in 1985, right in the heart of the storm. But I got there in the end, in my own way, and when I finally decided to write a drama for Channel 4 about AIDS in the 1980s, my mind turned to Jill. Her life and her actions. Her heroism.

It's actually a strange thing, to realise that your old mate is a hero. She's just always been there, in my life, being so much herself that I took her for granted. To me, she simply does the things that Jill does. It was only as I wrote, that I began to see her through others' eyes. That I realised how selfless and brave and unique she is.

One of the lead characters in *It's a Sin* was based so much on Jill's life that I couldn't even change her name! Every time I tried to type Alison or Susie or Jane, it clanged like a duff note. So Jill she stayed. Not that fictional Jill is anything like the real one. Oh, the actual woman is bawdier, funnier, madder, camper and even kinder, if you can imagine such a thing. I had to tone her down, or she'd have upstaged the whole show. And of course, the wonderful Lydia West brought such sensitivity and grace and insight to the role, that Jill Baxter is now a completely independent character in herself.

But it was really important to me, for Real Jill to become a vital part the production. So we offered her the role of Jill's mother. How lovely, how strange, how emotional, to see her on screen, being part of events, sitting in a recreated Pink Palace, acting out terrible events which had been reconstructed from her own stories.

One of the greatest joys of my entire life came after transmission, when people realised who Jill was. And celebrated her. Suddenly, my old friend was on chat shows, in newspapers, doing podcasts and charity launches. One journalist who interviewed her went through his own archives and found that he'd interviewed Jill Nalder on a sponsored bed-push around Leicester Square in 1994! I watched all of this unfold with amazement. Despite her profound and abiding modesty, Jill was carried shoulder-high for once in her life. Centre stage, at last.

The point is, people realised she's always been there, Jill and the thousands like her. The friends, the carers, the lovers, the unsung activists. Governments will always let us down. Jills will always rise.

And now this! Her own book. I'm so proud of her, and proud to know her. And I'm the lucky one because it's rare, in life, to get a chance like this. I can now say to my old friend, out loud, for everyone to hear: I love you, Jill.

Russell T. Davies
January 2022

# AUTHOR'S NOTE

*Declaration*

The book I have written is my own experience of the HIV/AIDS crisis in the eighties and nineties. It is how I remember it to the best of my knowledge. I have changed certain names, times and places for reasons of privacy and ongoing stigma, and I have adapted certain events accordingly.

*A Note from Jill*

Being approached to write a book was a huge surprise and, I must say, an honour. I had never imagined it, even in my wildest dreams, and yet here was an opportunity which was both scary and exciting.

I decided to accept the challenge, but was truly daunted by enormity of the project. What inspired me was the belief that the time when HIV/AIDS arrived in our lives is an important part of our shared history. In 2020 we were – and are still – living with COVID-19, but back then so many faced a different kind of pandemic: a disease that evoked hatred, stigma and horror. Following the success of *It's a Sin* and the conversations it engendered, I realised so many people did not know what happened back then. I wanted to describe to the reader what it was like at the time and how incredible the boys were – including my friends, who were stoic and simply wanted, like everyone else, to live their lives to the full. I wanted to tell their story alongside my own and to write about the joy and the fun they brought to the lives they touched. I wanted to write about their courage.

My friends were amazing, but so were so many people who faced this illness. To write about them, I believe, is a way to pay tribute to the superb doctors, nurses, healthcare workers, as well as the scientists, researchers and bold activists. There were many stories like mine, so many Jills and so many friends, families and partners who were by the sides of their loved ones when so many turned their backs.

I wanted to write with them all in mind and to try to do them justice.

I hope in some way I have managed to do that.

We were all part of the same fight.

# PROLOGUE

'Next,' said the man with the clipboard, hardly looking up from the magazine he was reading.

*This is it*, I thought, as I walked into the grey, musty hall. Three men of varying ages looked at me from behind a table, and I felt my knees shake. I had been petrified the whole way on the fast train to Paddington station. It had been a long journey, made longer by the continual butterflies in my stomach. As I stood there in my flowy dress, which I'd chosen because it felt a bit bohemian and very trendy, I tried not to think of the horror stories I'd heard from friends of mine about things they'd had to do at auditions. One of these concerned a very arrogant director, who had sat at the casting table, picked up a newspaper and said, 'I want you to surprise me. Do something to make me look up from this paper.' This did not sit well with the cocky young actor in question. Furious, he'd taken out his cigarette lighter and set fire to the newspaper. I wasn't sure how true this story was, but all the same, I prayed my experience would not be anything like as extreme.

'Name, please?'

I cleared my throat and said, 'Jill Nalder,' as confidently as I could manage.

A large man with a white beard gave a slight smile and said, 'Start when you're ready.'

I straightened my shoulders and tossed back a crazy amount of permed, curly brown hair. First was Hermione's speech from Shakespeare's *A Winter's Tale* (the play famous for the stage direction, 'Exit, pursued by a bear'), and next was a piece from a more modern play that involved my being daring enough to say the word 'tits'. I was then called upon to show some of my not-too-impressive dancing skills, before finally being able to fill the hall with my favourite song from *A Chorus Line*, 'What I Did For Love'. And then, suddenly, it was done – my first big audition. I prayed that I would be good enough; that I would get my chance.

All I could think of was how desperately I wanted to be part of all the excitement London had to offer: the tangible energy on every corner, the black taxis, the red buses, the theatre posters, the bars and cafés, the overwhelming chattering of the starlings filling Leicester Square – and all the incredible people. To my young eyes, everyone passing by in London looked attractive, interesting and sophisticated. I didn't stop thinking about it until a letter from Mountview Theatre School fell softly on the doormat of my parents' house, six long weeks later.

Up and down the country, all kinds of fellow dreamers were also anxiously waiting for this opportunity to begin their new lives, each of them in search of a place where they could be their true selves, and where they could find excitement, acceptance and love.

On the Sandfields estate, Port Talbot, in a small house belonging to a somewhat unmusical family, a shy six-year-old I would come to know as Jae had once begged his mother for a piano.

'Please, Mammy,' he said. 'I have wanted a piano for all my life.'

His mother, Margaret, turned to his dad and said, 'Alan, he's having a piano.'

Twelve years later, a letter arrived at that same house, offering him a place in a top London college. It had to be London, he felt. That was where it all happened; that was where he could flourish.

Meanwhile, in the tiny Scottish village of Coupar Angus, Derek felt stuck in a place where nothing thrilling ever happened. He was rebellious and naughty – and he wanted more. He was the youngest boy in his family, witty and funny. Behind the laughter, however, lay many secrets. He had always known he was gay, so when he was inspired by a friend to take a chance and move to London, he didn't need a letter. He was ready for the big city.

Three hundred miles to the south, another young boy, John – sensitive, creative and secretive – was growing up in Liverpool. A child prodigy marked for a career in music, he wanted to go somewhere where he would be able to be more himself. His eyes were on London, and a place at the Italia Conti Stage School.

Even further afield, four thousand miles away from the city where we would soon meet each other, a young man was being emotionally tortured in Dayton, Ohio. Born in Caracas, Venezuela, he had been sent to the heart of the American Midwest at the age of sixteen to study English – and he hated it more and more with each passing day. He had grown accustomed to secrecy, and his head was full of dreams. He put enormous energy into them, and imagined himself starring in Hollywood movies or singing on Broadway. The young man knew his aspirations lay outside the confines of Dayton or Caracas: he wanted London or New York. There, he thought, people were open-minded and creative. There, they would not laugh at his dreams. There, he would be able to be his true self. So *que fantastico* when, aged eighteen, a letter arrived offering him a place at a drama college in London. Juan knew his time had come.

Also longing for his chance to make it in the world was Dursley, a boy from the Isle of Man who was just sixteen when he received his offer of a place at Mountview. His parents did not stand in the way of his dreams. He was the youngest student the college had ever taken, and it was clear from the moment he arrived that he was destined for greatness. Enormously talented and ambitious, he possessed a wisdom beyond his years, and he knew he couldn't achieve his dreams on an island that considered his very existence to be illegal.

So, separated by land and sea, these hopefuls were set to take their first steps on a journey that would change their lives – and mine – in ways we couldn't yet fathom. As I tore open that acceptance letter at home in Neath, the words of my audition song rang through my mind: 'Kiss today goodbye and point me toward tomorrow.'

# CHAPTER 1

*Earth has not anything to show more fair:*
*Dull would he be of soul who could pass by*
*A sight so touching in its majesty.*
*This city now doth, like a garment wear*
*The beauty of the morning; silent bare,*
*Ships, towers, domes, theatres and temples lie*
*Open unto the fields, and to the sky . . .*

William Wordsworth,
'Composed Upon Westminster Bridge'

I had dreamed of living in London for as long as I could remember. Although born there, I grew up, from the age of six, in Neath, an old Roman town about a twenty-minute drive from Swansea. Even when I was young, I knew there was a bigger world out there. After all, Richard Burton was born about six miles up the road from my house, and he was in Hollywood.

At one time in its history, Neath's main attractions were a castle and, later, a really magnificent abbey. In the seventies, it had a lot of pubs, a couple of cafés, a Chinese takeaway and the Castle Hotel – and that was it. Far indeed from a buzzing metropolis. I knew there had to be events more enticing than walking into town from school in our lunch hour to buy faggots and peas in the old market. (In this context, I should explain that a faggot is a – quite awful to me, but very popular – liver-based meat ball. Suffice to say, I survived on the peas.)

In a world that is now so crammed full of stimuli, it is hard to imagine just how we entertained ourselves, or how we learned about life. We had no mobile phones, no internet, no daytime TV – no videos, even. We had cassette tapes to record the Top 40 from BBC Radio 1 on a Sunday night. We had parents who still called the radio 'the wireless', and we had grandfathers who had fought in the trenches.

We were certainly a unique generation: born into post-war optimism, but steeped in the fifties ideals of the husband as a provider married to the perfect housewife. I adored both my parents: they were supportive, loving and progressive. My mum was particularly open-minded and tolerant, and I think this came from her own life experiences. In the late forties in post-war London, Mum had been working as a teacher when she met a psychologist from Puerto Rico named Mr Moran. He was connected with her school as part of his research paper, which was called 'Roots of Prejudice'. Let's just say that, at that time, living in England, he certainly would not have been short on content for his paper. My mum told me that they became close, and that he was incredibly clever, and very handsome, but their relationship remained a friendship. It could not have amounted to more, even if they had wanted it to: interracial friendships between a white woman and a person of colour were rare enough, and they faced comments just by being close friends, let alone considering a romantic involvement. Race was the topic of many of their conversations, which fascinated and educated my mother. Growing up in the Valleys in the thirties had not exactly provided her with a multicultural upbringing, and so Mr Moran must have really opened her eyes to the harsh truth of prejudice and discrimination. She was incredibly forward-thinking and accepting anyway, but I think this sense of injustice over the racism and treatment people faced had always stuck with her.

So, when the time of civil rights marches and race riots in America came, President Kennedy and Martin Luther King were continually exalted in our house, and the fight for justice and equality was impressed on me from an early age. I learned to always be accepting of others for who they are, and never to turn my back on someone who needed my friendship, just because they were different.

My mum gave birth to me when she was thirty-seven, which was considered positively geriatric in the sixties. My dad tried to be present at my birth, which was not the norm at the time, but he was ushered out of the room because there were complications. My mum used to tell the story of my birth, so I knew I was born with dislocated hips – and I also knew I was lucky. 'The London doctors,' my mum would say, as if there was something particularly special about doctors from London, had noticed something was wrong. I was put in plaster for a year, and by the time I started to walk, all was OK.

Although I was lucky, I had also already experienced the first loss of many losses in my life – in the womb. My twin didn't make it. There is a strange, abstract feeling of loss being a surviving twin. I don't know whether people really believe it affects you, but I have always felt it does; a passing feeling sometimes that something is missing. I grew up privately wanting to know about my twin, but the hospital had given my mum very little information and she could only tell me what she knew. My parents didn't even know the sex of the baby they lost and so he or she was never given a name. I have always looked at twins and wondered how they felt, wondering what it would be like to have my own twin. When I headed off to school for the first time, I was very excited to make a best friend: that would be like having a twin, wouldn't it? I carried this hope with me to college. It was always important to me to find a true friend, a twin, a soulmate.

In my own eyes, I was a plain and quite nervous child, always a bit cautious, but enthusiastic and eager to do well. I met my first real best friend, Delyth, when I was eleven and we both passed the exam to get a place at the girls' grammar school. Delyth had a few close friends when we met, and I was accepted as one of the gang. We were united by the pop stars we adored. Together, we dreamed of our idols. We dreamed of the movies, of meeting them and of romance (just a kiss) with Donny Osmond. We would spend hours swooning excitedly over fan-club information, and we both craved some excitement, something to liven up our sleepy little town.

On one occasion when we were about thirteen, while walking through Neath's back streets, Delyth and I certainly got more excitement than we bargained for. As we strolled along the road, over the canal, we saw a torn-up copy of some sort of magazine, blowing wildly around in the wind. As we got closer, we saw that it was pages and pages of naked people: images of open-legged women and men with very large attributes. What had until then remained a mystery wrapped in plastic on the top shelf of a bookshop was suddenly right in front of us, in all its explicit glory, flapping around our feet in the middle of Neath. We dared each other to pick up some pages. Yes, we did it, and we hid in a corner of the street trying to piece it together, reading and shrieking. I can only say it was fascinated awe, teamed with a certain amount of disgust – we had never seen anything like it. We were in complete shock. I don't think we even knew then what a woman looked like from that way up, not to mention a man in full glory.

Fresh from the sex education made available to us by the West Glamorgan Education Authority, we pieced together the articles and took in the explicit pictures, reading a particularly graphic passage.

'What on earth is oral sex?' I asked Delyth, who was just as shocked as I was.

'Must mean talking about it,' she replied, very logically.

And so, we read on.

'No, no, no!' I gasped, pointing at a particularly graphic image. 'It is definitely not *talking*. No one,' I said, forcefully, '*no one* would or could do anything like that. That has to be a lie. Why would they do it? It doesn't make any sense. It's disgusting.'

At the time, I didn't realise that I was experiencing a small-town upbringing, because I thought everything was very open in my house. I knew if I asked certain questions, I would receive an honest answer (although I think my parents went by the law of 'Don't tell them till they actually ask'). They were both educated and tolerant. My dad was the only child of a tyrannically strict father and, as a result, took completely the opposite approach with his own children: he was very gentle and accepting. My mother was always happy to chat to me, and I was never afraid to ask a question. I suppose the problem was I didn't really know, other than the obvious stuff, what to actually ask *about*. It would never have dawned on me, not in a million years, to ask, 'Mam, what exactly should you do with a penis?' or, 'Mam, do boys have sex with boys as well as girls?' It just wasn't on my radar. It was all such a mystery: and I wasn't the only one who felt that way. One school friend told me she woke up one night and leaped out of bed to help her mother, who sounded like she was being attacked in her bedroom by what my friend thought must be a burglar. She was amazed to find only her father there, and no attack taking place. Another good friend told me recently that, as a young boy, his entire sex education consisted of a leaflet left mysteriously on his bed one day by his father (a doctor), after which the topic was never mentioned again. Sex was shrouded in secrecy.

It was at about this time that our religious education teacher (also, incidentally, our sex education teacher) inadvertently opened a door to me. She took a group of us to the theatre to see *Godspell* – and that was it. I became obsessed: with the show, with musicals, with plays, with everything and anything possible to do with theatre. I was in love with the idea of it all. That was when I knew I wanted to be an actor. I wanted to sing show songs, to be part of a world that was full of excitement. It would be my ticket out of my small town, all the way to London. I cannot count how many times we saw *Godspell* that year, but it became the carrot my parents dangled before me to ensure my O-level success: 'You can go and see *Godspell* if you pass your exams.' It was a simple bribe, and it worked.

There came a point when Delyth and I had seen *Godspell* so many times, we became kind of friendly with the cast and crew. We were just about at the age where you can blag being older than you really are. We used to love to try and get in to places we were not supposed to, and so we went to the pubs the actors would frequent after the show. We would listen to them talking, overhearing all kinds of gossip we didn't fully understand. There was one time in the bar that I overheard someone speaking about an older gay man, with the words: 'He's really only into chickens.' I had no idea that younger, attractive men were referred to in this way. I genuinely wondered what on earth he was doing with the hens.

We heard the words 'gay' and 'camp' bandied around rather a lot. We tried to understand who was actually gay, and who was camp – and what it actually meant. We started saying it ourselves, just to feel we were part of it all. 'Oh, he's camp,' we would say, feeling theatrical and grown-up, as though we understood. It was descriptive and seemed to be used as both a compliment and an insult. No one used the word 'camp' in Dwr-y-Felin Comprehensive, that was for certain. This new world we were discovering was much more colourful than anything we'd seen before, and the open-mindedness was intoxicating.

And so I went, persistently, to the Swansea Grand Theatre stage door, asking for a job. Within a year, I was granted an unpaid position: making tea for the actors during the intervals, then literally sweeping the stage at the end of the shows. Not a very glamorous role, but I didn't care: I was just so delighted to be there. Eventually, my employment status escalated to truly giddying heights, and I was offered the grand total of £12 a week to 'dress' the actors.

I learned about theatre as well as life. This unique, other world, steeped in centuries of tradition. I learned that you must always say 'Break a leg' instead of 'Good luck'; that you must never utter the word 'Macbeth' within the theatre, or bad luck will befall the show; and you must never, ever whistle backstage. I also learned what 'bisexual' meant. Steve, an incredibly handsome actor who had been dating one of the girls in the show, was helpfully telling me that the prompt corner was always stage left – and then, in the same breath, started talking about a boy he fancied, plain as day. I was a bit confused, but I admit to finding it really exciting. Next day, he told me he had a date with the boy. *That was quick*,

I thought, *he only told me yesterday that he fancied him*. Meanwhile, *I* had fancied Nigel Williams for three years and still hadn't got a date. I was actually very nervous when it came to dating boys myself. I was not at all confident, and, not being pretty (at least, not in a conventional way), I was never the first choice. This had always made me feel, I think, quite unattractive – but I held a hope that one day soon, I would definitely be fabulous.

Well, the next time I saw Steve, I asked him how the date had gone. He casually told me they'd had sex in the dressing room, and it was now very likely he would move on to someone else. Apparently, he had his eye on a few other boys and girls. I was shocked, but he didn't seem to think this was at all unusual. Girls' magazines like *Fab 208* and *Jackie* had sagely advised me that it was not a good idea even to hold hands until at least the second date. I didn't think it would be different for two men, but clearly it was. I remember thinking about how much I still had to learn.

Working at the Grand Theatre was fabulous, but I still believe I owe everything to the West Glamorgan Youth Theatre. The WGYT was a highly respected county drama group that held auditions annually, ran residential courses and put on all kinds of fabulous productions. It gave me the full theatre experience, life-long friends and the confidence and ability to get to London and chase my dreams. It was where I felt at home. Suddenly, it seemed it did not matter if you weren't the prettiest girl. Here, it seemed you could be part of the most popular group if your personality was right. If you had any talent, and if you were open-minded, you could be – and were – part of something special. Writer Russell T. Davies, my lifelong friend, was also a member, and has described it as 'a safe space'; looking back, it was exactly that. To me, it was a unique, joyous and camp place to find an extended family. Clearly, we all shared a love of theatre and performing, but it was more than that. We shared our own unique humour, our own language. We even had our own special greeting: 'La!'. It was a quick, half-sung, half-spoken way of saying 'hello', or 'goodbye', or 'I understand exactly what you mean.' 'La!' said it all. We were part of a special club and we loved it. We would never have imagined that our special phrase could possibly have captured people's imaginations the way it did when Russell used it for his characters in his television show *It's a Sin*!

At the WGYT, I also became firm friends with a fantastically talented and very pretty boy with Betty Boop eyes and thick, dark, curly hair. His name was Jae (a name he had given himself, as he was already working in the clubs with his own show), and he had worked semi-professionally since he was twelve years old, he told me. He was an amazing singer, and I thought he was surely destined for stardom.

Jae was that shy six-year-old from the Sandfields estate in Port Talbot (as the story goes, his father actually knew Richard Burton), and so he, too, had experienced a small-town upbringing. He'd been brought up a Catholic, which meant confession and a generous helping of guilt. At one point, he was severely reprimanded for saying such a horrific and dangerous word as 'pregnant'. He could certainly never have asked his parents what he should do with a penis that wasn't his own, nor could he have said something like, 'Dad, is it OK to sleep with boys instead of girls?' From a young age, he was a brilliant musician, and was desperately looking for some sort of outlet to express himself. At the age of fifteen, he'd found that outlet when he joined the West Glamorgan Youth Theatre.

Someone at the Youth Theatre came up with the fun idea of calling all the boys by their mothers' names – and I mean *all* the boys, straight or gay. So, in our group, Jeremy, Russell, Gareth, Martyn and Malcolm became Gwen, Dulcie, Joyce, Hazel and Marlene! The names have stayed with them all to this day. Being part of the WGYT allowed each of us to express ourselves, but some of these boys were discovering, for the first time, their true authentic selves: meeting people they could be honest with, and discovering a safe place to be gay. The doors to freedom were opening. Coming from an accepting home myself, I found it easy to be accepting of others, and I quickly learned that the camp, fun and open conversations we enjoyed together could open the way to real honesty.

I started to find myself becoming the keeper of secrets for boys who had been afraid to tell anyone they were gay. I had a feeling that it was special to be told such a secret by boys who I thought were so wonderful. I hated the idea of the prejudice they might face, and I wanted to support and understand them. It opened my eyes to the differences in my world, and I liked feeling that I was part of something unconventional and enlightening. I would continue to play this role with my friends for years to come. Jae had never mentioned his sexuality to his family, even though he had known it since he was ten years old, he told me.

Our involvement with the WGYT made sure we were on the right path when the time came to think of further education. I knew I wanted to act and sing, and I knew London was where I wanted to do it, but it was a topic that caused a lot of, sometimes tense, conversations in our house. My dad thought I would be better off getting a 'proper job' and suggested it would be wiser to aim for a good career in the Abbey National. My younger brother Colin was proving to be a highly intelligent young boy with a brilliant brain for all things scientific, and was clearly destined for a good university, so I trod carefully. I did not want to disappoint anyone with the words 'drama college'. Despite the debates, I knew my parents would support me if it was what I truly wanted, as long as I was willing to work for it.

So, with my A-levels under my belt, I was beside myself with nervous excitement when I was accepted into Mountview Theatre School to take a three-year acting course. I spent hours dreaming of what my new life would be like: where would I live? Who would I meet? Would I have a gorgeous boyfriend? Who would I thank when I received my first Tony Award? What would I wear? Would I ever get through the long list of, sometimes unusual, instructions sent to me by Mountview? Where was I supposed to buy fencing gear – and who on earth could make me a rehearsal skirt that would double as a Shakespearean cape?

# CHAPTER 2

*Friendship is a single soul dwelling in two bodies.*

Aristotle

It was the early eighties and, as a bright-eyed eighteen-year-old, I was poised for a life in the theatre in London, at long last. Totally unfazed by and delighted with the gay scene, and with my closest Youth Theatre friends also going to colleges in the city (Jae had a place at the Central School of Speech and Drama), I was ready for all the fun that lay ahead.

When I first arrived in London, my flat was horrible, cold and dingy, with a room next to my bedroom that the landlord kept locked unless he chose to use it with the various women he brought round. I was too naive to complain, but it was disturbing and uncomfortable. However, Mountview was warm and welcoming. Situated in Crouch End, north London, it was an old building with a traditional small theatre and a modern studio. The green room was cosy, full of sofas and old cushions, and the bar was always busy and full of all kinds of characters. I wrote home to my mum: 'We have it all here in London. There is such a brilliant mixture of people here on my course; Swedish and Italian girls, an Indian boy, two Welsh boys, at least two lesbians – and I'm sure lots of queens!' I felt like the world was coming together in one building. It was where it was all happening!

It was there in college, at the end of my first year, that I met that handsome dreamer from Caracas. He became one of the greatest friends of my life. His name was Juan Pablo, and we were brought together by a production of *The House of Bernarda Alba*. Juan had been described to me as the popular Venezuelan boy. The first time I met him, he was laughing heartily with a group of fellow students, and I adored him almost immediately. He had a loud, infectious laugh and a broad, gorgeous smile that wrinkled his chocolate-brown eyes. He was tall and handsome, but not intimidating, with a mound of dark, curly hair that you immediately wanted to ruffle. I approached him a bit shyly, because I wanted some help. I needed to know how to pronounce some of the Spanish words in the text. He, in an incredibly warm, all-embracing kind of way, responded by inviting me into the West End with him, to see a production of *Yerma*. Off we went, I didn't understand the show as it was all Spanish, but on the way back we found ourselves singing songs from *A Chorus Line* all the way up Crouch Hill.

We stayed up till four in the morning, chatting and laughing, and from that night on, I knew that Juan was a beautiful soul. He was passionate about theatre, passionate about art, and incredibly talented. He was also completely in love with Barbra Streisand, in a way that is unique to some gay men: something between a complete obsession with her and a desire to actually be her. He regularly tried to recreate the essence of his beloved Barbra from his Crouch End bedsit, belting out her hits in his rich, honeyed voice. Thankfully (for the neighbours' sake), Juan was a glorious singer, especially after a bottle or two of wine.

Juan was nineteen years old, and ecstatic to be living in a new city. This wasn't like his life in Caracas, where he'd had to keep so much of who he was secret from his parents. In London, he could finally be free. He loved life, music, sex, parties – and he had found a place where he could be completely open about his sexuality. His excitement was palpable, and it summed up his character perfectly. He always possessed an infectious sense of wonder and enthusiasm; it was one of my favourite things about him.

One morning in Juan's flat in Crouch End, we woke up to light that seemed unusually bright. There was a quietness that felt bizarre for London, and through the window, the world was white. It was the first time Juan had ever seen snow and he was so excited he nearly exploded. I remember him shrieking with delight, shouting: 'Jiiilly! Jiiiiiiilly, come JILLY! Snow, SNOW!' We rushed outside into the freezing morning air, and seeing Juan's face light up made me feel like a mother watching her child captivated by their first snowfall.

If Juan's sense of wonder was childlike, so was his naughtiness. Like a little boy who stole sweets from the table while your back was turned, he had what he claimed was a 'South American' lack of respect for authority. In Juan's case, this rebellious nature manifested as a peculiar desire to shoplift, primarily from the local shop in Crouch End. All the students at Mountview called this shop 'Mrs Busy's' for the simple reason that whenever you went in, the loveliest, friendliest Indian lady would always say, 'Hello, and are you busy?' in her soft accent. Juan would go in to Mrs Busy's for some chocolate or a bottle of wine, and come out with a tin of salmon or tomato soup as a bonus. He could never pass a newspaper stand without nonchalantly picking up a paper, as though it was a free gift. This kleptomania horrified me – and it didn't stop there.

There was the one occasion when Juan, with his persuasive charm, managed to convince me not to pay for a ticket on the Underground. 'Just flash an old ticket,' he said. So I did it, heart racing, and my face a picture of guilt. Of course, Juan's tactic didn't work, and we were stopped.

'Where have you come from?' the ticket officer demanded.

'Wood Green,' I said, sheepishly, nearly in tears. I hated getting into trouble.

'And you,' he said, more sternly, looking at Juan. 'Where have you come from?'

'Caracas,' Juan said gleefully, before running off and leaving me with a fine and a record. *Thanks Juan*, I thought. *You can tell my parents.*

He may have caused his fair share of trouble, but Juan and I would continue to spend our college years as best friends. We were young, carefree and having fun: doing shows, sharing stories of boys we fancied (he was always luckier in love than me), and taking chances to travel. Most of all, we were happy. My mum once said to me, 'I knew you had really left home when you told me about Juan.' Juan and I had such a close bond that I sometimes wondered if my real twin could have been gay. I felt it was a strong possibility.

If my first love in London was Juan Pablo, then my second was undoubtedly the Pink Palace. Throughout my first year, in an attempt to escape from the dingy den I was living in, I stayed in various places, including Juan's bedsit, which he made as lovely as he could. But in my second year at college, it was a different story. Me, Jae and our friend Martyn, (also from the Youth Theatre), decided we would live together, and so began the hunt. Even back then, trying to find a decent-priced, liveable flat in London was no small feat. But in September 1980, we struck gold – or, should I say, pink – and found a glorious new home.

It was a lovely autumn morning when I answered the phone to Jae, who was, not unusually for him, gabbling excitedly on the other end of the line. 'La! You'll never believe it, Jill. I'm with Martyn and he has seen in the *Ham & High* that there's a flat going on Finchley Road. It says: "First floor, two bedrooms, sleeps four." And – wait for it – it's £80 per week. It could be *fablus*,' he shrieked, sounding more Welsh than ever.

'That's cheap,' I replied. 'I wonder what's wrong with it.'

'Well, it'll probably be shit, but we're going to have a look anyway. It's only up the road from college; it would be stupid not to. I'll call you later,' he said, as he hung up.

We weren't expecting much for £80 a week, but when I went over to see Jae that evening, he was even more excited than he had been on the phone.

'Oh my God, Jill, you won't believe the flat,' he said. 'We were shown round by a very well-dressed man who told us he was a headmaster, and the flat was his elderly mother's. I couldn't believe my eyes when I saw it – and you won't either. I can't get over the fact that he's happy for students to live there. It's like a palace.' Jae was bursting at the seams. 'We've told him we would love to have it,' he said excitedly. 'It's got everything – you must come and see it.'

When I went to see the flat the next day, I was gobsmacked. As we say in the Valleys, it was lush. The place was everything

Jae had described – and more. The real shock came when you walked from the small but lovely kitchen into the lounge. It was enormous, with a large bay window overlooking beautifully kept gardens below. Not only was the room gigantic, but it was unusually – and absolutely amazingly – *pink*. Dark purple-pink carpets; an enormous, dusky pink Dralon sofa with matching pink chairs. The walls were covered in dark purple flock embossed wallpaper, and, to make it even more ostentatious, the room was lit by three glorious chandeliers. It was a palace, that's all I can say. So that's what we called it: the Pink Palace. We had central heating, silver service cutlery, a beautiful oak table, Susie Cooper coffee cups and lots of lovely crockery. It was more glamorous than anywhere any of us had lived, ever. It was clearly the home of someone very wealthy – and now it was for us. It was worth the huge amount of forty-two thousand pounds and it had a blue plaque outside, which we decided made it even more special, and probably haunted. It was totally captivating – and it was ours.

Our new home completely changed our lives in London. Our Youth Theatre group and college friends merged until we were all part of an eclectic, over-the-top bunch. We felt the world was our oyster, and the Pink Palace the pearl. It quickly became part of our folklore. It was soon a base for all our friends, with countless people coming to stay from all over the place, including Russell – and, of course, Juan practically never left. Life was great. We worked hard, played hard and showed off our Palace with pride by throwing legendary parties. We loved to dress up, drag up and stage cabarets for our guests. Martyn would perform comedy songs with his guitar, while Jae hired a piano to make these nights more 'professional' and exciting.

There was someone else who helped ensure that none of our

guests would ever forget a Pink Palace party. We called him the 'Wanker in the Window', and he earned the nickname by doing precisely that. On a Saturday night, regular as clockwork, he came to his window in the flat opposite ours and the cabaret began. We thought it was funny to invite people along for the floor show. For obvious reasons, it was a one-act play. After a while, we discovered you could quite literally time an egg to his antics. Of course, as the rumour spread, we had to throw a few more parties to prove it was true. Well, any reason for a party suited us.

When we weren't throwing parties in the Pink Palace, we made the most of being students in the city. We went to Heaven for the dancing and to Stringfellows for the glamour; to the Roof Gardens for the flamingos and to cheap restaurants for dinner. And, of course, we went to the theatre for the love of it. It probably goes without saying that there were the normal ups and downs: bad hangovers, bad choices of boyfriends, bad one-night stands – although the last one wasn't so true for me (well, only once). In fact, I felt I experienced the most love but probably the least sex of anyone in my year. I don't really know why, but I just never seemed to get the romance bit right. From his room at Oxford, where he was studying, Russell wrote to me: 'Who knows, perhaps you'll find the man of your dreams. But be careful, dear – knowing you, he'll probably be gay.' Clearly, I was getting a reputation, but the truth is I was drawn towards gay men. I never felt like having a boyfriend just for the sake of it. When it came to romantic relationships, I had a sort of blind faith that one day soon, everything would just work itself out.

Our time as students seemed to go by so quickly, but we really did live life to the full. Although, of course, we dealt with things like having no money and arguing over bills, there were also those wonderful parties, cabarets, suppers, Sunday lunches, music and singing, college productions and one glorious Christmas. Then, all of a sudden, it was 1982, and we were in our last year at Mountview, with two years completed towards a final degree in Performing Arts.

My last year in college was spent in one production after another, as a way for us student actors to prepare for the real world by experiencing the lifestyle of a true theatre performer. One of these productions took us much further afield than the West End – in fact, it took us all the way to America. Of course, our whole year group was incredibly excited. That is, until we discovered that we would not be making our Broadway debut. Instead, we were informed, much to Juan's profound anguish, that we would be travelling to Dayton, Ohio. Realising he would soon revisit the place where for three months he had been locked in his bedroom by his puritanical religious hosts in order to prevent wayward behaviour, he howled in horror. Poor Juan clearly felt the situation was too terrible to put into words, and spent thirty minutes having a panic attack on Crouch Hill, while passers-by told him to breathe into a paper bag. Unfortunately for Juan, the tour was compulsory: he had no choice but to return to the stiflingly repressive town he had hoped he would never see again.

Upon our arrival in Dayton, after many hours on a TWA flight, we were housed with local families. To my dismay, I was to be hosted by the Reverend Fenwick and his wife Lois, whereas Juan was placed in the care of two handsome men, the raven-haired and heavily moustached Tom and the blond, blue-eyed Kurt. They had an aura of being completely at ease with themselves, and definitely up for some fun. One look at these sexy boys and Juan quickly forgot his panic attack, forgot he had described Dayton as 'a damnation on me' to his brother Nelson – and totally forgot that I was his best friend – and excitedly embraced the different side of Dayton that lay ahead of him.

Having been cast aside by Juan, I took to heart the old saying about making lemonade when life gives you lemons. One of the girls in my year, who I got on with very well, was accommodated next door to me: gorgeous, popular Peg. We travelled to our hosts' homes together in an apartment-sized car, marvelling at the wide roads, manicured lawns and mansion-like houses with automatic gates that opened as you approached. Over the course of the tour, Peg and I spent a great deal of time together: the Geordie lass and the girl from the Valleys forming a lifelong friendship.

While Juan's hosts helped him to see Dayton in a more positive light than before, the rest of us soon witnessed the downside of staying there. It was a very hot Midwest summer, humid and oppressive – and I mean both the weather and the atmosphere. Our hosts were generally delightful, and my original dismay about staying with the Reverend was proved wrong as they were lovely, welcoming, open-minded people, but I could not say the same for the wider town. It was the time of the Falklands War, and we often got abuse related to that fact when we were out and about in the town. The locals would hear our accents and shout at the boys: 'Shouldn't you be in the Falklands?' And, more than once, while walking down the Midwest streets, we'd hear a cry of 'Faggots!' – and I presumed they were not talking about the kind from Neath market. Usually, this happened when I was walking – or perhaps I should say 'strutting' – down the main avenue with Duncan, who was very at ease with his sexuality. He was neat in every way, trim and manicured, a great dancer and a good laugh. He didn't seem to allow this abuse from strangers to affect him; in fact, he even seemed amused by it. He was bold and he took it all in his stride. If it made him feel a little nervous, he didn't show it.

Duncan may have remained unfazed, but I was taken aback. I thought I knew what a small-town mentality was like, having grown up in one myself, but the prevailing conservative attitude of small-town America back then really was something else. The whole country was so different from what I was used to. It was like an entirely different world, something we had only ever seen on the TV. And, speaking of TV, in America, there was TV every morning from 6am. There was also huge amounts of space, swimming pools in the gardens, endless supplies of food and beer, and huge cars. Even the theatre we performed in was massive.

We had shows in this enormous theatre every day and night, and our reviews were definitely interesting. Peg still laughs at what she remembers one local Dayton newspaper saying of our performance of *Once in a Lifetime*: 'The young theatre students took the words of Kaufman and Hart, spoke them, and hit them over the head with a hammer for good measure.' And that was one of the better ones. But we didn't care too much. All we really wanted to do while we were in Dayton was have fun – probably too much fun, if there is such a thing. Every night after the show, we partied from house to house and bar to bar. It is hard to describe what we did to that poor town. We were, no doubt, a bunch of the gayest boys and craziest girls that that part of the Midwest had ever seen.

When we left almost a month later, we were changed – and so was Dayton, Ohio. Monty's Bar, where we had become regulars, had changed into a gay bar called Mandy's; one of our girls was engaged to an all-American boy; and one of Juan's hosts had accused him of having an affair with the other, and threatened to walk out – although, thankfully, not before they had introduced us to the Broadway show *Dreamgirls*, playing us a recording one night in their living room.

26

So, all in all, despite the broken hearts, many hangovers, bad reviews and weight gain, we returned home excited and raring to go for our graduation, ready for the chance to get out into the wild world. We were desperate to get agents and start work, and maybe even get famous. We felt ready to face whatever was ahead of us. The truth is, on that hedonistic, happy and exciting trip, we had no idea of what was actually ahead of us – or what was possibly, patiently and silently, already with us.

# CHAPTER 3

_____

*What we know is a drop. What we don't know is an ocean.*

Sir Isaac Newton

One perfectly ordinary day in 1982, I was heading into Pineapple Dance Studios in Covent Garden to do a dance class. In the café there, I read a small article – it barely even had a headline, I just noticed it in passing – about a weird, fatal, flu-like illness that was affecting young gay men in America. The journalist even referred to it as 'gay flu'. It bothered me, not just because most of my friends were gay men, but also because I could not understand how an illness could recognise a person's sexuality. They were just men, like any other.

I had no answers of course, so I consoled myself with the thought that it was probably just a couple of cases of a particularly bad flu, and that it would soon blow over. I suppose I thought it wouldn't affect me or anyone I knew. So, as you do, I thought about it for a brief moment, then put it to the back of my mind.

I discarded the newspaper and went to my class and about my day as usual, sure I wouldn't hear about it again.

A few days later, though, I headed to a house party with the usual crowd. I was squeezing my way through the packed-out rooms when a particularly odd conversation between a group of people I didn't know caught my attention during a lull between the disco hits and dancing.

'There's someone with a political agenda writing things about a gay disease,' one of them said.

'It's just something put out there to frighten gay men,' another responded. 'Or it could be chemically engineered on purpose. They want to get rid of homosexuals!'

'I wouldn't be surprised if they did want to do that,' their friend agreed.

Before I had the chance to hear more, I was pulled into the next room for a dance. I tried not to think about what I had overheard, but immediately my mind went to the newspaper article and the 'gay flu' in America. *Oh my God,* I thought. *Juan's in New York.* He was there on holiday. I wondered if he'd heard about this mysterious illness, so I wrote to him the next chance that I got:

Hi Daaarlling!
Of course, you are having a gorgeous time in NYC and not thinking of *moi* here in cold wet London.
[. . .] I know you are loving New York, but London needs you back! Please don't make me too jealous by telling me you have seen *Dreamgirls*!! When will I ever get the chance?
Anyway, we are having loads of fun here as well!!
Lots and lots of love,
Jill x

P.S. Be careful pleeeease, 'cos I have read all about this illness, sort of like flu . . . but, Pabbi, it can kill you, apparently. Gay men are getting it in America, and they say it's possibly infectious! No one knows how you get it. I know that sounds weird, but have you heard about it?

Please hurry home!

*Te quiero mucho* xxx

I hoped he wouldn't think I was being fussy and telling him what to do, but when I heard back from him soon after, he didn't seem very concerned. He was far more interested in getting tickets to shows and meeting cute boys, and he assured me he was having a fab time on Broadway.

And so this strange American disease remained a rumour, something to gossip about in hushed tones at parties. As far as the general public were concerned, it was gay men who were affected, which meant people didn't worry too much about it. Besides, for us, America seemed a long way away, and the truth is that, after leaving college, it felt like there were more important things in our lives to worry about. So, we forgot, because now we were all focused on work, money and the next mountain to climb: getting an Equity card. This was the passport into 'the business', and it was like gold. An Equity card was proof that you were in the union. Professionally, it meant you were allowed to work. Psychologically, it made you feel like a real actor. To become a member of the union, you needed to have a certain number of professional acting jobs under your belt. The problem was that in order to *land* a professional job, you needed to be a member of the union. You even needed an Equity card to be an extra on film or TV. You couldn't get a card without a certain number of professional engagements which in total added up to thirty weeks of work, and you couldn't get a job without a card. That was the world of acting, then: a closed-shop industry and union. It made what was already a difficult profession even harder. It was great once you were in, of course, but trying to obtain the card in the first place was an arduous task. As we all heard many times from more seasoned professionals, 'You have to *really want* to do it.'

Getting that little red provisional card was pretty much all we thought about. Some young actors were very lucky as well as talented, and managed to land an Equity card with their first jobs (some theatre companies held two cards aside to give to new, standout actors, and that was a great way to get it). We were all thrilled when Martyn got his card and left the Pink Palace for a repertory season in Salisbury.

Poor Juan had even more of a battle ahead to get his card, because his visa ran out and he could not stay in London. Much to his dismay, he was forced to return to Caracas for a while, which drove him crackers. After the freedom of London, he was once more back in the closet. He could not cope with that for long, so he took off again, leaving behind his family and visiting his friends in America. We wrote to each other constantly, and I so looked forward to receiving his letters. It seems old-fashioned now, but it was such an exciting event to receive a letter, to see the familiar handwriting and to be transported into each other's worlds for a brief time. We made each other laugh whilst also sharing our problems. This time was to mark the beginning of Juan's endless struggles to get visas and work permits. Having trained and worked so hard for his dream, he was thwarted not only by Equity, but also by the Home Office. A 'South American' passport wasn't all that desirable in the eighties; something to do with someone called Escobar.

Eventually, Juan obtained a visa, much to his excitement.

However, I was less than thrilled, because it was a visa to study in France. Paris felt like a world away, and I didn't think there would be half as many theatre opportunities there as there would be in London. But Juan had looked into all kinds of avenues into the business, and this was his best choice. He insisted that once he had Paris as a base, he would easily be able to nip back to London for auditions. It would be no time at all until he found a job that would give him both a British visa and Equity. I decided not to share my doubts with him. Instead, I told him I thought it was a good idea. I did truly believe that with his beautiful voice, he would be bound to get a job soon enough. Besides, as we often said with much optimism when we were struggling: 'Don't worry; we have our whole lives ahead of us, anyway.'

My route into Equity was perhaps a little unusual compared to others – but it was a lot of fun. I decided that it was best to embark on the cabaret route, as getting gigs actually seemed possible. I knew Jae's professional cabaret act before college had put him ahead of the game, because he was already an Equity member. I needed to collect contracts to receive a provisional card, after which a further twenty-six weeks' work would be required before I was eligible for a full membership. One day, when I was browsing through my weekly copy of *The Stage*, I saw a job advertised: 'Singer required – Blue Angel Nightclub, Mayfair W1'. Nervous but excited, I went to the audition, dressed in a blue sequinned dress with shoulder pads (which I admit looked a bit out of place on the Underground at 9am).

The Blue Angel was a beautiful and elegant club, dimly but tastefully lit. The stage itself had an illuminated floor, which was rather fantastic. The place was smart, with an air of the Kit Kat Club in *Cabaret*, so I thought. I was somewhat daunted by all the other girls at the audition, all sitting at the tables watching the stage. I felt like I was at a cattle market, but I told myself that I just had to take the bull by the horns and get used to it. So, with a deep breath, I took the long walk to the stage to sing. I was called over to the bar afterwards, where I was told, there and then (to my delight) that I'd got the job. The audition was on a Friday and they told me I was to start on Monday, performing two shows every night, at 8pm and 10pm. The pay was £100 per week, which sounded like an amazing amount of money. I couldn't believe my luck.

I was so excited to start my first job as a performer. After the initial thrill, I spent the weekend frantically practising any good songs I knew, ready for the act . I enlisted Peg to help me, and she boosted my confidence by telling me that every song I did was marvellous. I arrived at the Blue Angel on Monday with all my cabaret glitz, ready to take on the world. I needn't have worried about taking on anything, though, as the audience was, to put it mildly, sparse.

'Who's in tonight?' I would ask Panos, the other act: a sexy Greek man with a trendy eighties moustache.

'Rosa,' said Panos.

I looked at him, confused.

'Rosa empty seats.' He laughed.

For the next three weeks, we played our acts to the bar staff and some random tourists (and of course Peg, and my mum and dad, who came down to visit). Some nights were better than others, though, and I learned a lot about being a 'real' performer. I also discovered that, at around the time Panos and I left the club at 11pm, the 'real' audience, mainly men, would arrive and the place would quickly fill up. The belly dancers started, and the Blue

Angel was buzzing: it was like the whole place suddenly came to life. I smiled, wondering if I was like 'Mama Rose's Hollywood Blondes' act in *Gypsy* – 'designed to keep the cops out'. I didn't care. I just needed the contract for Equity – plus I loved working, audience or no audience.

The Blue Angel as a club was actually pretty classy and I got on well with the staff. I would often sit and chat to the bartenders while the place was quiet, or when I was waiting to go onstage. One night, I was talking to one of the girls about her recent holiday in America when another bartender overheard and brought up that strange illness over there that was affecting homosexual men.

'Oh yeah,' she said, her eyes glinting as though she was sharing particularly juicy gossip. 'Well, people there are saying that you only get ill if you're gay, because it has to do with the *lifestyle*.' As she said the word 'lifestyle', her eyes widened and she grimaced. 'It's really down to the way gay men behave,' she continued. 'That's what's causing it.'

I felt myself getting irritated, but thankfully a customer took her attention, and as the bar began to grow busy, she was unable to continue sharing her opinions on the matter. I was glad the conversation had ended there, as it was upsetting, but I vowed to myself to find out more, wondering what it was about a *lifestyle* that would cause a gay man to get ill. I wondered if it was just the young ones, or whether older guys were getting ill too? Before I had time to worry, I was distracted by a horde of men piling through the door in eager anticipation of the night's belly-dancing show. This was my cue to leave, and I headed out into the night air to get the tube back to our lovely Pink Palace.

My time at the Blue Angel was short-lived – just a matter of weeks – but, nevertheless, I had one contract under my belt.

Only twenty-nine weeks to go! Job number two came along, and this one was even more bizarre in comparison to the Blue Angel. The Man Fu Kung, a Chinese restaurant in Leicester Square, were advertising for a singer. This time, brimming with confidence and experience, I went, auditioned, and got the job. I was thrilled. Two shows a day: one in Chinatown, then a quick sprint down to Leicester Square to the sister restaurant there. My slot was sandwiched between two beautiful, petite Chinese girls with very sweet voices. They spoke no English, and I spoke no Mandarin. So, when some cameras arrived to film, I didn't really understand what was going on. One of the girls said, 'Just for restaurant,' with a very strong accent, so I smiled, nodded and tried to fluff up my hair.

I never knew why the cameras had suddenly appeared or what it was actually for, until one afternoon in the Odeon Leicester Square. I was waiting for the film *Yentl* to begin, when I suddenly saw myself on the cinema screen, looking quite Amazonian beside the two petite Chinese girls. Then came the voiceover: it was a very basic advert for afternoon dim sum at the Man Fu Kung. There I was, smiling and singing away, oblivious to the pictures of dumplings and chicken chow mein that were now circling my head. Not the most glamorous big-screen debut, but at least I'd now completed two contracts. I kept going, and eventually I had more than the required contracts from showcases, town halls, care homes and parties. I delivered them by hand to Equity and waited – nervously. I hadn't been this anxious waiting for the post since the weeks when I was waiting to find out if I'd been accepted to Mountview. So I could hardly contain my excitement when I got home one night to find it there on the mat: that elusive little red card. I was now twenty-two, and a fully fledged professional artiste!

★    ★    ★

The arrival of my Equity card meant one thing: auditions. Auditions on top of auditions, as many as I could physically – and mentally – handle. Of course, lots of auditions meant lots of rejection. Thankfully, living with fellow actors meant that we were never alone in our struggles. In fact, we were never alone full stop. The Pink Palace was pretty full, as Juan had come back to London from Paris to live with us for a few months.

While I was auditioning for theatre roles in London, I managed to land myself a wonderful season at my old haunt, the Swansea Grand back in Wales. It was a proper old-fashioned repertory job amounting to five months of solid work. Rep seasons were how theatre had run for decades, and how many great actors had learned their craft. It was tradition to rehearse a new show in the day while playing another one at night, and to run each show for three weeks. It was my first full theatre season, and my family came to see all the shows. I felt that all their help to send me to college was paying off; it really seemed like I was getting somewhere.

During this time – and after failing to catch the eye of our company manager, whom I fancied quite a lot – I met John Hogg. We clicked straight away, laughing together from day one. Of course, it seemed typical of me to be able to meet a wonderful gay friend, but not a lovely straight man for a romance. But John and I bonded quickly, after one drunken night when we discovered we had completely identical hands. We decided we were twins, so we called each other 'Sister' from then on.

Sister was also based in London, and he had a unique sense of humour, huge talent and a handsome Italian boyfriend. Together, we appeared in a run of *Jesus Christ Superstar* that quickly became infamous. Had it been a television episode, it may have been known as 'the one where the Apostles are late for the Last Supper'.

The hydraulic lift below the stage failed, so the glorious twelve, dressed in pink kaftans, had no choice but to clamber up from the orchestra pit to the Garden of Gethsemane. Of course, the audience was in stitches. These technical difficulties meant that Judas barely made the kiss, and Sister got so flustered that he forgot a key costume change, and ended up helping nail Jesus to the cross while still dressed as John the Apostle.

Five months of performing passed quickly, and with the summer over, I drove us back to London. I quickly fell back into life in the city. I was so pleased that my friendship with Sister had lasted beyond our time in Swansea, and it wasn't long before he was very much part of our world. Everyone loved his quirky Liverpudlian humour and wild spirit. One day, we were getting the tube to Covent Garden to go out for lunch. I happened to glance at a copy of that morning's paper, which had been left on the empty seat to my right. My eyes were drawn to the headline 'Britain Threatened by Gay Virus Plague'.[1] Was this that same mysterious disease? Until now, we'd only seen brief mentions of it or heard hurried whispers. Now, here it was: front-page news in the UK. A plague? Was it coming here?

'Sister, can you believe it?' he said under his breath. 'It's not safe anywhere. What do you think it is?' He was taking care not to talk too loudly, trying not to draw attention to himself or what he was reading. Always polite and discreet, John was never a person to be outrageous outside his own circle. He was immediately aware of the danger an article like this held for a gay man.

I wondered if the article was just an example of the age-old prejudice with which we were painfully familiar, or whether this new disease had something to do with its particularly hateful tone. In the eighties, we all accepted the vilification of gay men as 'normal'. It wasn't unusual to read about people like Anita Bryant. She was an American anti-gay campaigner, openly calling gay people 'human garbage'.[2] Mary Whitehouse on our own shores, considering herself a 'moral' campaigner, took *Gay News* to court on blasphemy charges. She won! The QC defending *Gay News* described her fear of homosexuals as 'visceral'.[3] In her own book, *Whatever Happened to Sex?*, she wrote, 'Homosexuality is caused by abnormal parental sex during pregnancy or just after.'[4] Throughout the seventies and into the eighties she always made the headlines. To us, at this time, to see headlines like this was cruel, but unsurprising. Unfortunately, this was just the way it was.

Subconsciously, however, these homophobic articles had a lasting impact on the boys, and most of them felt it was wise not to be too open about their sexuality in predominantly straight spaces. They were open about their sexuality in the circles where they knew they were loved, but some friends, I felt, carried a deep-rooted insecurity just being who they were.

I thought back to how timid I'd felt when I first arrived in college, and how all those third-year productions had given me so much more confidence and experience. My friends were all just as confident and full of experience, yet part of who they were had to remain hidden or was judged. It felt so unfair to me. I realised how all the fun I'd had with my friends at the Pink Palace had cemented our relationships, and now we were all growing up and finding our feet. Feeling very much like a proper adult, I finally registered with a dentist, and then with the doctor – the latter of which led to the not-so-joyous experience of my first routine smear test.

When I entered the room, I was desperate to talk about anything that would ease my sense of impending embarrassment, and the first thing to come to my head was a topic that had clearly been rattling around in my subconscious for some time. I asked the nurse if there was any information in the surgery about this strange new disease affecting gay men. Somewhere I had heard that the disease damaged the immune system. I also knew some were calling it GRID: Gay Related Immune Deficiency. The nurse looked rather surprised; I suppose they weren't expecting questions on the subject, particularly not from me.

'We don't have any information on that, I'm afraid,' she said. 'But you certainly shouldn't worry about it.' She smiled, then proceeded to reveal an alarmingly large metal instrument. 'It's very unlikely to affect you. Now please lie back. Knees apart, ankles together.'

She didn't really understand what I was asking for. I wanted to be armed with information, not so much for me, but for the boys. I wanted to understand whether there was real danger.

It wasn't many months before I found out that there was.

Not long after, it transpired that American doctors had named the disease. They were now calling it AIDS: Acquired Immune Deficiency Syndrome. Once we'd heard it mentioned for the first time, it seemed like we were hearing it everywhere, again and again. It was a real thing – a thing with a name – and in 1984, within a year of the rumours starting, a bleak and frightening *Panorama* programme brought that name into the nation's living rooms. The name also confirmed the chilling truth that this was something you could catch. It was Acquired. Infectious. And if you could catch it, you could spread it. It was a horrendous thought, and it really did take some time to truly grasp the enormity of that fact.

In the early days of the rumours about the disease I had talked to Jae about it, telling him how worried I was about it – particularly about him, as he always seemed, to me, to be so laissez-faire in life, never really foreseeing any danger. He told me casually he'd heard the illness 'might be down to sniffing poppers'. But now, as more and more reports came out, I saw that it wasn't poppers that was making boys ill and ruining their bodies. It wasn't anything to do with the so-called 'gay lifestyle'. Anyone could catch AIDS – and spread it.

But *how* was it spreading? Well, that question was creating even more confusion. Surely, it wasn't airborne, otherwise all kinds of people would get it, and thousands would be dying by now. So how was it happening? Then, slowly, alarmingly, the news filtered through.

'I read that it's in the blood,' Sister told me. 'And possibly in *all* body fluids. It's terrifying. And, what's worse, that's how it spreads. Through blood, through needles . . . through sex.'

So AIDS was caused by a virus: a terrible one that was given the name HTLV-III/LAV. These complicated names didn't help clear the confusion, and still no one really understood the science behind it. All we really knew was that it was very scary. We kept hearing about huge numbers of people dying. Apparently, they were closing the bars, the saunas and the clubs in New York and San Francisco. There was talk of an epidemic – or, worse, a possible pandemic. It was true that most of the gay men I knew had many sexual partners, but closing meeting places in this way seemed to be very threatening. It felt like a kind of witch-hunt. We were scared that London would follow suit, and that gay men would be victimised even more so than they were already. Sister (the polar opposite to Jae in many ways), began to panic, saying to me: 'They'll close all the bars. What will we do? We'll be treated like lepers. You know how quickly people can change. This is terrifying.'

Fear grew, like a mist encroaching and surrounding us, creeping into more and more of our conversations. There were so many predictions of impending doom or the apocalypse ahead. Some women were infected, and then there was news that even some babies had contracted the virus. By now, we were being told that the virus was definitely in blood, semen and all body fluids. This information was coming from an organisation called the Terrence Higgins Trust (THT). In clubs and bars, you could pick up an information leaflet from THT. Through them, we learned that the virus was so deadly because it killed the cells that fight infections. To us, then, it seemed that anything could be fatal. We thought you could even die of a common cold. It was a truly frightening thought. But despite the attempts that were being made to educate, accurate information clearly wasn't spreading fast enough. Someone called into a radio show to ask if the disease could be spread to their dog if it were to accidentally bite a gay man, such was the level of anxiety.

However, even as these rumours of catastrophe began to spread like wildfire, the reality is that life just carried on. Despite the bleak news we were hearing, the world still seemed to be very exciting and full of possibility. Jae was working in Leicester on *West Side Story*, and it soon transferred to the West End. His career was taking off, and he became one of the youngest people ever to conduct that show. This was a source of great pride for us all, and for his parents especially. It played a huge part in cementing his career trajectory: he was now an up-and-coming musical director. Two of our college group, David and Duncan, also became part of the cast. Soon enough, landing a role in a West End show became the ultimate prize.

For me, an exciting development at that time was the formation of 'Jill and Jae', an ingeniously named double act consisting of, surprisingly enough, me and Jae. We worked between jobs, after shows, for charity nights, and for parties or special occasions, and it always went well for us. We sang in the Two Brewers, the Vauxhall Tavern, the Oriental in Brighton, Legends, the Dog and Fox, Roy's Restaurant and many, many more.

One of our most memorable gigs was a guest spot with Lily Savage (Paul O'Grady) at the Vauxhall Tavern in 1984. The Vauxhall Tavern had been attracting gay men since the end of the Second World War due to the female impersonators who performed there, and by 1975 the venue had two sections: a bar, which attracted local workers, and the lounge, which was a favourite spot for the local gay community. This often led to trouble at closing time. Eventually – and rather surprisingly – the local gay community won it for themselves. On the night of our gig, Jae and I rocked up to that historic venue with our show songs. That night, the snow was thick on the ground. We must have been the only people on the roads, but with our youthful, 'the show must go on' attitude, we set off in the car, valiantly skidding all over the place, shrieking and narrowly missing the first fox I had ever seen in London. We eventually slid up to the Vauxhall Tavern.

'It'll be dead, and we'll be cancelled,' Jae said miserably.

*A bit glass half empty*, I thought. We were due to earn fifty quid each, which meant a lot to two young performers living in London. We opened the door, expecting nothing but empty space. We couldn't have been more wrong. It was crammed full of men: smoke, leather and buckets of testosterone. In contrast to the lonely fox and the virgin snow outside, there was hardly a virgin inside. The massively popular Lily Savage was on form, as always. She slagged off half the audience, us included, and everybody thrived on it.

Playing in gay clubs and bars could be a challenge. As famous comedians have always said about performing in such venues, these gigs taught us how to deal with tough but brilliant audiences. Over time, these shows gave us great confidence – and, as a bonus, we got to know those wonderful drag acts who so coloured our lives. They were men from a different era; men who had discovered their sexuality at a time when it made them criminals. The Trollettes (Maisie and Samantha), Lily Savage, Regina Fong, Dockyard Doris and Mrs Shufflewick were among the gay scene's household names. They weren't just entertaining: they were trailblazers, paving the way for the drag artists of today who have hit the mainstream. Camp and wickedly funny, they were making a statement of their place in the world. In 2019, the winner of *Ru Paul's Drag Race UK* named David Raven, aka Maisie Trollette, as their inspiration – someone who has always been one of my own favourite people and performers. Maisie wore wild, excessive wigs, and layers of garish make-up that looked as though she had just thrown it up in the air and let it land somewhere on her face, finishing the look with huge, plastic eyelashes stuck on with Copydex. David made us laugh out loud with his stories. He told me that, one day, back in the sixties, he'd been rehearsing when he realised he was 'pushing it' to get to the bookie's in time to bet on his tip for the day. He rushed out and got there just in time, wondering why he was getting such odd looks. He glanced down and, to his horror, realised he was still wearing his Maisie stilettos. He walked out of the bookie's and back to the rehearsal with great dignity, as if size ten, six-inch glittery heels were an everyday occurrence in the bookie's on Streatham High Road.

David had had a difficult enough start in life, growing up an orphan and later being adopted – and that was before he'd had to come to terms with his sexuality. When David was onstage as Maisie, she (along with all the drag acts), showed people how to be true to themselves, to not be afraid to stand up and be proud of who you are. David is still performing today – at nearly ninety years old, he is the oldest drag act on the circuit – and he can still belt out a tune, my favourite of his being 'I'm Still Here' by Stephen Sondheim. I am always proud to call him a friend.

One night in the Vauxhall, there was a newspaper left in the dressing room. Over the previous few months, we had noticed many articles speculating about the sexuality of matinee idol Rock Hudson: was he gay? *That would upset Mum*, I'd thought, whenever it came up. She'd been hoping for a passionate affair with him for years. *She'll be livid to know Dad has a better chance.*

The newspaper that night showed pictures of him looking gaunt and frail, with the stark question printed beneath: 'Does Rock Hudson have AIDS?' Worse headlines followed: none of them caring, none of them showing sympathy, just an endless stream of barely disguised scandal and homophobia about a once-beloved actor.

This almost gleeful gossip continued to circulate in the press until 1985, when the truth was revealed in a statement issued by Hudson himself. He had AIDS, and was in France for treatment. The headlines now screamed of Rock Hudson 'Living a Lie and Dying in Shame', accompanied by images of the man who had once been the most handsome male star on the silver screen. It was awful. Then, four months later, there came another headline: 'Rock Hudson is Dead'.

The way his story had been portrayed had left many in no doubt that gay men were somehow responsible for this illness.

There were increasingly condemning headlines, such as, 'I would shoot my son if he were gay'.

'Everyone will blame us,' Jae said. 'It's ridiculous. Can you imagine what people will think in Port Talbot when they read things like this?'

The illness that had once been so difficult to find out about, that had made its debut in the British media in a small article about a strange 'gay flu', was suddenly everywhere.

At the beginning of the eighties, before the illness that had been lurking in the shadows for so long began to seep into the cold light of day, my friends and I had been so optimistic. We were living in a new decade, technology was changing all around us – and we'd felt that attitudes were changing, too, especially among young people like us. The gay scene was hedonistic and open, and women had more opportunities than ever before – the Prime Minister was a woman, after all. Everyone seemed to be making money, the West End was thriving with innovation, and musicals were filling the theatres. One day soon, the Berlin Wall would surely fall, and acceptance would abound. Could it possibly be true, then, that a tiny virus – one that could sit millions strong on a pinhead – would be the catalyst for headlines that threatened the chance for that acceptance to come to fruition?

There were no headlines full of care and compassion for those unlucky people who died so quickly and so young: no headlines like those you might see about cancer patients, or some other illness causing widespread suffering. Instead, the *Sun* printed a bold headline putting forth the perspective of a vicar: 'AIDS is the Wrath of God'. It was also the *Sun* that called gay men 'walking timebombs with the killer disease who are a menace to all society', and suggested, 'locking gay people up as they [were] an evil threat'. And it didn't stop there. The *Daily Express* published a comment from a reader who pontificated that 'homosexuals have brought this plague upon us [. . .] Burning is too good for them. Bury them in a pit and pour on quicklime.'

These articles – and many, many others – infiltrated the subconscious of our country. There was no internet, so newspapers, selling millions of copies every day, were the way most people learned the news. The articles written during those years left a deep wound that is still trying to heal.

Throughout 1985 and into 1986, everyone continued to talk – and panic – about AIDS, but still no one seemed to know any real facts. The Terrence Higgins Trust was asking for volunteers to help people who were sick. In most cases, people in hospital with AIDS didn't have visitors, because people were too afraid – or too ashamed – to be in the same room as them. Some nurses wouldn't even enter the room to give them food. Any visitors who did come were made to talk to their loved ones through a door or a window, and very often those infected were too sick to even respond. In some cases, people could only enter the room if they wore full hazmat suits. A friend of mine told me once that he had flatly refused to dress in plastic to visit his ill friend. 'I am going in to hold his hand,' he'd said firmly. Because of his defiance, he was called upon to sign a disclaimer, absolving the central London hospital of any responsibility should he contract AIDS.

I wondered about phoning the Terrence Higgins Trust and volunteering to help – that, surely, would be a good way to educate myself, and perhaps to fight off the growing feeling of panic that came from my own lack of understanding. My friends and I were still very naive and misinformed. 'Don't sleep with anyone from America,' I would say. Then clueless speculations would follow:

'I've heard it's dangerous to kiss.'

'Well, I've heard you can just dry kiss.'

'Yes, definitely – you can definitely do that.'

'What is that? What does that even mean?'

'No, no! If you want to be safe, you just can't kiss at all!'

'It came from monkeys, you know.'

'Well, I wouldn't kiss a monkey!'

'It's in saliva.'

'No, it's in spunk.'

'And blood! It's in blood.'

'Best not to get near anyone's blood.'

'Well, we don't have it here.'

'Yes, we do.'

'No, we don't. It's all a lie.'

'It's a conspiracy.'

'Have you heard of Terrence Higgins? He was the first person to die here after being in America.'

'How old?'

'Thirty-seven.'

'Wow! Pretty young.'

'Well, everyone seems to be young.'

'Some people can live with it for ages I heard'.

'It depends what you do in bed'

'Did you realise Rock Hudson was gay? He was so handsome.'

'He looked terrible. It's very sad.'

'Well, I've heard it's genetic.'

'No, it can't be genetic. It's a virus.'

'Oh my God. Best to just be celibate!'

'How do you know if you've got it? What are the symptoms?'

'Well, it's like flu.'

Only it absolutely, truly was not like flu.

*　　*　　*

Gay men everywhere were terrified – and people everywhere were terrified of gay men. One man I knew was worried that his own dear friend would not even allow him to touch her new baby, while my friend Robin suffered horrible abuse on the train. Dressed in his peach shirt and clutching his new Filofax, he was spat at and taunted for fifteen minutes for being gay and a 'carrier of AIDS'. Even shaking hands with someone 'suspected' of being gay became an issue. Then the government made a move. The virus had not only made the newspapers. Now, it had a major commercial.

Frozen to the floor in our living room, Jae and I saw an image of the Grim Reaper on the screen as the voice of John Hurt filled the room.

'There's a disease,' he said, his tone sombre, with just a touch of horror film. 'So far, it's confined to small groups, but it's spreading. Anyone can catch it. Man or Woman.'

Next came a tombstone, a bunch of lilies and a stonemason's chisel carving the letters AIDS above the words: 'Don't Die of Ignorance'. Leaflets arrived in everyone's homes, bearing the same message. It was scary. Although the ad did not directly refer to gay men, the prevailing mood of the time in the press and media was such that the chiselled words might as well have read: 'Gay men, be prepared for ignorance. *You* will get the blame. Anyone can get this virus, but it is *your* fault. You are not the innocent victims. Some people are innocent, but *you* deserve it.'

I often think back to one night in the Blue Angel, when a strange, middle-aged woman knocked on my dressing-room door and promptly let herself in.

'I am a clairvoyant,' she said. 'I see you onstage. You are smiling – but I see many tears around you.'

'Oh! Thanks,' I responded. I tried to laugh, but I was definitely

49

unnerved – what a weird thing to say. 'Does that mean I'm not going to get my Equity card?'

I didn't really want to talk to her, but maybe I should have. It's strange: since then, I've completely forgotten what she looked like. But I have never forgotten what she said.

# CHAPTER 4

_____

*Now is the time to understand more so that we may fear less.*

Marie Curie

The week began with the sun shining through our front window.
As Jae looked outside, he noticed someone familiar walking out
of the house opposite ours, and called me to see. It was a friend
from Jae's and my Swansea Grand days (and, incidentally, he was
also known to me even before that from the tour of *Godspell* that
changed my life): Paul (who we camply called 'Madge') Burton.
We rushed downstairs to catch him, shouting to get his attention.
When he saw us, we all shrieked in the middle of the street at
the realisation that we were neighbours. It turned out he and his
boyfriend Joey had been house-hunting, and it was one of those
quirks of fate that, of all the millions of properties in London
they could have chosen, they'd put in a successful offer and had
moved to our street. We began spending a great deal of time with

51

them, and it was through them that Jae and I got the news that there were plans afoot to open a new nightclub in the West End.

The club was born as a result of a New Year's Eve party in the Piano Bar in Soho, a regular haunt for anyone looking for a late-night drink after a show. Joey was the bar manager and Paul was the bar's pianist, so they were both very well known. On this particular New Year's Eve, however, they'd looked almost unrecognisable: they'd turned up in drag for the first time. Initially, Joey told us, he hadn't been too keen on the idea, but with his gorgeous Malaysian complexion and high cheekbones, he looked very beautiful. Paul, on the other hand, being of Tooting origin, looked more like Miss Marple. Despite the fact that Paul was not quite the belle of the ball, the partygoers lapped up this new drag duo, and Joey's new-found glamorous persona was particularly well received.

The party was a great success – and, as a result, the idea for a new nightclub, a glamorous drag club, right in the centre of town, full of diverse and wonderful people, was born. Joey was to be the hostess and would be dressed as the beautiful woman he had created. There would be cocktails and dancing, beautiful barmaids and fabulous shows. In keeping with the vibe of Soho, it would be called Madame Jojo's.

Of course, every great West End club needed great entertainment, and Jae and I were up for the challenge. We formed a new act, which we called the NightWalkers. A great name, we thought – catchy and naughty, but not too risqué. Just right for showbiz and Soho. There were six of us, including me, Jae and my 'sister' John Hogg. We were booked to appear nightly. Jae would play piano, and, of course, we would sing show songs. We thought we were sexy and fun, performing songs like 'Touch-a, Touch-a, Touch Me' and 'Sweet Transvestite' from *The Rocky Horror Picture*

*Show*. One of our favourite songs to perform was 'The Deadwood Stage' from *Calamity Jane*, as we changed the lyric 'whip-crack away' to 'whip Doris Day', thinking this was the most camp and witty thing ever.

With our setlist perfected, we were ready, and so was the club. Madame Jojo's was decked out in an indulgent colour palette of deep reds accentuated with silver sequins, lit by sparkling chandeliers that offset dark, intimate corners. Altogether, the club was a perfect balance of glamorous and seedy, and it was an immediate success. The stage was regularly graced by a plethora of divine drag artists, such as the inimitable Tiny Ruby (aka Ruby Venezuela), who was anything but tiny, and wore so much make-up it must have added an extra stone to her already ballooning physique. There was Ziggy Cartier, who sailed into a room looking as though a strong wind had blown in from the right, followed by a sudden freeze that fixed her hair in a solid mass on the side of her head. She towered above everyone, every bit of six foot six in her heels, with an enormous fixed smile that was so wide her lipstick touched both ears.

Then there were, as planned, 'the barmaids'. The Barbettes, beautiful, shapely boys in fishnets and stilettos, graced with glamorous names: Mitzi Martini, Astral, Scarlet and Poison Ivy. They served drinks and paraded their gorgeous bodies, generating jealous looks from the female clientele, who longed for legs that good.

Into this world came the NightWalkers, fully rehearsed and costumed. Each night for the next few months, it was Ziggy who introduced our show, muttering through her immovable lips into her lipstick-stained microphone and never quite getting it right: one night we were 'The Streetwalkers', the next we were 'The Nightriders'. It took her about three weeks to finally introduce us as The NightWalkers. Whoever we were, we put on a bloody good show.

After one particularly fun performance, a group of us – the NightWalkers, our friends and a few friends of friends – were sitting around the candlelit tables. The place was packed, and a haze of cigarette smoke hung over us as we drank a bottle of wine. We were all in great spirits, and Jae was talking about the show, as usual, when one of the Barbettes approached us and asked, 'Has anyone seen Kent recently?'

Kent was a pretty Canadian boy who frequented the Piano Bar and Jojo's. He had been in West End shows and was a great dancer.

The Barbette looked concerned, and as we all looked at each other, everyone shaking their heads, we realised nobody had seen him in a while.

'I saw him a few months ago,' one of our group said.

'No, it was longer than that,' a chirpy Barbette chipped in, as they set a fresh round of drinks on our table. 'I thought he looked thin, last time I did see him,' they added, holding the now-empty drinks tray to their chest.

'He seemed fine when I saw him,' our friend responded.

'Maybe he's gone back home to Canada,' someone else said. 'I don't think he was very well.'

This was met by a knowing look exchanged between us all, and I felt a pang in my chest. Our conversation dwindled as we absorbed what we'd heard. I could tell we were all thinking the same thing – there was only one thing that was causing boys to disappear without warning, or to 'go home' without a word. I had heard of it happening to strangers, but this was the first occasion involving someone I knew, even if I'd only known him for a short while. The thought produced a strange kind of loss, because Kent was not a close friend by any means – just someone who we saw often and liked a lot – and also because he was our age. Alongside the tangible cigarette fog, another invisible mist had seeped into the room, and now it hung heavily over us. We discussed whether he had a boyfriend, or whether his family knew, and the boys began to question what sort of sex he was into.

'It's more dangerous if you have rough sex,' a mutual friend at our table said.

'Leather queens are really at risk, 'cos they like rough sex,' came a stereotypical comment from another.

'Fisting is the worst!' one of our group sensationally announced.

'Oh my God – well, that's scary, anyway,' I said, with wide eyes.

'Can you believe all this is happening?' Sister said to me with his usual anxiety. 'I'm scared.'

'You can always get a test if you're really worried,' I responded gently.

'I've heard it takes ages to get a result,' he answered. 'And apparently they can get it wrong. And that is even more terrifying.'

In 1986, when the first AIDS tests, as we always called them, became available, all we knew was they could tell you if you had it, but they couldn't tell you how long you had. The whole criteria of testing for AIDS were confusing. The only test available was an antibody test. This meant that you needed to be infected for some weeks before you would get a positive result, as it relied on detecting antibodies in the bloodstream. On top of that, you needed to wait for another three weeks to get your actual test result. While a person waited, they lived in fear. With a positive diagnosis came the certainty of death, and these vibrant young men were simply told to put their affairs in order.

My dear friend Robin was told the bad news by a doctor in a simple, matter-of-fact, and horribly blunt way. 'If there is something you want to do, do it now,' he was told. That was it: no glimmer of hope, no counselling, no nurse on hand for support. The kindness of strangers was never more evident than on that day, when an elderly lady, smartly and expensively dressed, physically helped to lift him up from the pavement where he had collapsed, crying with shock. She said firmly, in a very English stiff-upper-lip fashion (as is the way of that tough generation who lived through the Second World War): 'Come on, dear. Whatever it is, it will all be alright.' Her attitude infused him with some sort of courage, and, normally a very pragmatic person himself, he did pull himself together enough to get the number forty-five bus home and attempt to face the world with his new truth.

The tests, we were told, could sometimes be inaccurate, and you might wrongly test negative – or even positive. A false negative meant when you were actually infected you could unknowingly spread it. It was also possible to carry (and spread) the virus for years before you showed any symptoms at all. The whole thing was a tangled web of terror and confusion. As is human, some people just chose to ignore it – to pretend it wasn't happening. And some people found out they were positive, and still chose to ignore it, unable to face their new reality.

Almost forty years later in 2019, millions of people across the globe were experiencing another virus, one that appeared just as suddenly, and came with its own troublesome method of testing. This virus, too, had the potential to provide false negative results, to lure some of its sufferers into a false sense of security with asymptomatic cases, and even to have some ignore a positive result because of ignorance, fear or denial. COVID-19 saw non-medical people begin to understand that a virus could affect each individual in a different way, with different symptoms. Millions began to understand the difference between antibody tests and PCR tests for viral DNA. A big difference, though, and one which I will never understand, was that there were no headlines claiming COVID-19 was the wrath of God.

# CHAPTER 5

*Benthyg dros amser byr yw popeth a geir yn y byd hwn.*

*Everything you have in this world is borrowed for a short time.*

Welsh proverb: Anon.

Juan was back in Paris by now, and Sister and I took an impromptu trip to visit him, as we had both recently finished our latest contracts and had some money to spare. (I had been in a tour of the musical *Annie*, while John had just finished appearing in *Peter Pan* at Theatr Clwyd in the 'Never Never Land' of Mold, north-east Wales.) Jae was unavailable to travel with us, as he was musical director of *The Mystery of Edwin Drood* in the West End. The show starred Ernie Wise and Lulu, and was based on Dickens's unfinished novel. I thought it was great, but sadly it achieved the dreaded bad reviews and only ran for about six weeks. So, with critics' quips like, 'Whodunnit? Why do it?' etched in his mind, Jae waved us off. Two trains and a few gins on the hovercraft later, John and I excitedly arrived in beautiful Paris.

Juan was, by now, infuriatingly good at French. Together (as this was my third visit) we showed John the sights. Juan had a particular way of introducing new visitors to the city that I was delighted to join in with: we blindfolded him, walked him to the centre of the Place de la Concorde and revealed the Eiffel Tower in all its glory and Sister was speechless. We visited Notre-Dame and irreverently joked in the confessionals; we took in the Sacré-Cœur and the Champs-Élysées. We explored stylish coffee houses, hidden little restaurants and great bars by the Seine. It felt as though we laughed the whole time – but it wasn't long before our spirits were dampened by some ominous-looking leaflets containing information about '*LE SIDA*'. There was no escaping the threat of the virus, although we did laugh that the French obviously couldn't seem to spell AIDS.

It seemed that the subject of 'safe sex' was never far away. Even in the Palace of Versailles, as a handsome man looked our way, someone had to mention condoms. Safe sex had become part of our everyday conversation by this stage. Everyone was constantly checking that everyone else was behaving safely in the bedroom, and never more fervently than when fun was on the horizon. After all, AIDS was a timebomb and unsafe sex was Russian Roulette.

'Make sure you have condoms with you tonight,' I said, as we got ready for a night out at a club called Le Piano Zinc. The three of us were in Juan's small apartment, with its billowing white curtains and a view of the old streets of Les Halles. I was intent upon making sure the boys were safe. 'There's a new thing called a dental dam,' I continued, speaking around the toothbrush as I cleaned my teeth. 'It's like a mouth condom. You have to avoid semen at all costs,' I stressed, feeling like an extremely open-minded mother.

While I encouraged the boys to practise safe sex, for me, sex had become more of a source of anxiety than fun. I had decided that I would only have sex if I was in a long-term relationship – it had to be love, otherwise I wouldn't risk it.

Juan had a habit of cupping your chin with his hand and turning your face towards him when he wanted your full attention. He did this now, and smiled broadly. 'Stop worrying, Jilly. We will all just have fun singing.' Then, with his mischievous South American twinkle, he added: 'But what if someone comes in my eye, Jilly? Do you think I could get it from that?'

'Yes,' I replied, taking my cue. 'Because you wouldn't see it coming.'

We laughed at our new normal, and were still laughing as we walked along the street, ready to enjoy the hedonistic French nightlife. As we made our way to the club, I pondered the weird reality that men now had to consider the consequences of sex, in the same way that women always had.


Following our trip, I needed to earn some money. Luckily, Peg was working at the Hampstead Theatre, where she did two things: met the love of her life, and got me a job filling in for someone in the box office for two weeks. I had not done any of this sort of work before, so I prepared my outfits with care. I chose and ironed all my clothes for the two weeks to make sure I would be looking smart. I got to the lovely Hampstead Theatre on my first day, where I was left alone in the box office. I had hardly been there three hours when I received a message from the main theatre office to call my dad immediately. I phoned him right there from the box office, which was not really a good idea, as a customer was waiting to buy tickets. I remember my dad's voice, very anxious, trying to tell me the news. Never very eloquent, he did not really know how, and his choice of words could not have been worse.

'I have to tell you,' he said, 'your mother is in hospital.'

'What do you mean? What happened?' I asked, feeling scared, my mind racing. This was completely out of the blue. The customer waited patiently.

'Well, they've had to test a lump or something a bit odd,' he said.

'What do you mean, a bit odd?'

Then came the real shock.

'They already know,' said my dad, 'that it's cancer. She's had it all taken away, but they – well, we – don't know if this is the end of it all.'

There is a particular feeling, a freezing, falling, isolating chill that overcomes your entire body when you hear this sort of news. Thoughts scream frantically inside your mind, while the world around you is surreally calm. I ran out of the box office, leaving the expectant theatregoer with his money in his hand, and rushed outside into the cooling air. In my head – or perhaps physically, I can't remember which – I walked around myself in a circle trying to decide what to do, too panicked to make a decision. I didn't know much, if anything, about cancer. I didn't understand the treatments. All I did know was that thousands of people died of it.

I remember crying, I remember running and I remember trying to find Jae at his theatre. I remember getting to Paddington station, still crying. The tears didn't stop until I got back to Neath. I could feel sympathetic glances on the train, but I was beyond any sort of embarrassment.

It was the first of my experiences of a journey to a deathbed, but, sadly, it would not be my last.

When I got home, I heard the full story, which made me feel much calmer, but I realised I had been kept completely in the dark, and it really did take a while to sink in. My mother, it turned out, was not on her deathbed. They'd actually known about this pending operation for weeks and had kept it secret, hoping it would all be fine. She had gone in for a biopsy and, naively, had given consent for a mastectomy if they found cancer – never believing for one moment they would. My dad was still waiting to hear back from the hospital, so when he'd said, 'We don't know if this is the end of it all,' he'd meant the end of the treatment, not the end of her life. I felt myself breathing again as hope flooded back in.

I went to visit my mum in the hospital on Tuesday morning, and just seeing her made me feel happier. However, this feeling was short-lived. I woke up to a grey Wednesday and watched miserably as our gorgeous brown-eyed Shetland sheepdog, Lucky, lost his balance and fell on the lawn as he went for a pee. I knew something was horribly wrong.

'I'll take him to the vet – you go to Mam,' I said to my dad.

The vet soon confirmed the worst, and it wasn't long until I was holding Lucky's little honey-coloured paw as I watched him slip away in front of me. I was astonished at the simplicity of death: a last fluttering whisper of an exhalation, a tiny kind of woof, and fifteen years were gone, just like that.

For the second time that week, I was completely devastated. Realising I didn't have any money for a taxi, I carried our beloved pet for the half-mile journey home, covering him in an old blanket, determined to keep him dry from the soft drizzle that was beginning to soak me.

My lovely mum saved me the agony of breaking the news to her as she got ready to leave hospital. 'Don't worry,' she said to me, out of the blue. 'I know about Lucky – I can tell.' She always amazed me: I can only think that, as a mother, she had some unique intuition.

During this strange time, we all entered a different world: the world of cancer, full of scans, tests, follow-ups, anxiety and treatments. My mum was, on this occasion, one of the lucky ones, and was given a treatment regime of tamoxifen – one tablet a day.

When I returned to London, I arrived home to all my beautifully ironed outfits hung up exactly as I'd left them, ready for my smart box-office job – but I was looking at them now as a changed person. I had learned at least three very important things. One: the world of medicine is infinitely complicated, and it is better to be fully informed and to educate yourself as much as possible. Two: empowered with the truth, you can make better decisions. Three – and perhaps the most important of all: never waste time ironing your clothes for the weeks ahead, as you may never get to wear them. *Carpe diem.*

# CHAPTER 6

*Laughter is not at all a bad beginning to a friendship . . .*

Oscar Wilde

It was a cold, windy evening in January 1988, and I was headed to the Leicester Haymarket Theatre for the closing night party of a beautifully peculiar musical. I was dressed in a metallic grey trouser suit and actually felt quite slim, as, by eating only vegetables for a week, I had managed to get my weight to ten stone. This was the first night I met Derek. It was one of those occasions when you meet someone and know immediately that you just have to see them again.

Derek was a tall, wiry young man, with a dashing smile, a mop of immaculately blow-dried brown hair and a strong Scottish accent. I was introduced to him as part of a crowd, just as he was telling a joke. It was clear he was completely in his element, and everyone was laughing, even before the punchline. He had a knack for making the characters in his stories come to life, with extravagant gestures and over-the-top facial expressions, even offstage. Having already seen the show, I knew he was an excellent singer, and I discovered as we chatted later that he was also a recording artist. He recorded commercials and demos, sang for radio regularly on *Friday Night Is Music Night*, and, by the age of twenty-something, he had worked with the best. He was able to adapt his voice to all kinds of styles, from theatre to pop, and even opera.

The musical was called *Fat Pig*, and carried with it an air of excitement, as it was directed by musical theatre royalty, Mark Bramble. In the world of *Fat Pig*, the cast played various animals on a farm, ranging from glamorous baby chicks to Tusk and Snorter, the wild boars, and Shaun, the friendly sheep. Derek was cast as a Scottish cockerel Rooster MacBrewster and his was the opening number – after the overture from a band who were, bizarrely, dressed as bananas. Jae (as the musical director), was the top banana. Derek was to give the wake-up call to the audience, but apparently, he was far from happy with how he was expected to do so. He was never afraid to speak his mind, and in rehearsals he had been bold enough to discuss the original lyrics he was given with the composer, complaining emphatically that, firstly, they were not 'Scottish' enough; secondly, they did not suit his character; and thirdly, he would not be able to wake up even a dormouse with such a song. Under normal circumstances, this might seem a reasonable part of the creative process, but on this occasion the composer of the show was none other than Henry Krieger, the Tony Award-winning writer of *Dreamgirls*, who was adored and revered by all.

'It's just not right,' Derek had said, vehemently. 'It's just not *Scottish*! There should be bagpipes – and I need to be bright and lively!'

That was how bold Derek was – he told *the* Henry Krieger

how to improve his show. And Henry Krieger obviously enjoyed learning from a real Scot, as the award-winning composer had taken Derek's thoughts on board and, amazingly, by the following morning, had adapted the number to suit him. The new song was colourful and certainly fun – 'Och the Noodle Noo!' (Years later, I spoke to Henry Krieger, and he told me how much he'd loved Derek's performance.)

When we got talking that first night, I soon discovered that Derek was an incredibly intelligent and open person – in fact, his honesty took me by surprise. He threw into the conversation, quite casually, that he'd had cancer – and then he just as casually assured me that he was doing absolutely fine. He just said, 'I've had cancer,' as lightly as you might say, 'I had soup for dinner.' I was shocked and upset that someone so close to my own age had dealt with something I had so recently lived through with my mum. I understood more than I would have done a year previously, and he was quite matter of fact about it, saying he had been treated and had lots of tests, but he was OK.

Derek told me he had received his cancer diagnosis while he was in Manchester two years earlier, just after landing a fantastic job on the first tour of *Evita* – as is so often the case, life can give with one hand and take with the other. From the sounds of it, no one would have suspected he was poorly, as he told me he'd taken it in his stride and was determined to be positive. I admired his bravery and tenacity immensely. In fact, from speaking to his other friends later, I learned that, on that tour of *Evita*, Derek was known as someone who was full of zest and energy, and was forever making people laugh. He could have you laughing until you could hardly breathe. Some people have great discipline, and some don't. Derek (ever mischievous) was one of the latter. He was inspired and ambitious, but this did not stop him picking up the head of Eva Peron as she lay in her coffin for the requiem at the opening of the show and tossing it up in the air like a football. For this behaviour, Derek was summoned to the company office and hauled over the coals. However, no one seemed to have noticed that he had also positioned a large penis peeking out of her shroud.

Around the time I met Derek, I was also on stage as part of a touring version of the West End production of *Nunsense*. During rehearsals and performances, I couldn't help thinking that if Derek was so mischievous and naughty in a production of *Evita*, God knows how badly behaved he would have been as part of the cast for this play. *Nunsense* was a highly camp and tremendously fun show. It opened with the lyrics 'Nunsense is habit-forming,' and continued with lines like 'Drop-kick me, Jesus, through the goal posts of life' and songs like 'Tackle That Temptation with a Time-Step'. It was totally crazy and really very good. After originally starting in the gay clubs, it had become a bit of a cult hit off-Broadway.

The job came at a good time for me, as it seemed like all my friends were progressing in their careers, and I'd been feeling like I was getting left behind. I was at a stage in life when it was easy to fall into a bit of an existential crisis – especially when, as everyone does at times, I was finding the business difficult. Sometimes, showbusiness can feel like endless rejection, and then things change overnight. In a way, that's what makes it exciting.

*Nunsense* told the story of five nuns trying to raise money to save their convent by putting on a show. We toured for three months, and everywhere we went, real nuns came to watch it. It was irreverent, but they seemed to love it; we often found ourselves invited to their convents for tea and cake in the afternoons. They had loved the scene in the show called 'baking with the

BVM (Blessed Virgin Mary)' and they laughed heartily when the nuns delivered Mary Magdalene tarts. I always took along Sister Mary Annette (marionette), a bright-eyed, foul-mouthed glove-puppet nun who swore a lot on stage. We could never believe how much the real nuns adored her.

That year, Jae and I made the momentous decision to buy a new flat together in Balham. We had always lived in north-west London, but Balham was an affordable place to buy. We took on a mortgage together as friends – unconventional, we knew, but we were happy to defy all the conventions for the chance to actually own our own place. We had all our figures worked out, and we took the plunge for what we felt was the scary amount of thirty-two thousand pounds. It would have been so wonderful to buy the Pink Palace, but we sadly could not even afford to put in an offer. After saying my goodbye to our fabulous flat, I sat on the Northern Line going south feeling very emotional. I was on the way to pick up the keys to the new flat and open the door on a new chapter, but somehow I knew that the Pink Palace would never be forgotten.

We adored our new home. It was modern, with newly painted magnolia walls. We had more space now, and so a friend of ours from the Youth Theatre, Philip (who we affectionately called Miss Pinky of Penllergaer), moved in. It was supposed to be for two weeks, as he was just beginning a job for British Airways and hadn't yet found anywhere to live. It took two years for Miss Pinky of Penllergaer to move out and buy a flat in Brighton, and during that time we spent a lot of time laughing. Pinky would return home from a trip to the other side of the world, and even if he arrived home late at night, he would wake us up and recreate the voyage, telling endless stories of the passengers' antics – and his own. There was the time when he decided to clean the gangways on his hands and knees, with a scarf round his head and an unlit fag in his mouth, happily scrubbing and singing 'Someday My Prince Will Come'. Then there was the flight when he announced on the Tannoy that someone with car registration ATV 134A had left their lights on in Heathrow car park C: 'We can't help you,' he said, 'but just wanted to let you know, you will need the AA on your return.' Best of all was the story of him serving the first-class passengers while wearing fishnets and six-inch stilettos, just to prove no one would notice. The passengers didn't – but the crew were in hysterics.

As fate would have it, my new friend Derek had recently bought a flat in Streatham, not far from our new stomping ground in Balham. He now owned a gorgeously decorated apartment with impressively expensive furniture, thanks to a hefty discount from a 'friend' who worked in the world of interior design.

As our friendship grew, Derek revealed more of his life story to me. He told me he had made it to London at the age of twenty-three via a job in Dundee, influenced by some actors he had met during the rep season there. Derek had reached London with all the energy of a supercell, finally hitting the ground like a released tornado. He'd gone out every night, drunk on his new-found liberty, adoring the gay life all around him. This sense of freedom was something he had not known in his small home town of Coupar Angus, where everyone knew everyone else's business. He had kept his true self a secret for a long time.

Derek was a great addition to our little family. He continually proved himself to be a live wire, a force of nature. He knew he was funny, a natural comedian, and poor Jae, always able to laugh at himself, was often the stooge for Derek's jokes. With Derek in Streatham and Miss Pinky in residence life was never dull. Thinking back, it was the best of times.

While we were almost always in fits of hysterics together, we also, inevitably, talked a lot about AIDS. It was unavoidable, a continuous source of conversation and, in some cases, gossip. This was primarily because more and more boys simply 'went home', which caused a lot of speculation. We never seemed to know the truth – one minute they were around, and then the next they weren't. As the cases mounted, so fear grew; the symptoms monopolised our conversations, and marks and blemishes were checked obsessively, again and again. Black humour abounded, like using playful euphemisms – anything to avoid actually saying AIDS:

'I have a mark on my foot, what do you think it is?' a friend might ask.

'Oh, definitely the cat flu,' someone might say.

'I have a cough!' someone would announce.

'Oh, fucking hell,' came the reply. 'Have you slept with anyone who knows the lovely Ada?'

All over the world, people did the same thing: in South Africa they called it 'getting Slim'; in parts of the USA it was called 'The Magic' (referring to the case of poor Magic Johnson). In Zimbabwe, they didn't beat around the bush. They would say, 'Have you been given the red card?', meaning it was game over.

On one occasion, Sister went to the doctor because he had a rash, and the doctor randomly asked him if he was gay. He confirmed that he was, and the doctor then became fixated on his sexuality and on Sister having an HIV test. There was no counselling, no explanation, no concern; the simple confirmation of his sexuality led the doctor to lose any intuition and focus entirely on HIV. This was the very worst thing anyone could have done. He was already anxious about catching the virus and this blinkered approach from the doctor led him to experience a great deal of stress. It also, indirectly, led to the medical condition he was actually suffering from, Coeliac disease, going undiagnosed for decades.

Sister had no symptoms, no recent partners who showed any sign of AIDS, and was in a long-term relationship with a boyfriend who also had no symptoms. However, like many others he couldn't face a test, being too terrified of the outcome. Every twinge he felt became a symptom. This continual anxiety so many people experienced was part of the increasing cauldron of misinformation and confusion.

So, anxious to show support and ease the confusion, one night I persuaded Jae and Derek to attend a Terrence Higgins Trust event in a restaurant in Greek Street in the West End. It was the gay community, not the government, who were trying hard to raise some money and educate people about the virus. We were sitting at our table, laughing among ourselves as usual, when a man walked into the room. He was probably only a few years older than us, but you would be forgiven for thinking he was decades older. We tried to continue our conversation, but found we couldn't. It was as though someone had sucked the air out of the room. None of us spoke. It was our first actual experience of seeing someone in the flesh with the visible manifestation of AIDS.

He was pale and gaunt, and so very brave to walk into that room, with hundreds of eyes upon him. His face was covered in Kaposi's sarcoma, or KS as we came to call it. His nose was black and swollen, and purple lesions covered the rest of his face, distorting his features. He walked delicately on the arm of a strong man to a seat near our table. We tried not to stare, but it was hard not to see – and to feel – the horror of the illness's worst disfigurement. Derek turned visibly pale and excused himself from the table, supposedly to go to the bathroom, but he didn't come back. We thought this was a terrible reaction to seeing someone who was suffering so badly; it seemed like Derek wasn't truly supporting the cause. I found out later, though, that looking at the man had made him feel sick with fear, and he had gone outside and vomited. The fear was too much.

After that night, it wasn't long before the inevitable happened – one of our friends was diagnosed HIV positive. It was Duncan, from college: the boy who used to strut down the street with me in Dayton without a care in the world. At first, I prayed it was a rumour, but then the truth came straight from the horse's mouth at a *West Side Story* reunion. He simply stated: 'I have AIDS,' and then, with his usual ironic humour, followed up with, 'It's very fashionable; everyone is getting it.'

That was it. It was here, among us, and the realisation was like a cold hand squeezing your stomach. There was to be no escape. It was this feeling of helplessness, of knowing that it was likely to cause the death of people I loved, that drove me to look for a way to be part of the growing movement. I joined a small group of volunteers at the Westminster Hospital. On paper, I was just doing a tea round, but really it was much more than that. I was to be a visitor, a friendly face, a non-judgemental person who didn't feel the need to dress in plastic to hand out some scones or wear a mask to pour a coffee.

There were boys on the ward for whom there was no hope of a cure. The smell of antiseptic hung heavy in the air, adding to the melancholy atmosphere. I saw a lot, very quickly. Many young men, (and at this time, I really did only see young men), lying in rooms in silence, waiting to die. What little energy they had left was stolen by the virus, day by day. There were so many different things the medical staff had to deal with, and they never knew what the next day would bring, but at least there were nurses and doctors there who were determined to give dignity to those who were facing their final days. It was common for patients to have breathing problems, diarrhoea, seizures, confusion and blindness. I didn't understand all the science, but during those visits I could tell it was infinitely complicated, that people did not really understand what they were dealing with yet. One thing was for certain, though: you could not help but be aware that the disease was infectious. Gloves, aprons and masks were donned to take blood. I was told it was done to protect the patient as well as the medic, which was true, but these measures still felt abnormal and disconnected, even to the medical staff. The basic comfort of touch was denied to many patients for fear of contamination.

Very often, as I walked into a room to offer a cup of tea, I would barely get an answer, but sometimes I would find a patient in a stronger state. I came across a young boy whom I shall call Tom who was surprisingly lucid, and he tried to chat to me for a while, although he had some difficulty forming all his words. He was very thin, but his face still had a gentle prettiness, although his dark hair was thinning and looked dry and dull. His family had been horrified to find out about his diagnosis, and he told me they could not face the hospital. His sister had been to see him, but it was a long journey, and his parents were ashamed of him, he said. What broke my heart was his complete acceptance of this shame.

It was obvious that Tom could no longer walk, and he had had a brain infection, so things were not going to improve. When I eventually left his bedside to continue my tea rounds, I went with a very empty feeling. It hadn't really occurred to me until then that because they were ashamed, a son might not be able to tell his own mother or father he was going to die.

Here at the Westminster Hospital, the ground was being laid for the AIDS wards of the next decade. In place of the nurses who had originally shown fear when faced with the virus were nurses who were learning and helping to create new methods of care. It was clear that the visitors on the wards were friends, partners and lovers more often than family members. It seemed those who could put aside the shame and fear surrounding AIDS were becoming part of a segregated world.

# CHAPTER 7

*A letter always seemed to me immortality because it is the mind alone without corporeal friend.*

Emily Dickinson

It was Christmas, and Jae and I were going to sing Christmas carols on the ward at the Westminster Hospital. We were in the day room, starting to set up. There were cups of tea and mince pies for anyone who fancied any refreshments, and some tinsel and a small tree to make things look festive. There was no doubt in my mind that this would be the final Christmas for any young man in the hospital. Some men walked in, and some were brought in by wheelchair, but all of them had the same gaunt, sunken look that made their teeth seem too large for their faces, with sallow or blemished skin and drips attached to their arms, or oxygen masks to help with their breathing. We were determined to bring a cheerful Christmas spirit to the room, but I was worried that might be easier said than done, given the circumstances. That is, until Jae quite loudly asked one of the nurses if he could have a stool by the piano. At this point, with wonderful black humour, one witty queen piped up, 'Don't ask for a stool in here, dear – you won't like what you get!' A fabulous line that made everybody laugh. By the end of our hour of singing, the mood was lighter. There really was a lot of love in that room.

In 1987, the following year, Lady Diana opened the first dedicated AIDS ward at the Middlesex Hospital. It was still a time when many people would not even touch an AIDS patient and would often throw away glasses or cups that they had used. It would be another three years before Lady Diana famously hugged a child with AIDS in New York, a moment that was captured on camera and made front-page news. It seemed crazy that something as simple – and human – as giving someone a hug could be so newsworthy, but it was. That hug made a lot of difference to so many people. It helped the movement to fight back against cruel misinformation, and the search for truth that was gaining momentum, slowly but surely. As Diana said herself: 'Shake their hands and give them a hug – heaven knows they need it.'

That same year saw AIDS become the rumoured catalyst for the closing of a West End show. *La Cage aux Folles* was a spectacular and brilliantly staged musical by the legendary Jerry Herman, who had been diagnosed with HIV in 1985. It was a stunning theatrical extravaganza, but it featured gay characters and a chorus line of divinely frocked boys. This was considered part of its downfall. Scott St Martyn, one of those original boys, described to me how the show continually received hate mail, filled with baseless claims about audience members risking catching AIDS from the seats, and that shows with such profanity and flagrant homosexuality should not be tolerated at the London Palladium. Unsurprisingly, the press added fuel to the fire, with such headlines as 'Quite

Right to Take This Folly Off the Stage' written by John Smith (who called himself Man of The People), in the *Daily Mirror*.[5]

A letter was even sent to the *Stage* questioning whether *La Cage* was *spreading* AIDS, and Scott stated that there was the lack of confidence felt by people in having the words 'gay', 'AIDS' and 'London Palladium' in the same breath.

Jerry Herman died in 2019 after living for an incredible thirty-four years with HIV. He received life-saving medication after being brave enough to volunteer for a drugs trial. He was told by his doctor that the trial was looking for people who were not doing well. Herman didn't hesitate. In spite of all the honours he received for his work, he said of being part of the protease inhibitor trial and those subsequent results being sent to the FDA (The United States Food and Drug Administration), for drug approval: 'I think it is the best thing I have done for the world.'[6]

Misinformation really was a terrible – and very dangerous – problem. The lack of widespread information from the government or health officials meant that some bizarre notions were being passed around. At one point, there was a wild claim doing the rounds that drinking your own urine could help recovery. There were hundreds of rumours about potential 'remedies', some of which were extremely dangerous, such as drinking bleach. Worst of all, in some countries, having sex with a virgin – or even a baby – was proffered as a way to cleanse the blood of the virus, leading to instances of terrible abuse. This lack of knowledge was a recipe for disaster.

In our own circle, the boys began to search for answers of their own. For Jae, this happened on a Tuesday in the summer, when he decided in his impetuous way he'd had enough of fear and wanted to get a test. The sun shone on the rose garden in Regent's Park, but it was difficult to enjoy the beauty as we arrived at the steps of a private clinic that provided HIV tests with same day results. The thought of waiting days or weeks for the result was just too stressful to bear, so Jae paid for the privilege of knowing within hours. A nurse took his blood before a matinee performance of *Cats* he was conducting at the time.

They informed him the result would be back by about four o'clock – just a few hours away. That gave him just enough time to do the show, Jae believed. I suggested he call in sick.

'No. I'm doing the matinee. What else will I do if I don't do the show?' he said. 'Even if I find out I'm positive I'll do the show this evening too.' Responding to my look of distress, he added in his best Mrs Slocombe voice: 'Those pussies need me, my dear.'

I tried to persuade him that this might not be good idea, but he was adamant. This is the pattern of our relationship: he always thinks everything will be fine, while I work through and imagine every possible outcome, and try to be prepared.

That was his final decision. While he was in the pit, I tried to kill time by window-shopping in the West End, but all I could think about was the fact that, in just a few short hours, our lives could change for ever. The hours felt like days as I paced the streets, until, after what had felt like the longest show ever – even longer than *Fiddler on the Roof* – we headed back to the clinic, not saying a word to anyone at the theatre about where we were going.

When Jae's name was called, he went in to get the result alone, while I sat outside on the steps, trying to hear anything through the door. I steeled myself for the worst. I was planning not to cry – I wanted to be strong and hopeful – but at the same time, I kept thinking of just how difficult it would be to tell his family (who did not know, even then, that he was gay) and even my family (who did know) that Jae was going to die.

I bit my nails and sat, listening to my own breath. Then,

suddenly, I looked up – and there he was, at the top of the steps with a big smile, clutching the negative result in his right hand. We were both overjoyed and hugged each other. He went back to the evening performance and felt, in his own words 'elated' and so did I.

Although this was brilliant news for Jae, I could tell we were all thinking the same kind of things. At this time, we still didn't fully understand how the virus was transmitted, so we questioned how Duncan could have caught it when Jae didn't. We were in the same circles, after all. We hung around the same sorts of people. We didn't think Duncan was any more promiscuous than Jae – so was Jae just one of the lucky ones? Or, rather, was Duncan just unlucky?

What we did know was that he was sick, but for now he seemed to be doing OK – at least, we hadn't heard the worst. Peg had bumped into him in the West End and told us that, true to form, he was incredibly open and honest. 'He has a permanent tube in his chest now, to deliver some kind of medication, and he was flashing it around like a new accessory,' she recalled. This was blasé, even for Duncan, but Peg said that being so open was helping him cope. I suppose that all his life he had faced stigma, name-calling and abuse – he wasn't going to give in to that now.

It was this bravery and apparent ability to take things in his stride that made everyone in our circle realise how much they truly admired him. The neat and very camp boy who had sash-ayed his way through life to this point had become a man with a heroic heart and Herculean inner strength. He was taking the bull by the horns. He was the first boy I knew who admitted his diagnosis in those early days – and one of the very few who did, with many others keeping their illness a secret.

*　　*　　*

Meanwhile, Juan was back with us in London. After the worrying news of Duncan's diagnosis, he had heard from Jae that he had tested negative, and it seemed to give him some confidence. He was thinking of booking a test of his own when he returned to Paris, just in the hope that it would ease the worry. If Jae was OK, then surely there was a good chance that he, too, would be fine.

Juan had been very busy indeed over the past few months. He had been back to Caracas for a while and discovered that, unsurprisingly, he still hated it. He wrote to me explaining that although the noise of the traffic there drove him mad, the main problem was the fact that he had argued quite a bit with his mother as he had made an attempt to discuss his sexuality with her. It sounded like his efforts hadn't been met with much understanding, but I was amazed he had at least tried to be honest with her.

His mother was a neat, glamorous, dark-haired Venezuelan woman with an infectious laugh and an ability to drink strong black espresso all day while seeming totally unaffected. We had all met her and loved her. She spoke only Spanish; one day she arrived back at the flat to announce she had been shopping in 'Toonpikkalaanay', which Juan eventually worked out was actually Turnpike Lane. He, wickedly, spoke English in her company when he was saying something he did not want her to understand. 'Look at that boy's cute bum!' he would say, and then revert back to Spanish. (This could work the other way too. Once, on a bus in Caracas, he'd heard two American girls on the seats opposite him. Assuming he could not understand what they were saying, they were chatting about how cute they thought he was. 'Why, thank you ladies, but you're not quite my cup of tea,' he'd said, in his best posh English as he got off the bus, leaving them quite red-faced.)

As usual, during Juan's visit to London, he was trying to make up his mind as to where was best to live. He was still hoping for his dream job – the chance to be on a West End stage. He had been haunted by work-permit problems for so long, but, as luck would have it, he'd managed to land a rather important job via Venezuelan contacts. His language skills allowed him to work as a translator for diplomats, which gave him a permit to work in Europe. He worked hard in this new-found role, but all the while he yearned for a singing career. Still dreaming of getting his big break, he arrived at Heathrow airport. I drove to meet him in my new little car, which I had affectionately named Audrey after *Little Shop of Horrors*.

I always loved meeting him at the airport. There is something so heart-warming about the arrivals hall, and I adored seeing Juan appear through the doors, waving excitedly like a big kid, dressed in the de rigueur black and brown colours everyone was wearing in Paris, swathed in one of his stylish scarves.

He shouted across the hall: 'Jilly, I'm back!'

I'd had to wait a while for this reunion because, as usual, he'd spent a long time in customs – this time, they'd even read his diaries. But finally, there he was, in front of me and ready for fun.

'Juan, darling, we're all definitely coming to your showcase tomorrow night,' I said as I drove Audrey back to the city. He was appearing in a showcase at the New End Theatre in Hampstead – I think it was called *Get the Hook*. It was a funny idea based on the old Vaudeville tradition where the theatre manager stood in the wings with a long hook. If you were a good act, you were allowed to finish your spot – if you were horrendous, as per Vaudeville rules, the hook would come out and pull you offstage and into the wings. It was like a very early interpretation of reality TV. Juan, of course, came onstage and sang beautifully. The hook made a brief appearance, poking out from the wings for fun, but the audience cheered and the hook disappeared. It was a great laugh. We had a brilliant few weeks together, and then I was off to start a new job in Nottingham in a production of *Oliver!* at the Playhouse, while Juan returned to Paris and to his new love, Frederic. Juan was sure this latest relationship was the most special in his life to date. I had heard this several times before in relation to Juan's boyfriends, but Frederic seemed to be the first man who had really understood Juan. Everything seemed to be going so well.

For the next few weeks, I was busy rehearsing for the new show. It was proving to be a completely fabulous experience with a crowd of people who got on famously. The father of one of Fagin's gang was in the world of horse racing, and the cheeky seven-year-old continually had good tips for a winner. One of the stage crew had won £2,500, and this led to us all constantly pressing this small child for tips and rushing to the bookie's.

But all the time, I was aware of a nagging worry that it had been very difficult to get hold of Juan. I knew that he had been planning to move flats, and I wondered if his new relationship was all-consuming, so I thought he was probably just distracted – but I also couldn't stop thinking about the fact that he had said he might take *the* test. I was filled with dread. Surely he would have called me if the result was negative. But then, perhaps he hadn't had the courage to go to the clinic? Or maybe he simply had nothing interesting to tell me? For a few days in a row I called, but couldn't seem to catch him. Perhaps the phone was broken. Perhaps they'd had to move again, or maybe there were family issues. Just like the horses, my mind was racing – I didn't know what to think.

Eventually, a letter arrived. It was chatty as normal, talking about a record producer he had met and telling me all about his cabaret. For a moment I breathed a sigh of relief – until the last page.

'Unfortunately, Jilly, I am antibody *positif*,' he wrote in his own beautiful mix of languages. It was the same way he talked, only this time with no frills.

Those last two words were so simple to read, but so chilling. I was suddenly freezing cold and frozen to the spot. I read and re-read the letter to make sure I was understanding what he meant: 'antibody *positif*'. He continued describing to me his trauma: not wanting to face reality, how his moods were unbearable, telling me Fred was an angel, and that he would appreciate it if I would not say a word to anybody. He wrote with courage and concern not for himself but for me, ending the letter:

It does not mean I shall die tomorrow. In fact, I can probably survive the whole thing. I'll be alright. I've got too much energy and need to live. That virus won't hit me. I shall wait for your answer – don't take it bad, darling.

He had underlined the 'me' like he really meant it.

Juan's diagnosis was an emotional upheaval for me and he occupied my every thought. I desperately wanted to speak to him, to hear his voice and confirm he was well. I was back in London for the Sunday, and had to find a time to call him when neither Jae nor Philip were around so they wouldn't overhear. Eventually, I went to a call box, with as many ten-pence pieces as I could find, and I finally got hold of him. The coins went through the phone like water down the drain, as Paris was bloody expensive to call.

He told me his immune system was holding up – apparently, they could measure the number of immune cells in the body now. T-cells were the important ones, and Juan was OK. We didn't completely understand it then, but a T-cell blood count needed to above 200 – the magic number. Below that, the diagnosis was full-blown AIDS or ARC (AIDS Related Complex), and any illness could strike at any time. A healthy T-cell count should be anything from 500–1600 per cubic millimetre of blood. I asked him if the doctors were good in Paris, and if they had any new information. He assured me his doctor was OK. I frantically wanted to go to Paris and be with Juan, but until my show ended, it was impossible. It struck me then that life had lost its shine. Once again, we would have to live with a new normal.

# CHAPTER 8

*Regardless of how you feel inside, always try to look like a winner.*

Arthur Ashe

Just as it seemed that the Fates had contrived to take Juan's future, he finally landed a job he loved, seven years after finishing drama school. *Cats*, the show Andrew Lloyd Webber created from T. S. Eliot's poetry, had been a London sensation since 1981. Now, due to its success, the show was heading to Paris. As is common for such physically exertive musicals, the production needed some local booth singers – vocalists who add to the sound on stage from a recording booth backstage. Blessed with size-twelve flat feet and a little extra body weight, Juan was never going to be able to land a dancing role in *Cats*, but he could certainly sing anything he wanted to, so the job was his. Being a booth singer was a great job, and one that people often didn't know existed unless they worked in the business. Brilliant session singers like Derek (who often sang in the booth at *Starlight Express*), and now Juan, sat there comfortably, out of sight, having great fun and singing the score live, conducted by the musical director on a small screen. Juan was absolutely over the moon. It was his chance to be part of the musical theatre revolution with one of the shows he loved.

*Cats* ran in Paris for more than a year, which gave Juan security, money and lots of joy, but, most importantly, it also helped him to finally land an onstage role as Old Deuteronomy, the non-dancing 'Big Daddy' cat in *Cats: Das Musical* in Hamburg. I went to Hamburg to see him and was so proud of him. He sang brilliantly in German (although I did laugh at him singing *'Jellicle Katzen'*) – his fourth language – and looked phenomenal in the make-up and costume. We had so much fun partying with the cast and seeing the sights. For a short while, it was as though the diagnosis hadn't happened.

For a long time, I was one of the few who knew Juan's secret. His family had no idea, and he chatted with them on the phone as though nothing was out of the ordinary. He felt it was important that no one in the show knew, as he didn't want to be treated differently – and he most certainly would have been. People did not look at those who were HIV positive in the same way once they found out. He wouldn't even admit to feeling normal amounts of tiredness, because he was worried people would think he wasn't fit to work. He worried that his fellow performers would not want to share a dressing room for fear of infection – and he was always afraid that he could infect someone, even if there was just a tiny amount of blood from a paper cut. On top of this, there was the medication to consider and hide. Juan was given doses of AZT (Zidovudine), which was the very first treatment for AIDS. It was originally a leukaemia drug that had been given up as ineffective against that disease, but brought back to life by Wellcome as a treatment for AIDS.[7] AZT brought some hope, but the science was still so new that it was all a bit of a minefield. However, at least taking something dispelled despair and worked to reduce the feeling of helplessness. Due to pressure for treatments, AZT was given a fast licence, but controversy reigned. There was a lot of publicity due to the toxic side effects and bone marrow damage it could cause, and some refused to take it. In fact, a friend of mine, Boyd, who lived in the Church Street (gay village) area of Toronto in the eighties, vividly described how at certain times an unexpected shower would happen: not of rain, but of gay men (who had reached a limit of endurance with the side effects) wildly throwing their medication from apartment balconies. For a few brief seconds it would rain tablets onto the sidewalk below. Juan embraced it, however, and although he said it made him feel fatigued, he persevered. It was said that the drugs were killing people as quickly as the disease itself, but at that time, there was nothing else available. Just as in America, the UK government seemed to have little interest in AIDS. The potential for AIDS to spread to the wider population was being ignored, and because most sufferers were gay men or other marginalised groups, there was little financial attention paid to the pandemic. AZT was the only certified treatment and gay men were, without doubt, the guinea pigs, willing to try anything to live even a few more months.

Some years later, in 1993, I was fascinated to discover that Wellcome had had to delay an initial trial due to a shortage of a vital ingredient needed in the manufacturing process. Somewhat incredibly, that missing ingredient was herring sperm.

In the early days, AZT needed to be taken at regular four-hourly intervals, and I have since read that the real money lay in making the bleepers to remind patients it was medication time. So many people persevered in desperation, that one article from about this time states: 'In New York in the late eighties, opera performances were punctuated by bleeps.' The drug was prescribed at many different stages of immune damage at the discretion of individual doctors, and often even they really didn't know what was best. So much was uncertain, but Juan was determined to fight.

Back in college, when we would sit up late talking and drinking, Juan would sometimes tell me, ominously, 'I shall die at thirty-three, Jilly.' I would always laugh, but he really seemed to have a strange feeling about that age – he thought it was linked to his Catholic upbringing and the death of Jesus. Now, when I left Juan and returned to London, I was desperately hoping that this premonition would not come true.

I carried with me an uneasy sadness. Whatever time we did have together was more special than it had ever been, and I started to feel I couldn't help him enough because we lived in separate countries. I worried about him constantly, and I couldn't even confide in any our mutual friends at home, because I had been sworn to secrecy. I couldn't even speak to Jae about it. I was haunted by the fear that each time I saw Juan would be the last, and although this could be true of any relationship, at any time, AIDS made it more a question of probability than chance. I told myself not to be stupid: time and modern science were on the case; new treatments were just around the corner. But, even with no particular religious belief, I found myself praying to some kind of higher power for a cure, for help of any kind. However, as so many people know, nothing in medicine ever seems to happen quickly – and prayers are not always answered.

# CHAPTER 9

*And both that morning equally lay*
*In leaves no step had trodden black.*
*Oh, I kept the first for another day!*
*Yet knowing how way leads on to way,*
*I doubted if I should ever come back . . .*

Robert Frost, 'The Road Not Taken'

Early in 1988, when we were twenty-seven years old, Jae was thrilled to be chosen as the musical director for an incredibly popular new production of Stephen Sondheim's iconic show, *Follies*. The show was magical and moving, portraying the nostalgic reunion of a group of once-famous performers who laugh, reminisce and revisit life's regrets, trailed by the ghosts of their younger selves. It was instantly a sensation and received rave reviews – anybody who was anybody went to see it. I remember being very proud of one of those ghosts in particular, recognising him as a blue-eyed golden boy from Mountview with an unusual name: Dursley.

We had known each other moderately for many years, but had never really been close friends, mainly due to the fact that I was four years older than him. But the showbusiness circle in London is really quite small: something of a village, really. Everybody knows everybody, to some degree, so we kept up with each other. There was always gossip on who was doing what show, and of course who was going out with whom (or who was doing what to whom, in or out of bed). On top of that, Dursley was a genuine success, so everybody talked about him. I knew him as the one boy in a thousand who'd left a small town and actually become somebody. As luck would have it, it turned out that he and Jae were sharing a dressing room, and so, to my delight, we began to see much more of each other.

I was always in awe of Dursley. It was fascinating to see him at cast parties, surrounded by friends and strangers alike. People just loved to be around him, but it was not just his looks or his tremendous talent that left people enamoured with him. He was incredibly charismatic, with star quality and sex appeal all in one, which meant he was able to charm everyone, men and women alike. He could certainly hold court and recount stories. One of his favourites was how he got his unusual name. 'It's a town my father went to during the war,' Dursley would say, and he'd always get a laugh when he followed up with: 'Good job it wasn't the next town, or I would be called Uley!'

I never knew so many people could fall in love with one person, but they did; he just had a natural ability to make anyone he spoke to feel special.

One of the many things I loved about Dursley was his way of keeping everyone happy by organising things to do: dinners, trips, days out, parties, and all kinds of fun. He was always right there in the centre of things. He had a natural flair for partying, and would take us to the most wonderful clubs, the best restaurants, and the funkiest bars. As Dursley and I became closer, we went clubbing quite a lot, mainly because he loved it so much – and he was never short of attention. I loved to dance, and it was wild on the dance floor in the eighties and early nineties. The shirts would come off, and sometimes all you could see was a sea of flesh. It was hedonistic and sexy. (The downside was getting home and climbing into bed with loud music still ringing in my ears and the smell of cigarettes thick in my hair, spoiling my clean white pillowcase.)

On the nights not spent clubbing we would, more often than not, be in one of our favourite places: a restaurant called Joe Allen. Named after its founder, an entrepreneur who'd already opened a famous restaurant of the same name in New York, the place had been a theatrical institution since 1977. The walls on both sides of the Atlantic were papered with show posters of all kinds: hits and flops! I adored it. Live music from Jimmy on the piano welcomed you as you arrived, and rather beautiful 'resting' actors made up the fabulous team of waiting staff. It was one of the few restaurants you could go to after a show and stay there till two in the morning, and I loved to spot the faces from the theatre posters on the walls eating at the red-and-white gingham tableclothed tables.

As the place was full of all kinds of celebrities from the world of theatre, film, art and fashion, there was a strict 'no picture' policy in case the stars wanted privacy. A shame, really, as I would have loved a photo of the time Richard Gere popped over to our table from his and asked if he could borrow a pound, or of the night when Lauren Bacall gracefully popped out of the cubicle next to me in the ladies' loo. The one thing I would not like to commemorate is the amount of money we spent there between us over the years – probably enough to buy a small yacht. We were not alone in this: years later, at Jimmy the pianist's memorial service, Chris Biggins told of being quietly approached by his accountant, who asked if he was being blackmailed on account of an extraordinary number of cheques being made out to one Joe Allen.

Dursley was on track to become just as renowned as one of the famous faces spotted at Joe Allen. It was showbiz icon Liza Minnelli who said: 'Anything is possible in this world; I really believe that,' and it seemed like Dursley was one of those people who was not only ready for his lucky chance, but whom luck was ready to find. He had ambition and tremendous talent, and his ability to make the world fall in love with him without even trying meant that networking came to him as naturally as breathing. He knew everyone. Despite his success, though, he remained the thoughtful and lovely boy he had always been.

His family liked to tell stories of him as a child. He always knew what he wanted and was rather adventurous. He was inclined to wander off, and this of course caused alarm, so his mother made the unique decision to sew bells to his slippers so she would always be able to hear him. Neighbours and family members would hear the bells and return him home and all the while he charmed them all.

It was no real surprise to us that success came quickly. Aged twenty-three he won an amazing film role, *Just Ask for Diamond*, in which he played Tim Diamond and acted alongside Patricia Hodge, Saeed Jaffrey, Roy Kinnear, Nickolas Grace, Susannah York and Jimmy Nail. Along with his family, he invited us – including my parents, whom he adored – to the premiere. I had never been invited to a film premiere before, and I felt so thrilled to be there – especially with the star. He had even managed to get two of his sisters, Melanie and Tracy, into the film as extras, so it was a family affair. He took it in his stride, of course, but it was really an honour, and such an exciting event. It promised to be the beginning of a fabulous career.

Dursley had talent, looks and personality, as well as a great agent. From the outside looking in, he had the perfect life, but the reality was that, for years, a chilling feeling had been brewing within him. He was completely aware of the changes in the world; aware that he had slept with and played with many beautiful, high-flying boys for many years, from both America and the UK. He put off getting tested, telling himself that he was busy making a movie or a TV series – but inside, he knew it was because he was terrified. It was the little things that nagged him at first: a rash on his skin, the way his hair didn't look quite as shiny as it always had, a query from a friend – 'You look a bit tired, darling, are you OK?' – or a comment from a director: 'I want the lighting to be slightly different here; your skin's looking unusually pale.'

Try as he might to ignore it, the thought was always there, festering in the back of his mind. He had been close with boys who had become sick, but his most recent, most passionate relationship had shown no sign of illness, so he told himself he wasn't at risk. However, there was one boy he had been close to who concerned him: a boy who had disappeared from the cast of a show a few years before; one of those beautiful boys who 'went home' and never came back.

Throughout our friendship, Dursley and I had had numerous conversations about AIDS – by the time we became friends, in the late eighties, it was impossible not to. However, these conversations were always about someone else, or the wider state of the world. They were never really about him – that is, until one fateful night, at a corporate event we had been working at together. We'd been doing various themed musical performances at the Guildhall in the City of London, and this occasion in particular had been a very hot and hectic night. Jae was organising the music and we had all had fun laughing at each other in elaborate medieval costumes, especially sister Hogg, who was wearing some very dynamic pantaloons. Dursley looked worn out by the end of the evening, so we went and sat on the steps outside the building, just to get some air.

We were sitting in silence, enjoying the cool breeze on our faces, when, all of a sudden, he looked at me seriously (or as seriously as he possibly could while dressed in a medieval jester's costume), then looked away and blurted it out: 'Jill, I think you ought to know that I have AIDS.'

I don't know why he chose that moment. It was surreal, but I know I remained very calm. It was the first time someone had told me this terrible news to my face, so I shakily replied, 'OK,' then made some vague attempt at positivity, saying something like, 'Well, you seem strong at the moment.' Not much use, really, but no one prepares you for what to say in that situation.

So, I just told him that if he needed help, he could always ask me. He told me a couple of people knew, and asked me not to tell anyone else.

'Of course I won't,' I said. Half of me felt overwhelmed with a mixture of horror, loss and sadness all at once, while the other half felt a sense of privilege that he trusted me with a secret so intimate. But with such a secret comes a great deal of responsibility. In truth, it was a nightmare, as I couldn't tell Dursley about Juan, or vice versa, no matter how desperately I wanted to. I was anxious to share information, but I was trapped in a web of untold truths.

It was the boy that vanished from that touring show, a boy he'd had a relationship with, that forced Dursley to finally face his fear head-on. In the autumn of 1990, at the age of twenty-six, and with a shining future within reach, he put on his new blue jeans and a plain white T-shirt. Looking gorgeous, 'Paul James' headed to the tube, and took a long and lonely ride to the Royal Free Hospital. He could never give his real name – he knew that. We'd all heard the rumours, and knew that once this was on your medical record, you were labelled for life. He had also heard that in order to get information about Freddie Mercury, the press had dressed as doctors and tried to get photos of a dying man. Dursley was from the Isle of Man, where, at this time, homosexuality was still illegal. If the worst was true, and the newspapers found out, his family would be heart-broken.

He waited, all alone – and then it happened. Just a few words: 'I'm sorry to tell you this, Paul, but your test has come back with a positive result.'

His life, a life of great joy, of excitement and promise, a life of adoration and sexual freedom, a life of auditions, dinner parties, trips and sexual conquests would now become something different: a life of rigid adherence to safe sex; a life of hospital visits, blood tests and medication – and always, always secrecy.

# CHAPTER 10

*Out of the night that covers me,*
*Black as the pit from pole to pole*
*I thank whatever gods may be,*
*For my unconquerable soul.*

William Ernest Henley

Dursley had a different view of the world now, and I had a different view of Dursley. Our relationship changed. As well as his outward beauty, which, of course, everybody was able to see, I now learned that he radiated an inner beauty and depth that he shared with just a few people. Thankfully one of the few people he included in his diagnosis news was Jae. That was a huge relief to me because it was so difficult to maintain the secrecy at home, but it meant that Jae had a burden of his own to deal with, and a degree of guilt when speaking of his own negative status.

Dursley had an intense love for life, and he was utterly determined to make the most of every minute he had. His fighting spirit was inspirational, but he knew he needed to rethink some things. He made a decision to cut down on the number of auditions he was doing, simply because the stress on his health would make it difficult to compete with the same vigour.

However, he was never one to slow down for very long. He began to move into the other side of the business: producing. Now, of course, Dursley wouldn't work for just any producer – they had to be the best. Cameron Mackintosh gave him a job, meaning he was part of the production team for some of the biggest shows in the world. For the first time, Dursley had job security, and he found that his charm made him a very popular member of the team. In short, they loved him. He was working with a crowd of trendy, exciting and gorgeous people, and he loved them right back.

He was having fun. He was in charge of organising the casting of the production of *Moby Dick, A Whale of a Tale,* a new show which was due to open at the small theatre in Oxford called The Old Fire Station. It was a St Trinian's-type romp with lots of outrageous ideas. Inspired by the success of the Chippendales, it had been decided that the parts of some security guards in the show would be played by muscle men who, at some point in a musical number, would remove their clothing. Dursley called Jae. 'Could you help out, Jae? The musical director isn't free on the day. You would have to watch some boys do the dance routine, which involves them stripping down to their underwear. Is that OK?' Jae paused for about a millisecond, before casually saying, 'Of course, Dursley, I will try to make myself free and I would be *more* than happy to help.' Naturally, they had a whale of a day.

While Dursley's new job took him offstage, I was performing in a touring production of *Annie*, starring Elaine Smith. She was one of the cast of *Neighbours*, the TV show that made Kylie Minogue a household name and was a huge success at the time. She played Daphne. In true soap style, Daphne was a stripper, then owned the coffee shop, then gave birth on a picnic blanket by a lake, before finally dying in the arms of her husband, Des, after a terrible car crash. Elaine was a massive TV star but, more importantly, she was – and still is – an absolutely fabulous person. We got on brilliantly. Elaine was anxious to get all she could from her time in the UK, and spent much of it in London. I enjoyed being at home and commuted to the show when I could, and so we spent time together in the city. It took a girl from Australia to introduce me to some of the sights of my own country – and to teach me that Leeds Castle was just up the road from the capital and not, as I told her, three hours up the M1.

Because I was at home a lot, Dursley and I often met for lunch. He had two favourite haunts: there was a trendy little café, full of healthy food and not far from his office, which he affectionately referred to as the Lesbian Café; or there was First Out, the first gay daytime venue, which he insisted on calling 'First Up Your Bum'. As we sat in both places, we gossiped about everyone and put the world to rights. Although he had blood tests every few weeks to monitor his immune system and keep track of his T-cell count (which would indicate how much damage there was to his body), Dursley seemed pretty fit and vibrant, and everything appeared to be going rather well.

However, it wasn't long before I realised how hard it was for Dursley to actually hide the truth. One weekend, some of his family and a few friends came to visit him at his flat. He had a gorgeous flat in a lovely area not too far from the Pink Palace, where I had so many happy memories (each time I visited him, a part of me wished we had never left).

The week leading up to the visit had not been great, as together we were discovering the smaller problems that HIV and low immunity could dish out to its sufferers. There was an endless list of infections that, while not life-threatening, were hideously unpleasant infections: thrush, impetigo, molluscum, giardia, and cystitis, to name a few.

This time, for Dursley, it was a very bad bout of shingles. His whole back was a scarlet-red colour and covered in large, watery blisters. Not only was this a worrying reminder that his immune system was under attack, it was also just bloody painful. On top of that, there was the added risk of spreading shingles to anyone else who might be vulnerable, so we had to make sure he was well covered at all times. He tried paracetamol, which did little to help with the pain. We tried calamine lotion, which didn't do much either. So, on the advice of Gudrun (Dursley's faithful and inspirational alternative therapist and homeopath), he began eating loads and loads of grapes and garlic. It may not have been a cure, but in his mind, it helped him: so, while he usually smelled beautiful (with Ralph Lauren's help), he was definitely not going to be attacked by a vampire anytime soon.

Of course, we both knew that Dursley needed proper medication, but at that time all he wanted to think about was organising this special party. I truly don't know how he did it. I was standing in the kitchen as people started arriving, and I saw him grimace with pain whenever someone gave him a big hug – but not one of the guests suspected that something was wrong. If anything, Dursley seemed to be high in energy, perhaps compensating for the stress of secrecy, and he didn't complain once. Talk about acting! I spent my time trying to organise the food, running back and forth in an effort to save Dursley's energy. By the end of the evening, I was completely shattered, but he was so relieved and happy that everyone had had a good time (and that his secret remained intact). The night had been a great success, and I was coming to realise just how determined he was not to be defeated.

AIDS is not really an infectious illness in the conventional sense. Instead, it defines an acquired, rapidly developing, devastating and truly sinister destruction of the body's defences. The human immune system has gone through millions of years of remarkable evolution to make it as perfect as possible, and this disease sees it aggressively hijacked by these microscopic viral entities on a mission to reproduce themselves. They're not even defined by science as truly living organisms.

The nature of the disease means that there is no clear set of symptoms, so each and every person will experience the HIV invasion in a different way. That's why Dursley came to believe a person's 'attitude' was fundamental to their quality of life and survival. He told me how he had worried for at least three years before he took the test, whereas now that he knew, he felt strangely uplifted. The burden of uncertainty had been removed, and he was ready to fight with all the strength he believed was within him.

Dursley's tenacity was incredible. It inspired me, as I had been trying for a while to convince my mum to look into alternative health regimes to help her recovery. Now Dursley was clarifying some thoughts that had been in the back of my mind for some time. Lovely Derek, too, I saw as a shining example: he had faced his cancer head-on, and was now a survivor.

Dursley was fired up with one goal: to remain as fit and as

strong as possible because, as he often told me, 'I know the cure is just around the corner.' Juan, too, clearly felt he could survive the whole thing. Neither he nor Dursley were ever *victims* of AIDS. They were People With AIDS (PWAs) – and they were going to fight.

There has been some debate about the expression 'PWA' and its origins. However, I agreed wholeheartedly with the consensus of those who had previously been labelled AIDS victims, relayed at the Denver Health Conference in 1983: 'We condemn attempts to label us as victims, a term that implies defeat . . . we are people with AIDS.'[8]

Certainly, with my friends, 'PWA' was the preferred abbreviation. Inspired by something I had read about the importance of seeing the person, not the disease, we also used the description 'living with AIDS'. It was certainly a more positive outlook. Unsurprisingly, then, 'positive thinking' became a very important phrase in my vocabulary.

# CHAPTER 11

*Fan the sinking flame of hilarity with the wing of friendship;
and pass the rosy wine.*

Charles Dickens

In January 1991, we had a brilliant party in our flat for my thirtieth birthday. We set up a small stage, hired a spotlight and hung a glitter curtain. Miss Pinky arrived from Brighton, decked out in her pink sequins and pink wig, ready to perform. We were on target for a night reminiscent of the cabarets we'd so loved when we started life in the Pink Palace days. Martyn would be there with his guitar, Jae and I had planned a few songs, and Dursley (who, among his many talents, happened to be a fully-fledged magician) would do his magic act – maybe the 'disappearing cigarette', or maybe sawing Miss Pinky in half. Juan arrived from Paris, ready to sing à la Streisand. So, to borrow Russell's favourite phrase, it was sure to be 'a hoot!'

Pinky regaled us with more astonishing stories, the latest being how he had spotted four policemen escorting Nelson Mandela and his bodyguard on to the aircraft. In the galley, preparing the food and drink for the flight to Johannesburg, was Miss Pinky herself. *She* headed for the unsuspecting Mr Mandela and served him his meal, all the time chatting away, even managing (whilst kneeling in the aisle) to ask him about Robben Island and his time in prison. Mr Mandela was the ultimate in charm and respect, and even told Pinky how pleased he was to see such diversity among the staff, all working together on the aircraft. But even superheroes, it seems, can become exhausted by the chatter of an over-excited Welsh drag queen, and that noble man, who was almost sainted for his courage, humanity, tolerance and forgiveness, eventually turned to his bodyguard and said, 'I need to get some sleep now. Will you talk to him? Because he won't shut up!'

At the end of the party, Jae and Derek presented me with a large white envelope. 'Happy thirtieth birthday!' they cheered in sync, laughing as they watched me open their present. Inside, I discovered the promise of a flight to the Canary Islands and an apartment in Playa del Inglés for the three of us. I was thrilled.

'Well, you deserve a treat,' said Derek. 'And really, it means we can have fun with the boys in the bars! Especially Jae – they'll all be fighting over a short Welshman with little legs.'

Jae laughed as he usually did and said, 'They'll all be fighting over more than the legs, dear!'

I agreed with the treat idea! I had just finished a few hectic months in *Sugar*, the musical based on the film *Some Like It Hot* at the West Yorkshire Playhouse: it was a wonderful show, starring a very young Andy Serkis in the Jack Lemon role of Daphne.

I thought I deserved a trip, and couldn't wait for us all to escape to the sun.

\* \* \*

A few weeks later, the three of us arrived at our lovely white-washed apartment in Playa del Inglés. After setting our bags down in the hallway and claiming our bedrooms, we headed out to our balcony and immediately began planning a night out. It was a busy, gay-friendly island, and we knew that we would end up in the bars in the centre, but there were lots of lovely restaurants to choose from before that. Before we could leave, however, we had to spend thirty minutes photographing Derek, as he'd decided to indulge in a photo shoot, posing and pouting while dressed in my skimpy black and silver bathing costume. Still laughing, we headed out into the glorious balmy evening.

On the hill near our apartment we found a large, noisy restaurant called La Casa Vieja, where we enjoyed some traditional food: *patatas bravas, gambas y pescado*, or, as the very handsome waiter translated with a wink, potatoes in sauce, prawns and fish. After drinking quite a lot of sangria, we left, skipping down the streets and singing hits from the seventies like 'Chirpy Chirpy Cheep Cheep' and 'Fernando'. Thinking we sounded rather fabulous together, we decided we should resurrect the NightWalkers when we got back to London, this time just the three of us.

We ate, drank and danced our way around Playa del Inglés for just over a week, dressing up each evening, visiting different restaurants and ending the night in the most popular gay bars, where we danced till the early hours. Unsurprisingly, we sang lots of show songs in a bar called Centre Stage, and received great applause when we donned wigs and attempted to recreate *Dreamgirls*. However, the trip was not all glitz and glamour: we also spent a day riding camels across the massive, man-made sand dunes. This was particularly memorable as Jae, always a little nervous around animals (he had already spent a hysterical ten minutes trying to cover a cockroach with a saucepan at the apartment), fussed around his extra-large and angry-eyed camel. He annoyed the poor creature so much that, to Derek's delight, the disgruntled animal spat right in Jae's face.

The whole holiday was such a lot of fun, and there were times we could actually forget about AIDS for a while, although, as always, I went on about safe sex like a stuck record. (There was also plenty of information in the gay bars, which were mainly run by the ex-pat community.) Jae seemed to be able to stay out until the last glass was put away in the clubs, holding court and maybe even getting lucky. I would plead with him, 'Jae, please take care. You know how scary it is out there.' He would laugh it off and ignore me, of course, never giving up until the bitter end when the lights came on, whereas Derek and I would often throw the towel in a little earlier and go back to the villa. Derek seemed more interested in a good night's sleep and the fun of the next day rather than looking for casual fun with the boys in the bars. I was pleased, as I was not likely to get lucky either (gay bars weren't exactly the best place to pick up the sort of man who would be interested in me). So, we kept each other company as we flagged down taxis and tried to explain where we were staying in our broken Spanish, laughing as we did so because we weren't really sure how to get there ourselves. When we eventually got home, the two of us would sit chatting with a coffee on our little balcony, enjoying the buzzing of the cicadas looking for love. After our nights out drinking, those quiet moments on the balcony led to some intense conversations about love and life.

Derek told me about his mother, and how their relationship had changed since he had attempted to broach the subject of him being gay. He was hurt by the fact that she had never wanted to speak about it since; for him, it felt like there was always something unspoken, a wall between them. It certainly wasn't easy, but

Derek would always pretend to brush things off quite quickly. He preferred to be the clown, but I liked this deep-thinking side to his personality, as it meant we could have honest, open conversations. One night in particular, he was very philosophical. Despite not being a religious person, he said that he imagined that when a person dies, there must surely be something else out there.

'In fact, I think that, as a person gets older, their brain alters and kind of prepares them to be ready for this big adventure,' he told me.

'That's very profound, dear,' I said. 'I remember my dad reading me *Peter Pan*. Isn't it he who says, "To die will be an awfully big adventure?"'

'So people are ready and happy when they die?' asked Derek.

'I suppose it could be possible,' I said, without much certainty.

'But I don't think the brain is so prepared in those who die young,' he said.

'No. I don't think so, either,' I said. And with that thought hanging in the air, we went to bed.

# CHAPTER 12

*I am not afraid of storms for I am learning to sail my ship.*

Louisa May Alcott

When I got back from Gran Canaria, I headed to see Dursley as soon as I could. I discovered that he was determined to research and experiment with any treatment he could find that might help fight the virus or strengthen his immune system. Each time Dursley talked about some potential new remedy that would help his health in some way, I was straight on the phone to my mum, saying, 'You must try this meditation, Mum, it's good for relieving stress,' or, 'Eat this kind of food, Mum,' or, 'You should try getting a regular massage, Mum. It's all good for you, it's all about keeping the immune system healthy.' She probably thought I sounded like a parrot on speed, but she knew where I was coming from as, with his blessing, I had told her about Dursley very recently. He knew that she was non-judgemental and accepting, and her compassionate reaction left him feeling encouraged that he might be able to tell his own mother some-time soon.

I really truly believed that all these alternative therapies could help. There were many self-help books at the time that talked about the power of the mind and the ability to heal yourself, and I became obsessed with the idea. I was desperate for it to be true, and tried to learn as much as I could, surrounded as I was by illness in people I loved. Dursley had one goal, and that was to survive long enough for the cure. With the power of his mind, he believed, one hundred per cent, that he was strong enough to do so. His incredible courage filled me with such admiration for him that it is difficult to put it into words, but I was passionate about him and the fight, because his soul carried a strength that inspired people to love him.

I was desperate for Juan to have the benefit of some of these ideas in Paris, but although he and Dursley knew each other from our college days, their shared diagnosis remained a secret, and had to stay that way. This meant that a lot of the time, I would research alongside Dursley, and then share the information over the phone with Juan as if I had discovered it of my own accord. So many of the treatments were fascinating to me – like the power of the placebo effect when testing medicines. For example, I learned that if someone who is ill takes a pill that they *believe* will work, it will help them to a degree, even if there is nothing more in that pill than sugar. More amazingly still, if the pill is red, the effect is even stronger. The most powerful placebo of all, achieving the maximum effect, is an injection given to a person by a doctor – but said doctor must be wearing a white coat. Incredible people all over our planet with different diagnoses were beating the odds even when facing death, and living long, happy lives. Was AIDS any different? Maybe not.

Dursley collected all kinds of vitamins and homeopathic medicines and immune-boosters. In addition to helping him concoct his various potions, I tried many of them myself, as Dursley loved for everyone to share the benefits. I tried acupuncture, aromatherapy, reflexology, acupressure, shiatsu and Tai chi. Together we experimented with meditation, harmonisation, creative visualisation – in fact, if there was an '-ation' on the end of a word, we thought it was worth a try. There were always health spas with saunas and steam rooms, of course, but I think that might have led to a different sort of relaxation – as well as another kind of '-ation' altogether. The only '-ation' we really wanted to avoid was hospitalisation!

We tried flotation tanks and faith healers and herbal concoctions of all kinds. In my opinion, the worst remedy we tried was a packet of dried medicinal herbs bought from a mysterious and colourful herbalist in Chinatown. They were very expensive – and they absolutely stank – but they were supposed to help to calm the skin and stop it itching. For months and months on end, Dursley would find his skin felt horribly irritated, experiencing something akin to prickly heat, with masses of raised bumps all over his body. It would drive him to distraction. The herbs had to be stewed with water, and the resulting concoction was like a witch's brew – a few years later and Professor Snape might be teaching his students that this potion would be strong enough to rid the wizarding world of Lord Voldemort.

When I stayed at Dursley's, I would prepare the medicine and boil the mixture for twenty minutes each morning, following the instructions we'd found on a tiny scrap of paper stuffed in with the herbs. It smelled somewhere between tar, sulphur and decaying wood, with an acrid touch of rotting vegetables, and it became darker, thicker and more evil-looking as it boiled. By the second week, I could barely pour it into the glass without gagging, but

Dursley drank dutifully large amounts every morning in the hope of an improvement. Miraculously, his skin did stop itching for a while, but I couldn't help wondering if it actually was the herbs, or if this daily infusion worked in the same way as an injection from a doctor in a white coat might have done.

After a while, it seemed that Dursley was on every treatment under the sun – although thankfully not any of the crazy-sounding ones we had heard of other boys trying. I had grown used to him doing well. His regular outpatient tests and results kept coming back OK, and he had always been well enough to take himself to the appointments. That's why his first admission to hospital came as such a shock to me. We had been out to a Greek restaurant in Camden Town called Andy's Taverna, a favourite of Dursley's, but he was not feeling great, so we headed home earlier than we'd planned. I stayed with him at his lovely flat, just to keep an eye on him, although I genuinely believed – or, perhaps, naively hoped – that he was OK. He seemed a bit wobbly, so I helped him to his room and lay next to him on his double bed.

'You feel hot,' I said, concerned, feeling his forehead.

'I think I just need to get some sleep. We can call the doctor's in the morning, OK?' he replied.

I didn't really know what was best to do, so I agreed and decided I would sleep beside him.

By 4am, he was significantly worse. I felt his forehead again, but I didn't really need to – his entire body was exuding heat like a radiator, and he was so drenched in sweat that the bedsheets were damp.

'Dursley, darling, I think we need to go to A & E,' I said, trying to hide the growing panic in my voice.

'No. I want to wait for Clinic 9 to open,' he said, through chattering teeth.

Clinic 9 was where he was going for his tests and check-ups. The doctors there already knew he had AIDS, meaning he wouldn't have to share his secret with any more strangers.

By this point, I was really scared. He seemed short of breath and was beginning to have fits of violent shaking. I know now that this is called rigours, but I had never seen anything like it before – only on the television if, for example, some brave adventurer caught malaria. I'd always thought that it was a bit of overacting. I realised now that it wasn't.

We waited a few more hours at Dursley's insistence, but it got to the point where he was too poorly to make a decision. Somehow, I managed to half-carry him outside and put him in Audrey's passenger seat. Thankfully, he lived very close to the Royal Free Hospital, where, with great relief, I left it to the doctors to make the right choices. Dursley was admitted to the Garrett Anderson ward. I had no idea what was wrong; I thought he was dying there and then. I sat waiting, with my head in my hands, and my thoughts began to spiral. What should I do now? Did I need to call his family? I had no clue. Everyone else seemed calm, though, and the doctors were lovely, which helped to ease my mind a bit. They put a clip on his finger, which they told me would measure his oxygen levels, then they gave him tablets for the fever. Two hours later, he was on antibiotics for pneumonia. They said he would be OK and should be home by the end of the week. I breathed a sigh of relief and felt a weight lift from my shoulders. For the moment, Dursley had fought and survived.

That morning, I called Nickolas Grace. Niko, as everyone called him, had had a long relationship with Dursley. In simple terms, Niko was his ex, but it was much deeper than that. They had met in 1986 and had a love affair that had lasted nearly three years. Although the relationship had ended, they still had a very strong bond, and it had been Niko who Dursley had turned to the day he had discovered his diagnosis. Niko remained loyal and caring, putting aside his own pain at the end of the relationship to support Dursley in the dark days following the terrible news.

# CHAPTER 13

*The tender heart, the simple soul, the loud, the proud, the happy one?*
*All, all are sleeping on the hill.*
*. . . in a search for a heart's desire,*
*One after life in faraway London and Paris*
*. . . sleeping on the hill.*

Edgar Lee Masters

As the AIDS crisis worsened, film-makers, playwrights and various creatives responded by shedding light on the incredibly difficult position in which gay men, and those that loved them, found themselves. *The Normal Heart* was written in the early days of AIDS, and depicted the different attitudes towards the unfolding pandemic. Its evocative title was taken from the W. H. Auden poem 'September 1, 1939'. The play's writer, Larry Kramer, was a trailblazing but controversial activist aiming to shame everyone (including secretive gay men) whom he felt should be standing up and fighting to prevent thousands of unnecessary deaths due to inaction. The theatre company Gay Sweatshop produced Andy Kirby's *Compromised Immunity*, which looked at the relationship between a dying gay man and his straight male nurse. *Philadelphia*, an Oscar-winning movie written by gay activist Ron Nyswaner, looked at homophobia and fear in the workplace. Randy Shilts, who died of AIDS at forty-two, left us with *And the Band Played On*, a book exploring the political mess that had allowed things to accelerate so badly out of control. *And the Band Played On* references the travesty surrounding the rumoured 'Patient Zero', who was believed to be an air steward named Gaetan Dugas. Gaetan was publicly named and horribly shamed as the man who brought AIDS to the Western world. This claim was later found to be incorrect.

Derek Jarman's *Blue* was a documentary portraying his experience as an AIDS patient with cytomegalovirus (CMV), a condition that in his case caused his fading eyes to see everything around him in shades of blue. Another documentary, *Silverlake Life: The View From Here*, provided truth and imagery so graphic that I watched it as if it were a horror film. At times, it felt like too much to be surrounded by the disease in our daily lives and then to watch films about it in our spare time. At the same time, though, there was a certain comfort in recognising that the life we were living was reflected back at us – if not for me, then certainly for Dursley, who wanted to watch everything he could. I believe it was a way of feeling part of the growing movement. With a lack of support in the day-to-day world, there was comfort and education to be found in the arts, and these creations provided a small window into the truth we were experiencing.

In the early nineties, a musical inspired by life in New York's Greenwich Village called *Elegies for Angels, Punks and Raging Queens* came to London. It featured songs and monologues inspired by the Names Project AIDS Memorial Quilt, which was a collection of panels designed and stitched together by loved ones of those who had died from AIDS. The piece was also inspired by *The Spoon River Anthology* by Edgar Lee Masters, a selection of short poems that act as epitaphs for a group of people buried in a fictional small-town cemetery. The Names Project AIDS Memorial Quilt is maintained to this day, some forty years after the beginning of the AIDS pandemic, by the 'Handmaidens of the Quilt'. In 2020, when COVID-19 brought the world to a halt, the handmaidens were struck by the similarities between these two terrible waves of illness. In response, under the leadership of Gert McMullin, they mobilised the use of quilting fabric to create masks for protection against the new virus.

The writer of *Elegies*, Bill Russell, said of his work, 'I was trying to show a canvas of the many types of people both infected and affected by AIDS.' The play was full of humour as well as tragedy, and famously cued a musical number with the line, 'T-cells dropping, it's time to go shopping!'[9]

At the time, as I've explained, a patient's T-cell count was the all-important marker of their chances of survival, with 200 being the 'magic number' above which they could feel relatively safe. Facing this T-cell count was a huge mental hurdle, and most of the boys I knew used humour as a coping mechanism to help them deal with the stress. Dursley, for a laugh, decided that if his count dropped any lower, he would be able to name his T-cells individually. With his count scraping around seventy T-cells per cubic millimetre of blood, he was one of those patients who needed immediate help to prevent opportunistic infections. Miraculously, a new treatment became available right at the time he needed it to fight one of these infections. The treatment involved Dursley going to the Charleson Centre at the Royal Free every fortnight and using a nebuliser reminiscent of a fighter pilot's mask to breathe in a drug called pentamidine (or in some cases, as an alternative, Septrin) for half an hour. Wealthier countries with good access to HIV treatment seemed to be adopting this prophylactic treatment which worked in place of a healthy immune system, not to cure AIDS, but to prevent one of the extreme infections, pneumocystis carinii pneumonia (PCP), caused by fungal spores which remarkably failed to proliferate in the presence of these antibiotics. The treatment was life-saving, as a patient who developed PCP could die in less than a week.

However, I also sensed and feared a slow growing feeling among some government bodies and healthcare officials – and perhaps even some activists – that there was little point in keeping people alive with prophylaxis only for them to simply die six months later from advanced Kaposi's sarcoma or lymphoma. To us, however, prophylaxis was a lifeline, because it meant *time*: the chance to finish a job, see a show, go for dinner, have a laugh, achieve an ambition or fall in love. Above all, it allowed you to hold on to the hope that the cure was near, that it might be possible to live to see it, to receive it. It also meant that I was just that little bit further away from having to face an unspeakable reality.

The Charleson Centre was a new development at the Royal Free. Ian Charleson had been a patient and had died there. He was one of the first famous people to be brave enough to ask the media to speak honestly of his diagnosis when he passed. In his last weeks he played the role of Hamlet. His performance, described by Sir Ian McKellen as a 'near miracle', was overwhelming, as the character spoke lines about the meaning of life and death.[10] The Ian Charleson Centre is a fitting tribute to his memory.

\* \* \*

Since I had first started volunteering at the Westminster Hospital, I had been learning more and more about the vast array of manifestations, problems and complications that accompany such an infinitely diverse illness, and this new inhalation regime was one of the few advances that filled me with hope. It was a small triumph, giving rise to massive life improvement, and Dursley, who was always positive and cheerful, saw this new treatment as an affirmation of his concrete belief that a cure was just around the corner. During one session, just before Charlotte (one of his favourite nurses) slipped the nebuliser over his handsome face, which was slightly pale and no longer so robust and full, he fixed her with his enigmatic smile and repeated his mantra: 'I just need to fight it long enough for the cure, and I'll be fine.'

This nebuliser treatment had proven so effective that similar prophylactic treatments were now being expanded for some of the other horrendous opportunistic infections often seen in AIDS patients, such as toxoplasmosis. This fairly common infection can easily lie dormant in the brain. In AIDS patients it can reactivate, causing all kinds of dreadful issues, and often resulting in severe damage to the central nervous system. A drug called co-trimoxazole was used to prevent it recurring in patients unlucky enough to have developed it in the first place. It was a defining infection in the early days of AIDS, and we knew it was advisable to avoid eating undercooked or cured meat and unpasteurised products, as they often harboured the 'toxo' parasite. However, we had also picked up some less-than-complete information about it being spread by cats. While it is true that the parasite is very common and lives in the faeces of infected cats, I didn't really understand the minutiae of the disease, and, proving the point that 'a little knowledge is a dangerous thing', I developed a borderline phobia of cats getting anywhere near the boys.

Juan was allergic anyway, so generally he kept his distance from cats, but I vividly remember one occasion where I was left panic-stricken by a super-friendly kitty at a dinner party. Cats always seem to head straight to the person that wants to stroke them the least, and this one was no exception. It was very soon sidling what I thought was its potentially contaminated rear end in the direction of Dursley. Of course, nobody at the party even knew Dursley was ill, so I couldn't even explain why it absolutely mustn't go near him. Instead, I leaped up, saying, 'Oh, I must give your cat a cuddle,' grabbing the poor creature and entirely overreacting with enthusiasm at its gorgeousness, while at the same time shooting a knowing look at Dursley. Although I could see he was trying not to laugh at my hysteria, he also breathed a quiet sigh of relief and whispered, 'Thanks.'

Luckily, cats were relatively easy to avoid, but I felt as if Dursley and I were in a constant battle against vicious germs. I boiled water and overcooked food, terrified of cryptosporidium or salmonella; I disinfected surfaces to make sure there were no bugs hanging around; we gave a wide berth to anyone I passed on the street who had a trace of a cough, in case there was a chance of tuberculosis; and I tried to drive Dursley around as much as I could so he could save his energy. Altogether, I took it upon myself to ensure that everything was as safe as it could possibly be. I was certainly overcautious, probably because it was difficult for me to understand that the infections that could cause many of the complications of AIDS were probably already inside the body of the person affected. It was more often the case that, rather than being outside the body waiting to get in, the dangers were already lying dormant within the body, waiting for HIV to weaken the immune system and give them the chance to thrive. But I could only fight the germs on the outside. There was just one piece of advice I heard that I felt we could easily adhere to without making too many changes to our current lifestyle: 'Try to avoid handling pregnant sheep.'

Dursley and I regularly received all kinds of advice and updates from his doctors about different trials that were being conducted. I was really surprised the first time the doctor in charge, Dr Margaret Johnson, included me in one of Dursley's regular consultations. She opened the clinic room door and welcomed him in, before popping her head back round the door to me and saying, 'You can come in as well, if you like.' I had never expected to be allowed to share in the consultation, let alone spoken to by someone who understood the anxiety I felt because of the situation. This was my first indication that, in specialist units like the Charleson Centre, medical care was beginning to change in response to HIV and AIDS. Friends were being treated as family, and nurses like Charlotte and her wonderful colleague Sian were becoming our friends. However, outside of these units, people with AIDS were not always treated with the same compassion, to say the least.

# CHAPTER 14

*Absence of evidence is not evidence of absence.*

Carl Sagan (attrib.)

The end of 1991 saw Jae in his element (albeit briefly), in a new show called *The Hunting of the Snark*, written by Mike Batt, the composer of the Wombles' theme tune and the beautiful song 'Bright Eyes' for *Watership Down*. The show starred the unique comedian Kenny Everett, who was a well loved company member who had privately and bravely been battling HIV since 1989. The show was based on Lewis Carroll's nonsense poem about a crew of ten whose initials all begin with the letter B (for example the Bellman, the Banker and the Beaver), who are hunting for a fictional creature. No one really understood the show, and the response from the audience was sometimes luke-warm – with the exception of one night when the entire audience was sold out to Mensa, that small percentage of the population with an IQ of over 140. That night, the crowd laughed, gasped, shrieked and applauded loudly – they really loved the whole thing.

The title of the song that rather forebodingly ended the first half was called 'Dancing Towards Disaster', and that of course was a gift for the critics – in fact, it was exactly what Jack Tinker of the *Daily Mail* said in his review: 'Dancing Towards Real Disaster With The Snark',[11] deeply disappointing the whole company. One hundred years earlier, the poem itself had received reviews from critics that had simply said they found it strange. Personally, I enjoyed the show, and we were very proud of Jae, who remains the only musical director in the West End to have actually sung the opening number, which he did dressed in a blue and gold jacket while conducting a fifty-piece orchestra from the stage.

During those weeks of *Snark*, as we called it, Dursley and I spent a lot of time going to the movies or seeing shows, and really becoming kindred spirits. Sometimes, Dursley would suddenly get unnervingly exhausted and need to lie down. Where else, then, but in Jae's dressing room? It was a long way up the stairs to the room, and Dursley would lie down the moment we got in there. He seemed to be getting fevers. Jae would come up from the show and find me at his mirror and Dursley sleeping on the floor. Clearly something was wrong.

I ran through the list of possibilities of potential illnesses in my head – a fever could mean pretty much anything, from a minor infection to something more sinister. So, once more, we headed to the Royal Free Hospital.

When we arrived, one of the lovely nurses, Debbie, who was always so reassuring, made sure we saw a doctor quite quickly. Much to Dursley's chagrin, the decision was made to admit him to the ward for some tests. His reluctance was unsurprising – once in the clutches of the hospital, he would face a barrage of tests: X-rays on the lungs, a colonoscopy, an endoscopy, cystoscopy – all kinds of '-oscopies' – to get to the root of the problem.

We sat together in the waiting room, waiting for a bed to be found. I tried to chat normally, but he was too tired. Eventually, they got him a bed on the Garrett Anderson ward, and he made himself comfortable. The nurses explained that they would keep him in and run some tests.

'He'll certainly be in for a few days,' the doctor told us. Then his pager beeped, and with an 'Excuse me,' he hurried away.

Worried, I went to sit beside Dursley. It crossed my mind that I was lucky I was not working right now, because I was free to sit here with him as much as possible – but I was also due to fly to Paris the following week to see Juan, so I was praying that Dursley would be OK and out of hospital in a few days.

I drove up to Hampstead each morning, occasionally crossing paths with Niko, who knew that he was on the ward again. The Garrett Anderson ward was on the eleventh floor of the 1970s cruciform tower block that is the Royal Free Hospital, and this was the ward that cared for the most poorly AIDS patients. Its position near the top of the building meant impressive panoramic views over elegant Hampstead Village and the Heath. An apartment in such a block would have cost a small fortune. If I had been able to lean far enough out of the windows I would have been able to see the Pink Palace, and I longed for my old home.

During my visits, I used the visitors' kitchen there to make Dursley's meals, because the hospital food was worse than awful. I was told the pre-packed meals arrived on the ward after being brought in from somewhere in Milton Keynes and were then put into regeneration ovens. They stank of sour cabbage, insipid potatoes and milky custard, tinged with some sort of low-grade fish – the smell reminded me of horrible school dinners. Good food can make such a difference to a person's mood, and I wanted Dursley's mind to be as strong and positive as possible to help him get better.

The kitchen itself was a place where friends and family found solidarity and comfort. Everybody there was helping someone with AIDS or was a patient themselves. Their stories were always interesting, and often tragic. I met a lovely and brave lady there called Rebecca Handel, who had helped to set up CWAC (Children With AIDS Charity) after pretty much being ignored by all the existing charities because she was a white, Jewish, middle-class woman who did not fit into the usual AIDS stereotypes. She was trying to make life a little easier for the even smaller minority groups: CWAC were there to provide some practical and emotional support to children with AIDS and their families. Rebecca herself had become HIV positive after a blood transfusion when she was pregnant with her second child, Bonnie, before blood was routinely screened for the virus. Both Rebecca and Bonnie eventually died of AIDS. CWAC continued its work for some years before closing down in 2014.

When visiting a hospital under usual circumstances, one might glance into the side wards and see any kind of person receiving medical attention: perhaps a large woman on a drip, or small man with his leg in a cast; perhaps an old man looking bruised, or a young girl packing her bags to leave for home. A perfect cross-section of society. But as I walked down the long corridor, I glanced around me and took in the disturbing similarity of all the patients. Emaciated young men, gaunt and pallid, reminiscent

Cabaret for Dursley's 29th birthday party – the theme was 'The Famous Ladies of the Musicals'. Jae was Dolly Levi, Dursley was Fantine, David Raven was (as always) the irreplaceable Maisie Trollette, and I'm *supposed* to be Judy Garland!

Dursley looking gorgeous

Jae and me, drinking champagne and waiting for the party to start

Sister and me, posing like the statues at the Palace of Versailles

*Les Misérables* Cares committee, clockwise from second left: Anthony Lyn, me, Shaun Kerrison, Jon Osbaldeston and Nigel Richards, alongside two of our *Les Mis* colleagues, Tony Rouse and Andrew Robbins

With Derek and Jae having a 'camp' laugh in Gran Canaria –
wigs are always a winner!

Derek and me on the night of the *Phantom* Ball, organised by
the *Phantom* cast for West End Cares

Mum and Dad in the early days – on holiday in Italy (I think) in the fifties

Mum and Dad arriving at the St Pancras Hotel, which was hired and styled as Olde London for the *Oliver!* opening-night party

Russell and me in the eighties, home from college and out to dinner in Swansea

Jae, me, Dursley, Mum and Dad on the London Underground, hired specially by Cameron Mackintosh to take us to the *Oliver!* opening-night party

Arriving at Death Valley National Park – one of the few photos
of the four of us together on our California road trip

Juan next to his beloved Barbra Streisand

Juan and me visiting his brother, Nelson (behind the camera), in Amsterdam, one week after Dayton, Ohio: the total opposite!

Last to leave Joe Allen's: Juan, me, Jac, Roger from the Youth Theatre, Peg, Dursley, Dad and Mum

Dursley and me on the beach in Cape Town

Colin Bell as the long-suffering Dreen, making a fabulous appearance
at Jae's birthday. She is, on this occasion, escorted by Robert Jon.

Inspired by *It's a Sin*, the WestEnders launch our charity single for the Sussex Beacon (of which I am proud to be a patron). Left to right: Stephen Weller, Jae, Linda Jarvis, me with Adrian Grove behind, Frances Fry and Jon Osbaldeston

Russell and me holding a National Television Award in 2021, the night *It's a Sin* won Best New Drama

of prisoners of war – not POWs, though, but PWAs. It was easy to feel weighed down by the sadness, but I tried to see the real people, not the patients.

On the left was an incredibly fragile yet beautifully manicured queen, dressed in a pale lemon-coloured track suit, with lacquered hair that could have stayed still in a hurricane. He lay on the bed with a huge gold chain around his neck so heavy it barely allowed him to lift his head from the pillow. I smiled at the man who was sitting devotedly at his bedside, just as he had been every day. The bed on the right was taken by a willowy, slightly older, elegant-looking man with soft blond hair, who was sitting up and reading. On the right, opposite Dursley's bed was a young boy, Ben, very dark and pretty, in his early twenties. He seemed to be finding it hard to move or sit up to eat or drink. It was difficult to see him struggle, and I politely said hello as I passed, while thinking, *Oh my God, he looks terrible*. I felt guiltily thankful that Dursley was not that ill.

As I approached Dursley's bed, I saw it was empty. I felt a flush of panic, but the willowy man to the right spoke up and said, with a strong South African accent, 'They took Paul for a test, he'll be back now now.' I smiled to myself: this is the South African equivalent to the Welsh, 'He'll be back now in a minute.' The doctors, nurses and everyone else on the ward called Dursley Paul, of course. It was the name he had used on his original test, and now it seemed he was stuck with it.

'Thank you, I'll just wait then,' I said.

'I'm Michael,' he told me. We chatted, and he revealed that he lived between London and Cape Town. His surname was Smuts, a famous Afrikaans name.

About twenty minutes later, Dursley arrived back on the ward.

'I had to have a biopsy on this swollen gland,' he told me from the trolley. 'They wanted to check it.'

This had been done with a 'fine needle', he said. It didn't sound so fine to me, and I winced as he gave a graphic description of the needle going in. 'It didn't hurt,' he said. 'But they put a long needle in and sucked something out.' Perhaps the results might tell us why he was so feverish.

I asked Dursley if he had spoken to the other boys on the ward much. Of course, he already knew everything about them, as he had been busy charming them all and gossiping away.

Manicured queen Barry was very rich and lived in a detached house in Wimbledon. He was always accompanied by his partner Rod, a hairdresser. Willowy Michael was a refined man who ran a successful textile business. We didn't know much about the young boy, except that his name was Ben. We thought he had some sort of brain infection, but we weren't sure. Toxoplasmosis? Whatever it was, it wasn't looking good for him.

Our chat was cut short by a commotion in one of the private rooms further down the corridor. I could hear lots of activity and people crying. Clearly, the situation was bad, and I again felt guiltily relieved that it was them, not us. We took a moment to silently acknowledge the elephant in the room, then carried on talking.

It was a Friday afternoon, and I was anxious because Dursley had already been there all week, and now the weekend was looming, when not much was done in the way of procedures. But at 4pm, a doctor came on to the ward. You can always spot a consultant: a tall, distinguished man, with glasses and a head of curly hair, he walked towards us with a nurse and asked if he could talk to Paul James. We hadn't seen this doctor before. He had an air of authority and gravitas about him, and I suddenly felt my stomach turn. He sat by the bed, and the nurse closed the curtains.

'We're sorry to tell you this, Paul, but the biopsy has revealed a lymphoma,' the doctor said, without preamble. 'A B-cell lymphoma – a high-grade malignant B-cell lymphoma. I'll write it down for you.'

He handed us those unforgettable words on a small scrap of paper.

I remember feeling numb, and not sure if I was actually thinking at all. Lymphoma: that was cancer, wasn't it? The doctor carried on talking. It seemed that they had a plan: they would start chemotherapy immediately after the weekend, and take it from there. The nurse asked me some questions. I don't recall much of what she said or what I answered, but I do remember these words: 'We think a patient would expect to perhaps survive a couple of months under the circumstances of such low immunity.'

In that precise moment, all I could think about was Dursley's mum.

My heart was broken. I was in a complete panic. *Fucking hell*. I had started this day expecting him to be alright, and now I was being told he had eight weeks to live. I was determined not to cry in front of Dursley, but when it was time to leave, I was in tears before I even got to the lift. A doctor who I recognised – and didn't much like – stepped into the lift just after me. He was not a regular doctor in the Charleson Centre, and I'd found him quite abrupt during our few interactions this week.

'Look at it like this,' he said. 'It'll be easier to tell his parents. Anyone can die of a lymphoma.'

Just a few blunt words, and all hope was gone.

★　　★　　★

When I got home, I was distraught. I was trying to explain everything to Jae, who was just as upset as I was. We discussed how on earth Dursley's parents were going to cope with it all, and it was a late night of many tears. The nurse had handed me a leaflet about infections due to AIDS, and I read it over and over. It detailed a list of possible infections, what they were and how they would be treated. The last on the list was lymphoma, from which there was no recovery. I kept thinking, *Why, oh, why did he have to have the last thing on the list?*

I didn't sleep. With the dawn, I headed across London, back to the Royal Free.

As I walked up to floor eleven, then along the endless corridor and across to Dursley's bed, I braced myself to be understanding and caring. I was ready to be supportive. As I arrived, South African Michael greeted me, then he turned to Dursley and said, 'Good luck.'

Dursley was out of bed and taking off his red dressing gown. He seemed to be packing to leave.

'What's happening?' I asked, confused.

'I'm going for a treatment,' he said. 'It's all organised. I'm off to Tunbridge Wells. I spoke to Niko yesterday. It's a new oxygenation therapy – I'm heading there right now.' He looked pale and thin, and the lump on his neck was large and visible, like an old-fashioned image of mumps.

He was determined, so I didn't say anything other than telling him to take care and that I would see him when he got back. I knew there was no point in being negative about it, and I didn't want to be, but I couldn't help thinking it seemed like such a waste of his precious energy. He was adamant that the treatment would give him a boost, ready for the chemotherapy. I was left wondering how he could have been this proactive with such a bleak diagnosis. He'd organised all this during a single evening, which I had spent sitting at home crying and reading a leaflet. Once again, I marvelled at his spirit. We left the hospital at the same time, with him heading off for his treatment and me heading home.

On Monday morning, I returned to the ward. Dursley had had his treatment on Saturday, and then on Sunday, he'd had a visit from Gudrun, the therapist. He told me he and Gudrun had chatted about the treatment, which she had recommended for him. He loved Gudrun and really believed the treatments were very important. He seemed bright and positive when the doctors arrived, bringing with them the prospect of chemo-therapy. I, on the other hand, was not feeling at all positive: it was as though they were coming with a bullet to load the gun.

The doctor examined Dursley, and then actually looked quite pleased. He stood back and said something neither of us were expecting: 'Paul, I think we will wait a few more days before we start chemo. The lump in your neck seems a little smaller – it may be regressing. We'll consider a treatment plan for the end of the week, but let's look at it again tomorrow.' He nodded goodbye and left the room, leaving me feeling dumbstruck. Whatever I had imagined, it certainly wasn't that.

Tuesday came and the lump seemed smaller again. Within a few days, it had all but disappeared. The chemotherapy was cancelled, and nothing was to happen until there were more blood tests. Dursley said he felt better, and he was certainly hungry. All of a sudden there didn't seem to be anything wrong with him. He was perky and laughing, and there were no signs of the fever that had brought him to the hospital in the first place.

By Friday, exactly a week after he'd been told he could expect to survive only a couple of months, he was leaving the ward behind and planning supper with friends. Not only had he defied medical science, he had changed the atmosphere on that small ward to one of hope and energy. There was no real medical explanation, no scientific proof the oxygenation was behind his miraculous recovery, and to me it was mystery known only to the universe; but Dursley had achieved the impossible and had, like Lazarus, been given another chance. Perhaps it was this remarkable triumph that gave us a special bond with the other guys on the ward. We all became friends, because of that one week. We exchanged phone numbers with Michael and Barry, and Michael kept insisting that Dursley should come out to South Africa and get some sunshine, if he ever felt the need to recuperate. Barry and Rod invited us to their elegant detached home in Wimbledon Village, which had a beautiful garden, an impressive automated sprinkler system and an indoor swimming pool. As we all said our goodbyes, we could all feel that it was the most unbelievable end to an unbelievable week. On this occasion, everyone had made it out of hospital, and even Ben seemed to be holding his own. It was almost like a normal ward, where people recover and don't come back. Indeed, it seemed like all the nurses had a spring in their steps as Dursley packed his bags to leave for the second time that week.

From the moment that Dursley became well, I felt that it was vitally important that we do as much as we could. I was so happy: Dursley's amazing recovery not only meant more time together, but also removed the need to worry his parents about the situation for the time being.

But there was another big issue that had been on my mind, although I had been pushing it away. I had a ticket booked to fly to Paris for a very important event.

# CHAPTER 15

*A person is a product of their dreams. So make sure you dream
great dreams. And then try and live your dream.*

Maya Angelou

After a nerve-wracking week with Dursley, my latest trip to Paris
was everything I could have wished for. On this occasion, I had
made the journey to see the first French translation of the British
production of *Les Misérables*. It was produced by Cameron Mackintosh, and featured none other than my beloved Juan, who had
been cast as the young revolutionary Feuilly. I was so excited both
to see Juan – and to see *Les Mis* – that I practically ran off the
plane when it landed at Charles de Gaulle airport.

When I got to the city, the sun was shining. I headed straight
off to meet Juan's boyfriend, the elegant and smart Frederic. He
told me we would be able to see Juan briefly before the show,
but it was going to be a busy and thrilling night. I went with Fred
to their apartment to get all glammed up for the evening ahead.

'Shall we get a taxi then, Fred?' I asked, when I had finished getting ready.

'No, no. I will drive!' he replied.

I happily got in the passenger seat, but as we got closer to the theatre, I wondered why on earth Fred had decided to drive. There was absolutely nowhere to park, except for one minuscule space that looked like it would barely fit a bicycle.

'Fred, it'll be impossible to get in there,' I said, as I watched him prepare to reverse into the minute parking space.

'*Non*!' he said, waving his hand. 'It is EASY!' He proceeded to edge his way in. His method of parking involved slowly bumping the cars on either end to make room. I squealed with each bump. I had never seen anything like it.

Eventually, and in fits of laughter, we walked arm in arm into the Mogador Theatre, which was full of the buzz of opening night.

The evening was sensational – I almost burst with pride when I saw Juan step out on stage dressed in a tailored blue brocade costume. His character sang some of the really touching moments on the barricade, including: 'Drink with me to days gone by.' He was brilliant – it was definitely his finest moment onstage. I knew what he had been through to get to this point, and as they sang the finale, it was impossible not to weep. I knew that time was not on his side, but he absolutely shone. He was in his element – and no one in the cast had even the slightest idea he was unwell. It was wonderful.

This magnificent show was followed by an equally magnificent party, which took place right on the Champs-Élysées. Champagne flowed all night, food was laid out from every region of France, from Normandy to Nice, and ultraviolet lights shone across a huge *Les Misérables* sculpture. Juan was already there when we arrived, and he rushed up to give me a huge hug.

'Did you love it, Jilly? Isn't all this fantastic? I am sooo excited. *Apúrate, mijita*' – hurry up, sweetie – 'we must have champagne!'

That evening was a particularly special one for me, not just because I got to see my best friend onstage, but because my love affair with *Les Misérables* goes back a long way.

Back in 1986, I had been cast as Candy Starr in a production of *One Flew Over the Cuckoo's Nest* at the Swansea Grand. At the same time, there were rehearsals going on for Alan Bennett's *Habeas Corpus*, and one day in the green room, I overheard one of the cast saying excitedly, 'I have an audition for the Royal Shakespeare Company – they're putting on a new musical.'

Of course, we were all immediately interested. 'What is it? When's it happening? Who's directing? What's it about?'

Nobody knew much about it, except that it was based on a novel by the French author Victor Hugo, a book he'd written about life in early nineteenth-century France. It involved the trials of an ex-convict, anti-monarchism and religion. Surely a pretty dreary subject for a musical – hardly 'tits and teeth', it was decided. 'It'll never run!' people told each other.

After that, we didn't hear much else, until the news broke that the show had run for an incredible five hours on its first night at the Barbican, and that, with mixed reviews, it was planning a transfer to the Palace Theatre. Intrigued, I bought the cast recording on a double cassette, read the lyrics on the tiny inset booklet, and fell in love with the music almost instantaneously. I couldn't stop listening to that little cassette, playing it ad nauseam to my boyfriend at the time: tall, handsome Paul, whom I had met in pantomime the previous Christmas and was still seeing. I'd had a lot of fun with him during the season, but had had a few problems at my digs in a rather smart district of Leeds. The landlord, Basil, had strict sets of rules, including no guests in the rooms. In conjunction with his career as a famous theatrical landlord, Basil had been an award-winning window dresser at Gladys Vollan's Curtain Shop in Vicar Lane, Leeds. His home was pristine, with the air of glamour from a bygone era. This was appropriate, as he had known Ivor Novello, and his love for music and theatricals was obvious: he was a true British original. This did not stop me disobeying the no-guests rule, however, and Paul often sneaked in to my room. In the morning, Paul's cue to leave was when I was in the bathroom (trying to be sparse with the loo roll, another of Basil's rules). Paul would listen out, and once he heard me break into a song from *Les Mis*, he knew it meant he had a clear route out of the property, avoiding the eagle eyes of Basil. Maybe Paul didn't like the music as much as I did, and we did eventually split up, but my infatuation with *Les Misérables* has lasted to this day.

By the nineties, this new type of musical theatre had become the hottest ticket in the West End. They were sung-through high dramas with sweeping scores, large orchestras and powerful singing and acting. These Leviathans, from *Jesus Christ Superstar* to *Miss Saigon*, didn't close after a few years, as so many had done in the past. Instead, they ran for longer than any shows had run before, thanks not to the critics, but to the power of theatregoers and word of mouth.

The musical was in its sixth year when I got my first audition, and I was unsuccessful. 'There is nothing for you this time,' the casting director said, 'but please come back in six months – we'll be recasting more parts.'

I was thrilled: within the six months since my first audition it had all happened for Juan, and I felt this was my chance to finally make it to the West End. I loved the show, and I knew I was right for it: no dancing, just singing incredible music and telling passionate, exciting stories. I was a woman on a mission, determined to do everything in my power to get a part in the show of my dreams, so I went to one of the top singing teachers for West End performers, Mary Hammond. The lessons were expensive, but I didn't care. I practised as much as I physically could, strengthening my voice each day and really, really working at it.

For the next six months, I practised day in and day out, even to the extent of taking Dursley's keys in the middle of an afternoon out with a whole group of people and disappearing to do my singing exercises in his flat before rejoining them later. The auditions were happening, and I was ready. I bumped into the brilliant resident director Matt Ryan in Joe Allen one night (where else?), and we chatted for a while. I told him about my plans to audition for the show, and how excited I was.

'Tell your agent to call and get you on the list tomorrow,' he responded, smiling. I was over the moon, and raced to relay the news to my then-agent, along with anyone else who would listen.

The next day, I went to the London Welsh Centre (one of a number of such spaces in London used by theatre companies as an audition and rehearsal space) and sat waiting with other hopefuls in the corridor. This is always one of the most nervewracking moments of any audition, because you can hear the people before you singing their hearts out, and no matter what they do, you always think they sound amazing. After what felt like a lifetime, I was called into the room, and once again faced with the daunting panel of casting directors. Shielding my nerves with a smile, I sang 'As Long As He Needs Me'. Thankfully, it went well. They recalled me, and this time I sang again two songs. I know it was one of my best auditions ever. I was called back for a third time, now with music to learn from the show – the parts were 'whore' and 'old crone'. *Glorious, couldn't be better*, I thought. I was seriously excited.

I worked so hard to perfect the music with Jae, feeling lucky to live with a musical theatre director, and planned to act the parts of 'whore' and 'old crone' for all I was worth. Derek came round for coffee and said, 'You'll not need make-up for that, darlin'.' We laughed, and he regaled us with a few stories from *Starlight Express*, where he was now 'depping' in the booth for some of the other singers and loving it.

I desperately hoped it would be a case of third time lucky – and it was. I got another recall, some more music and had to prepare for some direction and improvisation. Now I was seriously nervous: including my very first audition, this would be my fifth recall, so I knew I was close. I was terrified that the nerves would get the better of me. I was wracking my brain to think of ways to manage my rocketing stress levels when Dursley mentioned he had booked a flotation tank appointment – a treatment that, as well as allegedly boosting your immune system, was supposed to be great for destressing. So, when Dursley went for his session, I tagged along. Inside a small room in the treatment centre, there was a tank that looked a bit like a small shipping container. I climbed in and closed the lid. Inside, there was soft lighting, relaxing music and warm, thick, shallow salty water that smelled like the sea. It was a weird and wonderful experience. At first I wasn't sure about it, as some cold drips landed on me from the condensation, but after a while, I began to relax. It was impossible to sink in the water – it was like the Dead Sea – so all you had to do was relax and float. I fell into a deep meditation and had what felt like a sci-fi experience, as if I was floating through outer space.

I will never know if this helped with my final recall, where I performed with all my soul as a tortured and angry peasant, but three days later, the phone rang and I was offered the job.

I was about to start rehearsals. It was four months since I had been in Paris with Juan, and he was just as thrilled for me as I was for him. We were united by our shows, and although we hadn't been in a production together since college, doing the same show in different cities was the next best thing. We could gossip about the same problems and who was doing what, and we were linked by our shared love of the show. It was so nice to have something current and exciting to think about that was nothing to do with the virus.

Although I was glad that Juan and I could talk about something other than AIDS, I was also relieved to discover that Dursley was becoming more comfortable about sharing his status with others, which meant he gave me the go-ahead to share the truth that he had the virus with Juan. Juan was deeply upset by this news, but still didn't feel ready to tell Dursley his own truth. It was not Dursley himself; it was the fear of being labelled as unfit for work and of being faced with stigma and fear every time he went to the theatre. Dursley was now happy and comfortable in his job at the production office, and because he trusted people he worked with, he began to let his guard down as he described his incredible recovery from AIDS-related lymphoma. His colleagues really supported and admired him. With the weight of secrecy off his shoulders, he was feeling well – both mentally and physically – and seemed to be thriving. As ever, his perseverance through hardship and his sheer love for life made me love him even more.

Feeling grateful that I'd landed a job in my dream show, and was surrounded with wonderful friends who were living their lives to the full, I marvelled how precious life was. Wasting time became anathema to me. I learned how important it was to take every opportunity life throws at you; to make the most of every day. That realisation has never left me.

# CHAPTER 16

*We are a family, like a giant tree*
*Branching out to the sky*
*We are a family, we are so much more than just you and I.*

Henry Krieger, *Dreamgirls*

Rehearsals for *Les Misérables* began in early January 1992. Our director, Matt Ryan, was what is known as a resident director. Along with the company manager, the resident director acts as a go-between from the cast to the management, giving structure to what is, after all, a huge money-making venture as well as a thrilling piece of entertainment. This is a job in a long-running show that takes a special kind of person: a leader, an organiser, a diplomat and a creative talent, as well as someone who loves the show and cares about standards. They have to navigate the moods, the insecurities, the discipline, the dramas and the complicated lives of the people on whom the show ultimately rests: the cast and the crew.

As part of the cast, learning the music was wonderful. In my case, it was more about exploring the harmonies and perfecting the rhythms, because I certainly knew the tunes already. For me, the real revelation was the sheer amount of work that was involved in giving the show its required depth and unique style. We read the book and improvised from that for weeks: discussing and exploring how life might have been for the sex workers and the destitute, and the shame that may have been felt by those forced into situations they might find degrading. We tried to understand the desperation of those in poverty, and we tried to identify with the sick and forgotten in society at the time. Considering the ways in which my dear friends were being ostracised due to their illness, I felt it was possible I understood this more than most. To this day, whenever I pass a homeless person – of which there are many in London – the lyrics 'and the righteous hurry past' ring through my head.

During these rehearsals, I became close with one of the other cast members. He was a young, fresh-faced boy named Jon, with an acid wit and a beautiful baritone voice. He spoke with refined received pronunciation – unusual for a lad from Wigan – and possessed a rather grand surname: Osbaldeston. Jon and I always found ourselves chatting and laughing. He was six years my junior, but, he told me, I was so enthusiastic in rehearsals he'd assumed *Les Mis* must be my first show.

'No, darling,' I responded. 'I've been touring for years.' Besides, if we were talking about enthusiasm, Jon would definitely win the prize. I will always remember the time when he was so energised he ran forward with a battle cry, straight off the end of the stage and into the orchestra pit. He wasn't hurt, but he did smash a very expensive cello.

As well as Jon, I became very close with a few other cast members. Without even realising it, through sharing so much time, fun and creativity, we really did become like a family. Due to the very nature of the job, friendships in a show are made fast and become very intense very quickly. The times between entrances when you can chat, complain, gossip and laugh are times of bonding, and the friendships I forged there in *Les Misérables* have been lifelong.

Making such close friends in rehearsals added to an already unforgettable experience, and I cherished every moment. I phoned home and reported each day in excited detail to my mum and dad, telling them how happy I was. I knew they would be coming up to London to see my opening night.

Finally, after seven weeks of hard work – plus the technical rehearsal, which involved us getting used to the revolving floor – it was time. Any opening night in the theatre is full of a frantic, busy, super-glamorous buzz. People rush around, carrying wigs and costumes, and shouts of 'break a leg' are heard everywhere. Cards arrive with scribbled well-wishes from loved ones, and they adorn the dressing rooms, stuck up on mirrors along with other good luck tokens. There are hugs and kisses, lots of 'It will all be marvellous, darling,' lots of nerves, and message after message on the Tannoy calling people to the stage door to collect champagne or flowers. At the Palace on my opening night, I had bouquets arriving all day. It was one of the loveliest experiences of my career to date.

At about 6pm, after the technical rehearsal in costume in the afternoon, I was called to the stage door. Our stage doorkeepers were the legendary ginger-haired, diminutive Pearl and her colleague Dean, who was younger and rather handsome. So, the voices that spoke to us over the Tannoy each day were the voices of Pearl and Dean (you couldn't make it up). Thinking I was about to receive yet more beautiful flowers, I rushed to the stage door – and stopped in amazement. It was Juan! He had taken a couple of days of holiday, and there he was, smiling his gorgeous smile and shouting, 'Surprise, Jilly! I am here for your West End star performance.'

I couldn't believe it. Here we were again, united by the thrill of it all. I hugged him, cried a bit and shrieked a lot.

Then Dursley came to the theatre from Cameron's office and called in to see me. 'I'll watch the show as a representative of the office,' he said, with a laugh and hug. 'That way, I don't have to pay.' He handed me a big bunch of blue and yellow flowers from the flower stall on Seven Dials, always his favourite, then gave Juan a big hug and rushed off.

'Darling, you look gorgeous,' Juan shouted after him.

I felt a wave of sadness, as I knew what was on his mind – it was the first time Juan had seen him since hearing of Dursley's diagnosis. I pushed away any sad thoughts and forced myself into 'make the most of the moment' mode.

My parents arrived then, providing a perfect distraction, with my mum dressed in all her finery (she loved an excuse to wear her favourite jacket, which was adorned with gold sequins). She'd recently had her ears pierced after wearing clip-ons all her life. Now in her sixties, she was thriving and loving it.

'I don't get much chance to dress up going to get the faggots in Neath market,' she laughed.

I will always remember my mum telling me that the most exciting nights in her life were special occasions in the theatre with us, watching shows and concerts and sharing the excitement of opening nights. She loved it. After all my parents' support for me, I was delighted and emotional to be able to give something back.

The one person missing was Jae. He was on tour with a show

called *The Magic of the Musicals*, and was furious, as he loved opening nights – but he sent me a beautiful card and a crystal decanter engraved with the date and the name of the show. I had been to so many of his opening nights, and I knew how completely our lives were intertwined and how much we cared. I really wished he could have been in London.

So, there I was: after ten years as a professional actor, I was appearing in the West End for the first time, and in a show that was certain to run for a long time. This was the first of many firsts. It was the first time I could do a week's work and go home to my real home; the first time I could take time off sick without losing money; and the first time I could guarantee there would be a standing ovation every single night. I was in what was arguably the most successful show in the West End, in one of the most iconic theatres.

The Palace Theatre, which was the home of *Les Mis* for so many years, is – aesthetically – one of the best theatres in London. It is a glorious tribute to Victorian glamour. The auditorium, which seats fourteen hundred, is the epitome of grandeur: red plush seating, gilded walls and a vast proscenium arch. Below the theatre itself runs the River Fleet, and you could hear it running right in the bowels of the theatre, beneath the wooden mechanisms of the barricade. I always felt this unseen underground river added an incredible mystic dimension to the building – that, and the talk of the ghosts of Ivor Novello and the ballerina with no name, who were said to sit watching each show from the circle in the seats put aside by Andrew Lloyd Webber and Cameron Mackintosh. All this added to the sense of history, and made me immensely proud to be working in this remarkable theatre. Despite the fact it had no air conditioning, which could make it unbearably hot in the summer, I fell completely in love with it.

However, the Palace was certainly much more beautiful than it was practical, which meant that the situation backstage was pretty much the antithesis of how smoothly things seemed to go onstage. The dressing rooms were old-fashioned and shabby, but full of character and very cosy, with windows that looked out on to the lights of Shaftesbury Avenue and made you feel that you were in the beating heart of theatreland. The downside was that they were across three floors, with only two single toilets, shared by (counting wardrobe, wigs and crew) at least fifty people. In the corridor there were two freestanding plastic shower cubicles next to the payphone, and, as you got to know people, you could tell who was taking a shower – not just by any singing coming from the cubicle, but by looking to see whose feet were visible beneath the shower curtain while you were on the phone. The running water in the taps came from tanks, which were rumoured to be filled with lead – and the occasional dead mouse or pigeon – so, of course, no one wanted to drink it.

During the performance, some of the most chaotic moments were caused by the many costume changes. I had thirteen. Most of these took place in said dressing rooms, which involved climbing multiple flights of stairs, multiple times. If you were lucky and happened to get offstage quite quickly, you could grab a place in the scary, creaky old lift, which could take six of us at a push. It had brass accordion sliding doors and frequently shuddered, sometimes threatening to stop entirely, filling us with the fear of missing a cue and weighing up whether it was better to dive out and run up yet another flight of stairs. Our (very) 'quick changes' were set below the stage. This wasn't much better than scaling endless stairs, though, because on a Saturday night, men outside in the street would often decide not to bother finding a toilet, and would instead use the insets outside the theatre walls as their urinals. By the time we were changing after the barricade scene into our finery for the wedding, we would be greeted by the pungent aroma of piss as it leaked down the walls. On a hot night, to put it bluntly, it stank.

Sometimes we liked to moan, but of course we loved it all, really: the camaraderie, the constant excitement, the legacy of the theatre itself. It made me very happy to pass through the stage door each night, above which was engraved in the stone: 'The world's greatest artistes have passed and will pass through these doors.' I loved telling friends to meet me or leave me a message at the stage door. I felt like I was part of it all, and that success was mine, at last.

Each night I travelled home on the tube from Leicester Square to Balham. I could always be sure of bumping into other West End performers and having someone to chat to on the way home. One night, though, I met someone much more interesting: Rafael. Not a West End performer, but an extremely pretty Spanish man with big brown eyes. He invited me to go for a drink, and I thought, *Why the hell not?*

We went to a bar in Balham. Much to my disappointment, he was the perfect gentleman and walked me home – only to appear two days later at my flat with a bottle of champagne and an invitation to lunch at his place. I found myself at his flat in Battersea, where he served me a delicious lunch. Over lunch I had made clear my concerns over safe sex. Rafael had been very understanding so I was happy and excited. Of course, eating a large meal at lunchtime makes you tired, so we went to the bedroom to lie down. We exchanged a few kisses, and just as some clothing had been removed I looked over his shoulder to see water dripping through the ceiling. The drops quickly became a deluge, and suddenly what I'd been thinking might be a fabulous and daring experience for me was interrupted by two firemen bursting in, trying to find the source of the flood. I grabbed my clothes and dashed out between what seemed like half the London Fire Brigade. A cute fireman handed me my bra. I never saw Rafael again – he went back to Spain. Adios, mi amor.

My role in *Les Mis* was that of 'swing'. People outside the business might not be too familiar with the concept, but essentially it's an ensemble role that also involves acting as understudy or cover to every (female, in my case) member of the cast. You can be called at any time to play any role and you need to be at the theatre every night in case of any trouble. In a long run like *Les Mis*, people get ill, go on holiday or change roles to cover one of the leading parts. Pretty much every night, someone – and sometimes more than one person – would be missing from the show, so the swings covered everything. There were four swings in total, and two of us – me and Shaun Kerrison – were new to that contract. We worked together as a team: all of us had learned the entire show, and we were ready to jump in wherever and whenever we were needed. Some performers don't enjoy the stress of being a swing, but Shaun and I found the challenge exhilarating: we both felt privileged and loved every second.

Six months into my contract, two new swings joined the cast, one of whom was Anthony Lyn. He was thickset with a head of dark, curly hair, a very dry sense of humour, and a bright twinkle in his eye. He was full of drive and energy, with a huge passion for his work. About three weeks into his contract, Anthony and I were talking in my dressing room. Aside from the show, we found we had more than a little in common. Not only did we both come from South Wales, we'd both been part of the West Glamorgan Youth Theatre (although at different times). But what most united us in spirit and gave us a special kind of closeness was the secrets we both were keeping. We realised, after a while, that we both had dear friends who had AIDS – and that we had both been sworn to secrecy. I had not told anyone about Juan, nor for a long time about Dursley, and it was the same for Anthony. It was the root of some strange conversations. He had a friend who had recently tested positive and begged him not to say anything, and another who was already ill. We said 'my friend' each time, instead of actually using a name, and were careful to skirt around any issues that might identify who a person actually was. In this way, we were able to share some of the burden with one another without betraying our friends' confidences. It cannot be under-estimated what a comfort it was to me and Anthony to be able to talk about our fears for our friends, and the endless hospital visits. Before long, Anthony took to greeting me by saying under his breath, 'How is it going today, Nurse Nalder?', and that always made me laugh. Being able to laugh together, even for a moment, made all of it so much more bearable.

# CHAPTER 17

_To move, to breathe, to fly, to float_
_To gain all while you give,_
_To roam the roads of lands remote,_
_To travel is to live._

Hans Christian Andersen

All around the world, _Les Misérables_ was doing incredible business – except, that is, in the city that inspired it. After only eight months, the lights went out on the Mogador Theatre, and the show closed in 1992. Nevertheless, it passed through my mind how brilliant it was that Juan had managed to complete his entire contract, and I was also glad that he would now have some free time to recuperate and focus on his health.

By the time _Les Mis_ finished in Paris, I was quite a few months into my own contract. For the first time in my life as an actor, _Les Misérables_ had given me something incredible: something extremely rare in our profession, something so exciting and unusual that I lay awake at night making plans because of it. Not worldwide recognition or stardom or film contracts; not the chance to meet royalty. It was nothing of the sort. This rare and thrilling wonder was holiday pay. For the first time in ten years, I could have a holiday and not lose money, miss out on a job or have to worry about overspending and running out of cash on my return. I was over the moon.

Determined to make the most of it, I spoke to Dursley and he came up with an idea. Juan was not working, Jae was about to finish his tour of *Magic of the Musicals*, and Dursley could book time off work. We could all afford a holiday, and he thought we should all take one and go to America. This idea was at the very least questionable – and it was possibly downright stupid. However, our little family agreed that it was where we wanted to go, and nothing was going to stop us. It seemed such an exciting place, with so much to see, but the trip would require a lot of careful planning.

In 1987, Jesse Helms, an American Senator from North Carolina, had added an amendment to a piece of legislation directing the president to prevent people with HIV from travelling or immigrating to the USA. This was a man who was 'bitterly opposed' to financing research into and treatment of AIDS, which he believed was God's punishment for homosexuals, claiming that 'there is not one single case of AIDS in this country that cannot be traced to sodomy[12]'. This left the USA as the only first-world nation to ban people from travelling there based on their HIV status. The International AIDS Conference, which had been due to take place in Boston in 1992, was cancelled, and, shockingly, it took until Barack Obama's presidency in 2010 for this legislation to be reversed. If you were HIV positive, you had to apply for a special visa – that is, if you were to be allowed in at all. It was very upsetting, and completely fuelled the stigmatisation of people with HIV and AIDS, presenting them as being dangerous or wildly contagious. No other illness was restricted in this way – normally you would just pay for your travel insurance or medical bills – so why were people with HIV being treated like this? It was infuriating. I couldn't help but think it would have been a completely different story if it were white heterosexual men who were the main sufferers of AIDS. Even today there is extraordinary injustice relating to travel and people's HIV status. Cuba, the Dominican Republic, St. Kitts and Nevis and St. Vincent and the Grenadines all restrict long term stays, while Russia may prevent entry to HIV-positive individuals. Bahrain, Egypt, Kuwait, Lebanon, Oman, Qatar, Saudi Arabia and Syria deport visitors who are found to have the virus.[13]

We heard many stories of people being turned back at the US border because of their HIV diagnosis. It was alarming to hear rumours of such prejudice. It wasn't as though you could become infected sitting next to someone on a plane. But we also heard stories of people not being checked at all, which gave us hope. It was a bit disconcerting planning a trip with the fear that we would not be allowed into the country – and, of course, as British people, we were not used to the idea of being turned away at customs and we hoped this would be true of our American trip. Juan was more resigned on that front, as he had a South American passport and was used to being made to feel as if he had done something wrong by just arriving at an airport.

However, great comfort came from knowing that at least we were no longer keeping secrets from each other. Juan told Dursley about his own status soon after *Les Mis* had closed in Paris, and I broke Juan's news to Jae before we decided to visit America. Sharing their diagnoses was a weight off both of their shoulders and the need for discretion was completely understood. Again, Jae realised how incredibly lucky he was, and he accepted the responsibility of the journey ahead willingly. I was certainly relieved to no longer be the only gatekeeper for their secrets. I had got used to living with a continual low-level anxiety; avoiding conversations, changing subjects and shirking questions.

Despite our hesitations, and after some deliberation, we eventually just thought, *Fuck it*. Dursley would just have to take the bull by the horns and sort out his visa waiver. We booked our flights and made plans for a two-week road trip.

Dursley feared looking too ill to travel and being denied boarding in London. He began to get his paperwork sorted. 'I'm scared about putting it on any documentation and asking for special permission,' he said. 'I know I don't have a choice, but who knows what they might do?' He joked, 'Can't I just say we're bringing AIDS back to where it started?' We all laughed.

Even so, we knew this trip would require careful planning, so we did what everybody did back then: collected brochures from our local travel agent and browsed the glossy pages, choosing our car and looking at accommodation options in different hotels and motels along our planned route. It all looked glorious – and it would be, as long as nobody got sick. There was not a cat in hell's chance of health or travel insurance for Dursley or Juan, but in the back of my mind, I had an imaginary plan. If Dursley got sick I would have to call the richest person we knew: Cameron Mackintosh. I pictured myself in a call box on Sunset Boulevard.

'Hello, Cameron. Sorry to bother you, but Dursley is in hospital . . . No, not the Royal Free . . . California. We don't really have any money – would you mind paying the bill? It's half a million dollars. Hello? Cameron?' Of course, it could never have happened; Cameron didn't know a thing about it.

It was agreed that Jae, Dursley and I would fly from London to California, and Juan would fly from Paris and join us there. We were all very excited at the thought of seeing the places that we had grown up with in our living rooms. My mum loved the police dramas, and we watched them all: *The Streets of San Francisco*, *Columbo*, *Starsky & Hutch*, *Charlie's Angels* and *McMillan & Wife*. We would see Hollywood and Yosemite Park; we would dance in San Francisco and ride in a trolley car. It would be great – as long as nobody got sick.

Aside from actually entering the country, we were facing one other major problem: medication. Would it be possible to carry everything we needed with us? All told, we'd require AZT, DDI, amoxicillin and the metronidazole, as well as acyclovir in case of shingles, Imodium in case of diarrhoea and Canesten in case of thrush. Then there was Nurofen, paracetamol and codeine. I didn't know how we could possibly hide AIDS.

Who would have thought a group of semi-naked men would turn out to be our heroes?

\*      \*      \*

We had been hanging around in London with a bunch of guys from a show that was doing a limited season in the West End. They were from America, they were gorgeous and great fun, and they were called the Chippendales. Their show in London was a big success with everyone, especially with hen nights. They were world famous due to their fabulous calendars, and now they had a proper show, which they were performing at the Strand Theatre. By a strange quirk of fate, a friend from our Swansea Grand days had been employed to work with them on some of the scenes in the show, as they obviously needed some serious acting tuition before they ripped their clothes off. All the Chippendales, or the

Chips, as we called them, were stunning boys: tall, tanned, rippling muscles, six packs, flashing white teeth, pert bottoms and big 'personalities', for which they received enormous applause every night.

When Des informed us he could get us some good seats, we did wonder if perhaps it would be better for our minds to see Checkhov's *Uncle Vanya* at the Cottesloe. Ultimately, though, we felt Ian McKellen (who was playing Uncle Vanya) would have understood our decision, so we said, 'Yes, darling – we'd love to!'

The show was brilliant. They staged a revue in which each item started as a perfectly respectable musical number, and ended with a lot of flesh and baby oil. Our friend, Des, introduced us to the Chips after the show, and we all headed to Joe Allen together. Wherever the Chips went, they turned heads, and we basked in the reflected glory.

We hung out with them a lot over the following months and went to a lot of parties together – and I could not have been more delighted when one half-naked Chip turned up at my birthday do to present the cake. Some of the boys were gay, some were straight; some were singers, some were actors; but all were strippers. And, more importantly, the boys we spent time with were really lovely people.

One night, we were discussing our impending trip to America with Mark, one of the singing Chips. We were excited to tell him about our planned trip, and asked if he could recommend some places to us in LA. As it turned out, a few of the Chips had a house in Los Angeles, and, fabulously enough, they invited us to stay. This solved two problems in the blink of an eye: one was accommodation, because, as yet, we had nowhere to stay for the first few days; the other was the medication. It was perfect. Dursley packed up some gifts to send to everyone there and included medication in the parcel – 'too heavy for our baggage,' he said – and sent it to the house in LA in advance. Dursley had visible molluscum on his face: a low immunity-related skin infection. He despised it. He was not vain, but he felt continually marred by it. He bore it uncomplainingly, but it was always there. He was aware that people could be reluctant to touch someone with AIDS and he had a palpable fear that the molluscum, in combination with the discovery of medication, might mean he would be pulled out of the security line in London and shamed by the question: 'Do you have AIDS?'

The irony of all this was that, even when all their paperwork was in order, a gay man – or anyone with HIV, but especially a gay man, given the heinous nature of what Jesse Helms had said – could still be faced with unreasonable prejudice and hatred just for being ill. I thought again how brave and tenacious Dursley was in disclosing his diagnosis to do something as supposedly simple as taking a holiday. Of course, looking back nearly three decades, perhaps he was (like actors do sometimes) winging it. He had not wanted anything to spoil this trip, so maybe he was telling us what we wanted to hear when he said he'd filled out the paperwork? I am left to wonder still. I do remember the feeling of relief and excitement as we boarded the plane and sank into our seats ready for the next thirteen hours.

Flying in 1993 was very different from flying today, and although I was nervous in case Dursley should have so much as a headache during our thirteen hours in the air, the pretty endless supply of drinks and the pretty endless flirting with the pretty cabin crew (stewards as they were then), meant that we had a great laugh and we excitedly peered out of the windows as we touched down in LA.

On arrival I happily said to the US border officer, 'Yes, sir, I am here for a holiday, staying with the Chippendales.'

'Welcome, ma'am. I'm sure you'll enjoy yourself,' he said with a knowing smile. So, with the unsuspecting Cameron Mackintosh's number safely in my purse (and feeling very rich, as the exchange rate then was two dollars to the pound) we began our trip by collecting our pale blue open-top Cadillac and heading out on to the freeway in bright and beautiful sunshine. We all felt liberated. Jae was driving and still trying to get used to the roads when who should pull up next to us at the traffic lights but Rod Stewart? After that, we kept our eyes peeled like leopards on the hunt. Jae was probably the most excited of us; Dursley took it all in his stride, while I was busy hoping the next set of lights would deliver Patrick Swayze.

We drove to West Hollywood to the Chips' house, and spent our first night in LA just crashed out: jet-lagged, completely shattered and a little concerned, because Juan wouldn't arrive until tomorrow. The next day, we went to fetch him at the airport, and we all shrieked with delight when we finally saw him come through the arrivals door. Despite having AZT in his possession, Juan's papers were OK and, for once, not questioned. Apparently, a customs officer had looked at his pills, but the man, who Juan had suspected was gay, had merely smiled and said nothing. Juan felt that the officer knew, but we will never know the truth. Perhaps he didn't agree with the law either, or perhaps he thought the pills were for indigestion. It didn't matter. What was important was that we were all together in California – the fun was just beginning.

It felt like we were living life to the full, making the most of our time and doing everything we could: Venice Beach, the Hollywood sign and the magnificent homes of the stars. We found footprints and handprints at Mann's Chinese Theatre, and Juan lay next to his beloved Barbra Streisand's handprints for a photograph. We went clubbing with the Chips in West Hollywood, then, a few days later, we headed up the glorious Pacific Highway, stopping in Carmel in the hope of seeing Doris Day. Sadly it was not to be, but we were instead rewarded with the sight of the Mayor of Carmel, Clint Eastwood, in the Hog's Breath Inn.

When we got to San Francisco, although we loved seeing the Golden Gate Bridge and Alcatraz, and taking a ride on the trolley car, we couldn't help noticing the heavy atmosphere. It was as though the clouds wouldn't clear. We realised that the onslaught of the virus had done its worst. Sadness hung in the air – it was a city in mourning. The clubs were quiet, and we could only imagine what it would have been like there a decade ago, with the bohemian freedom and openness that the city had once been so famous for. We didn't go on about it, but we all felt it was subdued. It certainly wasn't like life at the start of Armistead Maupin's *Tales of the City*. We decided to mark our visit by seeing a show which was an institution in San Francisco called *Beach Blanket Babylon*, a long-running topical extravagant revue. Even the Queen (the real one), had been to see it.

After a night in a five-star hotel (organised by Dursley, who, as usual, knew someone who knew someone, who had booked it for us as a treat), we continued our journey. Jae was proving to be the most confident behind the wheel, and he drove us further and further. By nightfall, we had found our way to the glaciated silver mountains of Yosemite Park, where we stayed in the tent cabins in Curry Village (with an exhilarating view of Glacier Point), which had housed people since 1899. The still lakes were like enormous mirrors in the moonlight, reflecting the strikingly symmetrical incense cedars and sky-touching ponderosa pines. However, we spent the night not daring to go out after dark. Jae lost all that confidence he'd shown while driving, and, with his usual mistrust of wildlife, kept us awake all night, hissing: 'I can hear bears rummaging in the bins,' or, 'There are bears out there grunting,' or, 'Bloody hell, that is *definitely* a bear.'

Eventually, Juan said, 'Fuckeeeng hell! I will rather be eaten by a bear than listen to this sheet all night!'

The next morning – not having been eaten by bears – we drove on to our next destination, Las Vegas, which was much more Jae's style. On the way, we paused in Death Valley to take photographs. Stopping the car was quite a daring thing to do, as we risked an already hot engine overheating in the middle of the desert. It was close to forty degrees, but it was the dryness of the air that was so extraordinary. It stole the micro-droplets of water from your lungs as you breathed, and threatened to shrivel your skin.

Las Vegas was a bombardment to the senses: hot, noisy, lit with thousands of neon signs and alive with the promise of winning a fortune in the casinos. While the rest of us ran riot, Juan decided to leave Las Vegas early, as he had a friend in Chicago, a Venezuelan boy also named Juan, and he wanted to tell him the truth about his diagnosis. He took an internal flight and spent the next forty-eight hours with his friend. I knew Juan felt that this would be the last time he would see him, and he carried that sadness with him as our trip came to a close.

For me, the absolute highlight of the entire holiday wasn't the gorgeous boys on the beach in LA, or the hedonism of Las Vegas: it was a helicopter ride over the Grand Canyon. It was truly one of the most amazing sights I have ever seen on this earth, and one that really puts things into perspective. As we flew over a green forest, the earth suddenly fell away, and the enormous canyon revealed itself to us. As we tipped over the edge in our tiny helicopter, the sudden shock of the two-kilometre drop was awe-inspiring. We were speechless, but I was also filled with so much joy and excitement to be able to share such an experience with my dearest friends – even if Jae looked as though he was screaming in fear the entire time. Still exhilarated, I drove us back to Las Vegas. Impulsively, I stopped the car en route, pausing to wonder at the dome of the sky enveloping us. In whichever direction I looked, the pinpoint shine of millions of stars stretched all the way to the horizon, bright in a dry desert night sky. All my life, I have looked to the stars as a way to bring myself comfort: the enormity of the universe seems to diminish my problems. At that moment in the desert, and just for that moment, the monumental struggles facing my dearest friends were forgotten.

The next day, as we headed back to LA, it was deflating to know that our trip was coming to an end – but we knew we had made the most of every second. What's more, the only person who had needed any medical attention was me – I'd hit my head when the mat somehow slipped from under me on a waterslide at Water World. Dursley had collided with me, arms and legs went in every direction, and I'd ended up completely disorientated. Two nurses had both rushed to attend to me as I landed in a heap at the bottom of the ride.

As Dursley, Jae and I stood in the departures lounge at LAX, saying a bittersweet farewell to Juan, I felt overwhelmed with gratitude. I was thankful, we had spent precious time making wonderful memories for all of us, and I was relieved that, for a brief moment, we had all been able to think of something other than AIDS. The success of the trip felt like a triumph over the virus, however brief.

# CHAPTER 18

_____

*How wonderful it is that nobody need wait a single moment
before starting to improve the world.*

Anne Frank

I was back in our flat in Balham, carrying that feeling that always
marks the end of a holiday – a mixture of tiredness and deflation,
so I was hoping to get a good night's sleep before my first day back
to the show. It was exciting, though, to be going back with tales of
our adventures to share with everyone. I woke up, thinking, *Oh,
what a nice morning. I'll just get up and make some toast.* Then I looked
at my clock and shrieked – it was 3.45pm! I was gobsmacked and
I leaped out of bed, rushing to get some food, get a shower, throw
on an outfit and get straight into town for the warm-up.

I managed to get to the theatre on time, back in the mood for
the show and ready for the warm-up. It was one of those rare
occasions that Anthony and I were in the dressing rooms alone,
so the conversation moved, as it always did, to AIDS, and then on

to what we might be able to do to help the wider cause as well as those friends in our immediate circle we were already helping. We talked about raising money, promoting awareness and fighting for a cure for this terrible illness. The seed had been planted and the promise of an exciting collaboration was the fertiliser it needed to grow. That conversation was to be the beginning of a whole new phase in the history of the West End.

Anthony and I began to plan and discuss ideas every chance we could get – after rehearsals, in between shows, even in the wings offstage. One day, in our dressing room, Anthony and I discovered that Shaun Kerrison had recently returned from a trip to Broadway, and had brought home some important information about the recently amalgamated Broadway Cares/Equity Fights AIDS. This was the charity initiative on Broadway that was championed by Tom Viola, and would eventually earn him an honorary Tony Award for his achievements. This was the inspiration Anthony and I had been searching for. Shaun excitedly shared the information with us both, clearly just thinking I would be interested as an ally and a supporter of the cause – he was unaware just how closely involved Anthony and I really were.

'What they're doing is incredible, Jill,' Shaun said, fired up with enthusiasm for the things he had just seen. 'It's not just about the stars, it's about everyone – ensembles, dancers and musicians, crew, wardrobe, designers, directors – anyone can play a part. They've raised a huge amount of money using the power that was right there at their fingertips – the ability to put on a show and ask people for money for the privilege of watching it!'

I looked at Anthony, who smiled back at me, clearly sharing Shaun's excitement.

'Let's do it,' I said, with a sense of urgency. 'Let's set it up – just like Broadway, but right here in the West End.' I thought about the ghost town that had been San Francisco on my visit a few weeks before. 'Without some sort of action, the whole of the theatre world will be devastated,' I added.

'Exactly,' Anthony agreed. 'We need to do it quickly.'

'This year?' Shaun asked.

'No, quicker,' Anthony responded.

'This week, then,' I said, looking at them both, 'We urgently need a cure.'

They nodded in agreement.

'By Friday would be perfect,' Anthony decided.

That became our little catchphrase, an affirmation to keep us going, and keep us laughing. We would fundraise for a cure by Friday – and by some Friday, some time, it would be bound to happen. We started signing letters and notes to each other with 'Love and cure by Friday.'

Now that the idea had been born, we couldn't let it rest: we were on a mission. Young men should not be having to lurk guiltily in the shadows with people seemingly terrified of them, quivering at the thought of hugging, kissing or even touching them.

With the three of us already on board, Jon Osbaldeston joined the fight, along with another cast member, Nigel Richards. Together, we decided to form a committee: Les Mis Cares. We had a plan, and the next step was to get other theatres involved. We wanted to use West End Cares as an umbrella title, but the name had already been used for a couple of fundraising concert nights run by Crusaid. Crusaid was a charity that had been started to help people struggling with AIDS, and it was quite different from the Terrence Higgins Trust, as it managed a hardship fund that gave money directly to the sufferers.

I went to the pay phone by the stage door to speak to Crusaid about using the name. With a bunch of ten-pence pieces in my hand in case it was a long conversation, and with the boys waiting in the corridor, I called and spoke to one of Crusaid's cofounders, Geoffrey Henning.

'Hello, Mr Henning. My name is Jill Nalder,' I said, nervously twiddling the phone cord in my fingers. 'A few of us from *Les Misérables* want to fundraise for charity, but we would need your permission to use the name West End Cares.'

I explained our plan in more detail and was absolutely thrilled because the answer was Yes! Yes! Yes! – to everything. Yes, we could fundraise, of course; yes, we could use the name; and yes, they would look after the money. It was the perfect partnership: we could raise the money with our performances and pay it to Crusaid, who would then use it for their hardship fund for people directly affected by AIDS, as well as giving to areas of research and covering medical needs. It was wonderful, as we could get on with what we knew we would be good at – coming up with ideas to raise money and promote awareness – while Crusaid dealt with the rest.

By this point, at the close of 1992, the devastating impact on our community was, sadly, becoming well established. Among the first, *Les Misérables* had lost Ian Calvin and newspaper headlines had been anything but kind with 'West End Star dies from AIDS' splashed all over the papers by journalist Mark Souster. Well-known actor Geoffrey Burridge had died. Robert Locke from *Blood Brothers* had bravely fought a terrible AIDS infection called PML (Progressive Multifocal Leukoencephalopathy). His partner Trevor faced not only the immense difficulties of caring for him but he was an actor and, unable to find time to work, had gone down many routes to seek financial help. There was nothing forthcoming and they relied on understanding friends offering money to buy food. *Starlight Express* had lost Michael Staniforth and Tom Jobe. Michael Sundin (British and world trampolining tournament winner and *Blue Peter* presenter) was gone. Since he had left *Pajama Game* there had been rumours about the disappearance and sad death of the very popular John Chester. Sadly for us all, lovely Duncan from my year at Mountview, who had seemed so stoic when Peg had seen him last, had since lost his fight. Now the West End could see that AIDS was no longer some distant disease happening to others across the ocean. It didn't take much research to discover the enormous loss that Broadway had already experienced, and was still in the midst of. It was the devastation of a whole generation of brilliant dancers, singers, choreographers and directors. So many had died – and the deaths were continuing: handsome and talented Steve 'Lottie' Lubman from *La Cage aux Folles*, passed away in his early twenties, Richard Sampson, dancer, choreographer and all-round force to be reckoned with, left us all too soon and the loss of brilliant and decorated actor Denholm Elliott was well publicised.

AIDS was right here in the midst of us. Anthony and I knew we were keeping secrets – how many more people in our business were doing the same? I was consumed with the realisation that it was possible that AIDS could, in fact, kill all of us – and even if not me, certainly all my friends. What would my life be without them? A chance for positive action was the only way to hold back the panic.

At the end of the year something beautifully positive happened when Jae was offered the job of musical director for Gershwin's *Crazy for You*. The show had been a massive success on Broadway, and the production was now coming to the Prince Edward Theatre. For the second time in his career, Jae would be the MD, in charge of a show from the very beginning. Unlike the less-than-successful run of *Edwin Drood*, *Crazy for You* was certain to take London by storm and be a massive hit. Although the shadow of AIDS continued to loom and was nowhere near clearing, it felt like a piece of my world had fallen into place personally, as now Jae and I would be in the West End together, working on hit shows at theatres that were almost next door to each other.

The opening night of *Crazy for You* was the theatrical event of the year in London. From his prestigious position as musical director, Jae was able to ask as many of us to the event as he wanted. I didn't realise it at the time, but this glittering night, when we joined together to proudly celebrate Jae's success, would be the last time that the people most dear to me would all be in a room together. Juan had travelled from Paris, and we were joined by Dursley and his parents, Peg (who, by this time, was working as an agent in the West End), my mum and dad, Jae's mum and dad . . . everyone was there.

A short while before, Juan had decided that he would tell Peg the truth about his diagnosis. She was very emotional, and amid the fun and glamour of the opening night, she tearfully spoke to me about how exhausted Juan looked. As the night came to a close, and Juan and I travelled home together, I could see just how wiped out he was, struggling to find any energy. Before we had gone out that night, Juan had revealed something truly awful to me: a large Kaposi's sarcoma lesion on his back and another smaller one on his leg.

'I hate it, Jilly,' he'd said, visibly upset. It was horrible to see it, but I comforted myself (and Juan) with the thought that they were on his skin and could be treated externally. I kept the positive thought that being at the opening night had definitely been a tonic, though there was no getting away from it – it was cancer.

*Crazy for You* was full of talented young dancers. Among them was the Australian Craig Revel Horwood, who would later prove to be a staunch ally when it came to fundraising. Another was the lovely Colin Bell: a completely beautiful enigma who had twirled into the West End from Gorleston-on-Sea, Great Yarmouth, like Ann Miller on speed. He lived to perform, parading his divine camp spirit and extraordinary humour at every chance he could get. Colin loved being in the West End, and, due to his delightful *joie de vivre*, he was loved right back by everyone who knew him, including me and Jae. We heard stories of his outrageous behaviour; how he would dress up at the drop of a hat and how he (not unlike Miss Pinky) would go to extremes to get a laugh. Colin had the enviable talent of being able to portray an array of self-created characters, the finest being his alter ego, Dreen Wythenshawe. She had a whole incredible history and she was obsessed with every aspect of theatre. Dreen was an extravagant and over-the-top English luvvie. She had made it into showbusiness but she was forever destined to be the understudy that never went on. She was well rehearsed and ever enthusiastic, but she *never* got her chance. She was something of a West End institution. Colin loved to reject a party invitation but in the same breath he would say, 'But, if you don't mind, Dreen would love to come to the party.'

It was Dreen in all her glory who came to Jae's birthday party that year, bursting through the doors of the Lindsay House restaurant: gorgeous as always, dressed as the diva she believed she ought to be. Never one to miss the opportunity for a grand entrance, she had a tendency to arrive late for maximum recognition. There was never a dull moment if Dreen Wythenshawe graced your soirée.

★ ★ ★

A few days after the opening of *Crazy for You*, Juan returned to Paris, making me promise that I would come over for his birthday in March. He had always loved a party. Our college friends will remember the legendary cheese and wine parties he held in his Crouch End flat. He would try to convince us that the concept was sophisticated and European, 'Not like you British, darlings,' he would say, trying to be ironic. The idea may well have been sophisticated, but the result of everyone bringing a small amount of cheese and a lot of cheap wine meant it turned out the way any party did: a lot of drunk students, and Peg dancing on the coffee table! Juan's birthday party in Paris was pretty much the same, only we ate very expensive cheese and drank very good wine. We still sang and danced till midnight, though. He really seemed like himself that night; a *tour de force*. Those who knew nothing of his diagnosis would never have guessed, and he gave nothing away.

Someone said, 'Juan, you look great – you've lost weight.'

Juan winked at me and said, under his breath, 'Cancer, darling. Finally, I'm thin!'

I laughed at the black humour, but thought how brave he was at the same time. He had weeks of chemotherapy ahead of him, and here he was, playing the host and keeping everyone entertained.

On reflection, I knew Juan had always been brave – not just for the past five years, but for his whole life. From the moment he realised he was gay and accepted his own sexuality, Juan, like so many others, had to hide the truth. At the time of writing, there is still no legal recognition for same-sex couples in Venezuela, and homosexuality was only declared legal in 1997. Unable to be honest with his family, he was used to keeping secrets, so AIDS just became one more. Added to which, he'd taken on the challenges of learning English, coming to study in London and learning to act in a language that wasn't his own, before moving to France, learning French and desperately trying to find a place where he would be legally allowed to work in the world he loved. He had faced discrimination all his life, not only for his sexuality, but also due to his nationality. The stigma of AIDS, though, was the most shaming of all.

# CHAPTER 19

_There is nothing like a dream to create a future._

Victor Hugo

The five of us from _Les Misérables_ were taking action. Together, we composed a letter – which was typed on Jon Osbaldeston's new word processor, how _professional_! – and we hand-delivered a copy to practically everybody that we knew in the West End. It read:

Dear Friends,
We are writing this letter to you in a spirit of bonding and cooperation for a common cause . . . a cause that is very dear to all our hearts: the raising of as much money as possible to combat the cause, effect and spread of AIDS. We are inviting casts from every show to form a committee of people who are prepared to organise any kind of fundraising they can think of – be prepared to be a pest!

We owe it to our friends and colleagues affected by this terrible illness to do all we can.

Les Mis Cares – do you?

Sincerely,
  Jill Nalder, Anthony Lyn, Shaun Kerrison,
  Jon Osbaldeston, and Nigel Richards

To our shared delight, it turned out we had clearly chosen the right time – and the right place. The West End came out in force. The response was overwhelming – and a bit mind-blowing – and it inspired all of us. With the go-ahead from Crusaid, we formed a West End Cares Committee of the most enthusiastic people from each show, and planned to meet once a month to generate ideas. Alongside the five of us from *Les Mis*, there was Jae from *Crazy for You,* David Curl from *Grease* and Murray Lane from *Sunset Boulevard*. Murray had an amazing talent. He was the West End's favourite dresser, but alongside this work he was a gifted artist and he promised to design posters and flyers should they ever be needed. Dursley had recently made a dramatic decision to try working on stage again. He was (wonderfully) cast as understudy to Raoul in *Phantom of the Opera* (after an HIV diagnosis, pneumonia, a brush with death and a change of career), so he was right there at the helm with us, and back onstage where he belonged.

One sunny Saturday morning, the nine of us got together for a meeting at the Adelphi Theatre on the Strand before our matinee performances. Coffee in hand, I was raring to go – I felt like we were on the cusp of something truly important. I was thrilled and excited, and as the only woman there even more so, to be voted in as the chair. I was ready to rise to the challenge. Although we were a small group, we were determined to make a difference, and we knew there were people in other shows ready to support us as well. It had been no more than two weeks since we first sent out the letter, but due to the rate at which news travels around the West End, almost every theatre cast had heard of our plans. More and more casts began to approach us, ready to support the cause. *Miss Saigon* was on board, as were *Cats* and *Carousel*. The West End run of *Kiss of the Spider Woman* were also incredibly interested in what we were doing, which was no surprise as, being an American/Canadian cast, they had already been involved with Broadway Cares. Having witnessed first-hand the success of our American charity counterparts, the Spider Boys (as we nicknamed them) started to meet up with us often to discuss ideas.

The first idea we were excited about was the suggestion of creating late-night cabaret shows. The committee decided that we would start with a season of four shows held over four weeks. After that season, we would take a small break, then do another season – and so on. Broadway had an established tradition of after-show cabarets, but in London this was a less familiar concept. We didn't know how well it would be received, but we definitely had a good feeling about it. We decided that our first cabaret performance would take place on a Monday night in February 1993. We had the concept and the date – now all we needed was a venue.

Anthony and I started traipsing around the West End between shows to look for the right place to hold our cabaret. Finding a location was proving to be a lot more difficult than we'd imagined – and bloody exhausting. It was a pretty complex situation: it had to have a good focal point where we could erect a stage and good sightlines, and it needed to be somewhere with a late licence and the right atmosphere. We thought a restaurant would be the best option, as we would need a helpful manager and a chef who'd be willing to work late. Likewise, we needed waiters willing to support our cause. We tried what felt like a myriad of places until we eventually found Smiths Restaurant in Covent Garden. It was a great option: a long room with a low ceiling and trendy bare-brick walls. It felt like a New York cabaret bar. When we explained what we wanted to do, they said they were prepared to give it a go. Ecstatic with our success, and with the venue secured, we were ready to go – and who else should launch the project but the cast of *Les Misérables*? Les Mis Cares! We were finally going to make a difference.

About eight weeks after Les Mis Cares was born, rehearsals were well and truly under way – often going on while we rehearsed for *Les Mis* itself. Everywhere I looked, cast members were going through material and practising harmonies for the cabaret – in dressing rooms, along corridors, up and down innumerable stairs. It made me feel exhilarated and empowered to see everyone so committed and passionate about a cause that was so close to my own heart. Yet, as thrilled and excited as I was, I was also appre-hensive. After all, I had been a large part of the team that was persuading people to get involved in this, and I really wanted everyone to enjoy the experience. Even getting to Smiths was going to be tight, as time was so short between the end of the West End shows (especially *Les Mis* which was known to be the longest show ever) and the planned beginning of the cabaret. Nevertheless, the running order had been finalised and the wheels were in motion. It was almost time.

I had a book in my dressing room with the names of those who were coming, and in the week leading up to the opening night, I took dozens of calls from potential audience members, driving Pearl and Dean mad with the number of people phoning up. I used a table plan from Smiths to allocate everyone a seat. Their ticket money would be collected on the door and at the end of the night it would be given to us to add up before being handed over to Crusaid. We decided on the grand price of £5, and volunteers from Crusaid would be on hand to guide everyone to their tables.

Behind every show are the unseen heroes. For West End Cares, Bob West (affectionately called Uncle Bob by us) was our hero – and a true gentleman. He was one of the West End's most loved and admired company managers, and was always on hand to help us. He was in his fifties, blessed with a beautiful head of grey curly hair, kind blue eyes and a warm smile. He was always calm and helpful: just the sort of person you would want to go to for advice and encouragement. When he was in charge of a show, though, he expected a good work ethic from the company, and wouldn't stand for any cast member who didn't pull their weight. This was exactly the kind of leadership we needed, and we were so lucky to have him. He had organised lighting, staging and sound, and was full of enthusiasm for the cause. We had everything we needed to put on a show.

On the night of the first cabaret show, on Monday 3rd February, 1993, the standing ovation for *Les Mis* that night meant that the show only finished at 10.50pm, and we were a good ten minutes' walk away from Smiths. Anthony, Shaun, Jon, Nigel and I rushed up the stairs, frantically pulled off our revolutionary costumes and threw on our ordinary clothes, then grabbed the music, piled our cabaret costumes into our arms, checked the props, and off we went, dashing through the stage door, shouting and laughing at Jon Osbaldeston in his cowboy boots, who was saying, 'I should never have worn heels,' while Anthony – Mrs Lyn to us – replied, 'Come on, dear, faster! Work those fabulous calves.'

We ran across Cambridge Circus, nearly getting run over by the number nineteen bus, rushing desperately to get everything set up before the rest of the cast arrived and our audience started queueing at the door.

By 11.15pm, we were all there and the audience were arriving. There was an air of expectation and excitement, and before long, the place was packed full of friends, family, theatregoers and actors alike. Smiths was buzzing. To us, it felt like Carnegie Hall. It was the first time anything like this had been tried in London. I was very nervous, but Dursley was in organisation mode, helping with meeting and seating, and Jae was going round the tables, getting everyone enthused and excited, while not forgetting to look after my ever-supportive mum and dad. Everyone was raring to go. The only moment of terror was when somebody rushed up to me and said, 'Stephen Sondheim is at the door and he can't get a ticket.'

'Oh my God, that's incredible,' I shouted. 'Don't let them turn him away! Can someone FIND STEPHEN SONDHEIM A SEAT?!'

(A false alarm – it was simply an elderly man with a grey beard. Oh, well, you can't win them all.)

A little later than planned, but not too late, the lights went down in the restaurant and there was the familiar hush of a show about to begin. The first-ever West End Cares Cabaret began with our cast singing 'Hey Old Friend' from Stephen Sondheim's *Merrily We Roll Along*. Our hour-long show was a triumph, and we had planned what we thought was a powerful ending: German Lutheran Pastor, Martin Niemöller's 'First they came for the socialists, and I did not speak out . . .' read by one of the cast and ending '. . . then they came for me – and there was no one left to speak out for me.' It was met with a ringing silence. Then we finished with 'The People's Song' from *Les Mis*. The audience stood to applaud, whistling and cheering.

Over the next three weeks, more shows were put on by the actors from *Kiss of the Spider Woman,* then *Carousel*, and to close the first season the cast from *Phantom of the Opera* gave an incredible performance. Phantom Cares, as they were called, made a lasting impression on us all that night for two reasons. First, there was a magnificently sung rendition of Bernstein's uplifting 'Make Your Garden Grow' from *Candide*, which, with the low ceiling in the venue, nearly blew the roof off. Then, I watched from my table as Dursley, looking fragile, sang a torch song written by a friend, Carlton Edwards. It was a song that alluded to the fragility of life, and Dursley sang the haunting lyrics so beautifully, standing under the lights, looking every bit like a PWA, although he was yet to share his status with most people. It was a bittersweet moment. I was proud – not only that my beautiful friend was such a talented performer, but that, once again, he had proved he was tenacious and determined to live his life to the fullest. At the same time, seeing him stand there alone, looking like a shadow of his former self, made me feel so sad, and there was a moment when I couldn't help thinking, *I hope he has enough breath to hit the high note*s.

Unsurprisingly, there were a lot of tears – not just from me – but there was also a moment of drama, because someone in the audience, who had perhaps had a few too many drinks, was talking very loudly while Dursley was performing.

He kept on singing, even over the raised voices. People started to stare and say 'Sssshhh' in the direction of our celebrity table. Dursley valiantly carried on (it turned out he did have the breath), but now a full-on scuffle had broken out – and a chair was involved. As Dursley finished his song, one of the people involved in the scuffle shouted, 'Fuck off, you bitch' at another person in the audience. People were ushered to the door, and, in the heat of the moment, no one was quite sure what had gone on. That was, until a headline in the *Sun* the following morning said it all: 'Babs in Bust Up with Blonde'. None other than national treasure Barbara Windsor had been part of the scuffle. We were thrilled – the cabaret was the talk of the town. It was fabulous publicity, and a great point of gossip for the rest of the week.

With a celebrity bust-up narrowly avoided, our first cabaret season was a roaring success. The shows went from strength to strength as each cast performed to a captivated audience – the four performances raised around £2,000, and we were well pleased. It was a rollercoaster – and it gathered enormous speed. The cabarets happened on Mondays, and we counted up the money on Tuesdays at *Les Mis*, then walked to the bank to deposit it in the Crusaid bank account. It got to the stage where there was so much cash that we had to clear all the surfaces in one of the dressing rooms to count it all, down to the last penny. I felt like we were unstoppable, like we would truly be able to make a difference – and we did. We couldn't have imagined on that first chaotic night that this was the beginning of something that would last in the West End for almost thirty years, raising millions of pounds in the process.

While there might have been West End performers onstage, there were often bigger stars in the audience, all helping to raise our profile and turn our little idea into a West End epic: Catherine Zeta Jones, Nickolas Grace, Barbara Cook, Gary Wilmot, Petula Clark, Chris Biggins and Philip Schofield, to name a few.

Looking back, it feels as though there were too many nights to describe! Such an array of experiences, beautiful sentiments, hysterically funny ideas and wonderful performers who took to the stage of Smiths and our later venues (Centre Stage, the Connaught Rooms, the New London Theatre, Prue Leith's, Dibbens, and so many more). West End Cares just kept going. We sang, danced and acted; and musicians, musical directors and composers wrote songs and arrangements for us, and played their instruments in restaurants, clubs, bars and theatres. We held parties, special events and themed nights. We provided entertainment for the Walk for Life; we arranged bed races in Leicester Square, and we organised lotteries, bingo games, tombolas, raffles and auctions. The shops around theatreland donated prizes and the restaurants of Old Compton Street gifted meals. We borrowed and made costumes and wigs, and took in all kinds of props, all supported by wonderful wardrobe departments and staggeringly helpful stage management teams.

There are so many wonderful memories: the night that Petula Clark thrilled us by singing 'Downtown'; the winter's evening French and Saunders switched on the Christmas lights at Her Majesty's Theatre; Graham Norton compering with his incredible flair; a superbly clever one-man performance from Victor Spinetti; and an equally funny night from Tony Slattery, with Issy van Randwyck offering her quirky brilliance on the same bill. Long before *Mamma Mia!* was even born, the cast of *Les Mis* performed *MiserAbba*, a selection of brilliantly sung Abba songs with all kinds of styles and arrangements, closing with the entire ensemble joining to sing 'Thank You for the Music'.

A great memory for me is the casino night, which was organised in incredible detail by Anthony Lyn (who had become the resident director of *Miss Saigon* when he left *Les Mis*) and Jane

Salberg. Based on *Guys and Dolls*, it began with violin case-wielding gangsters dropping off invitations to a secret location at every stage door during the half-hour call. At the end of our show, everyone found their way to a dark warehouse somewhere in east London, laid out with casino tables. It was like walking on to the set for a Bond movie. We played with a stash of fake chips for prizes; the more we bought, the more money was raised. At midnight, the Salvation Army leader Sister Sarah Brown, played by Alison Jiear, entered, calling for abstinence and singing 'Follow the Fold' with her Army Band. At 1am, we suddenly heard sirens and a lot of shouting. It was a police raid. The gambling stopped, and there were yells telling us to put our hands in the air. Alarming? Well, it would have been – if the raid had not been led by Emmy- and Golden Globe-winning actor Sharon Gless (Cagney from *Cagney & Lacey*). It was a brilliant night and is still talked about to this day.

As fabulous as the casino night was, I think the best laugh came from Judi Dench, who was appearing in the National's production of *A Little Night Music*. She was just so divine.I heard of her telling a story about how she had nearly been run over on Oxford Street, and someone had called her a cunt. 'I think you'll find that's *Dame* Cunt,' Dame Judi had apparently shouted back. I don't know if it's true, but we loved it, and is part of our folklore forevermore.

Through all our highs and excitement, we never forgot why we were fundraising. This was something that always hit home for me and Anthony. Each of us were staunch allies, and we knew we were fighting against the clock when it came to helping those we loved who were ill. However, not long after we began West End

Cares, Anthony received the worst news possible. He came to a matinee one day, and I found him in the boys' dressing room, absolutely distraught.

I told him he should go home, that he wasn't in a fit state to work, but he refused. He said that being at home alone would make him feel worse, and at least working was a good distraction. He had just come from the London Lighthouse, which was the hospice that specialised in HIV and AIDS care. He had been to visit his friend Nils Seibeck, who was very sick at the time. Nils was a dancer, and he was beautiful, tall and blond. He and Anthony had worked together, become very close friends, and enjoyed many a laugh with their shared 'naughty' sense of humour. On this particular day, Anthony had gone to Nils' room as usual, only to find that his friend wasn't there.

Confused, Anthony asked the nurse in charge, 'Where's Nils?'

'Oh, I'll take you to him,' she said with a smile, and led Anthony to a different room.

Anthony looked at the new bed and then at the nurse. 'This isn't him,' he said.

'Yes, this is Neil,' she replied.

'No, not Neil,' Anthony said, panicked now. 'Nils, my friend. Do you know him – the beautiful Swedish boy?'

At any other time, a simple mix-up of beds might cause no anxiety at all, but seeing this Neil (whoever he was) sitting comfortably in bed when Nils, the boy that Anthony loved so much, was nowhere to be seen, made him feel sick.

The nurse's face dropped, and she looked mortified. 'I'm so sorry, Mr Lyn,' she said. 'Did nobody tell you? Nils died in the night.'

The hospice had informed Nils' family, but not Anthony. Not Anthony, who had visited day after day, week after week, month after month. He didn't even get a phone call. The young nurse had no idea that Anthony *was* family to Nils, and now he was gone – with no warning. Anthony was left with the image of this stranger, Neil, in the place of his dearest friend, as the nurse's words, 'I'm so sorry, Mr Lyn. Did nobody tell you?' rang in his ears.

Anthony left the hospice in a daze and came straight to the theatre. There were many tears on the barricade that night.

Rest in peace, beautiful and mischievous Nils Seibeck.

# CHAPTER 20

*I am what I am, I am my own special creation.*

Jerry Herman, *La Cage aux Folles*

AIDS ripped the heart from the gay community. Beneath the surface, though, a cauldron of angry energy pushed through stigma and prejudice. Things were changing. Partners, lovers and friends, along with the more accepting of the mothers, fathers, sisters and brothers, could not and did not stand by in silence while those who were sick and dying found themselves isolated by pain and rejection. All across the world, the word 'family' was changing and expanding. So many friends found that their relationships were becoming something they could never have imagined, and they strove not to let down those they loved.

When Colin Bell had started rehearsals for *Crazy for You*, we discovered he was already carrying the burden of an HIV diagnosis.

Jae and I invited him for supper one night, and he felt comfortable enough to talk with us about it.

'I've got AZT, but I only take it when I remember,' he said.

I tried to stress the importance of being consistent with his medication, and suggested he might also try some alternative therapies. 'Dursley tries so many things,' I told him, 'and some of them seem to really help.'

Jae joined in. 'I'm sure there's a treatment round the corner. The show can't go on without you, dear.'

Colin, who seemed a little vague, suddenly announced: 'I've always wanted to stay at the Grand Hotel in Brighton.'

Jae and I laughed.

'Well,' said Jae, 'that glamour would certainly suit Dreen.'

We were surprised when, within a few days, Colin had booked a room at the Grand Hotel and travelled to Brighton alone. Once there, however, he suddenly lost his confidence, deciding he couldn't stay at the Grand, and called Jae to ask if he knew someone he could stay with. Our friend Stuart came to the rescue, and invited Colin to his lovely, calm home. The kindness of friends in a time of need is seldom forgotten. Colin spent the next few days at Stuart's house. He rarely came out of the bedroom. Instead, he slept and slept, not really seeming to know what time of day it was – one day he even appeared at 7.30am, ready for supper.

Colin's state of mind left him feeling very nervous about making the train journey back to London. Stuart drove him to the station, and Colin eventually found the courage to board the train. Soon after his Brighton escapade, Colin's health seriously declined, and he was diagnosed with Kaposi's sarcoma. Unable to find the strength for his second contract with *Crazy for You*, Colin was forced to vanish from the life that he had loved so much.

I travelled the long distance across London to the North Middlesex Hospital in Enfield, where Colin was now a patient. It was the bleakest of buildings: long, grey, lonely corridors, with what felt like an abundance of small side rooms. The nights were long, but Colin was rarely alone: he was loved, supported and cared for by his best friend Jonathan, who spent hour after hour at his bedside, often until the early hours of the morning.

The hospital staff were amazing and extremely caring, but even they could not dispel the lonely utilitarian ambience of the place, so Colin decided to return home to his mother Margery. It was a relief in many ways, although tinged with an inevitable feeling of grief. There was only ever one reason that boys 'went home'.

With Jonathan at his side, Colin told his mother the devastating truth: he had AIDS, and did not have long to live. Jonathan was family to Colin: it was Jonathan who'd told Margery that Colin was gay (up to this point, she had always described him as 'theatrical'). For those last few weeks of Colin's life, Jonathan lived and breathed the cruel illness alongside Margery.

Terrified of AIDS himself, seeing Colin in these last days reinforced Jonathan's deepest fears. Colin's emaciated body was entirely covered with Kaposi's sarcoma lesions. His energetic, creative mind was confused. One day, he asked Jonathan for his clean, lemon-coloured pyjamas. He put them on and settled down to watch a video of one of his favourite Disney films, *Dumbo*. At some point during the heart-warming story of the elephant that can fly against all the odds, Margery walked in and discovered that her son had quietly flown away into everlasting sleep.

After Colin passed away, Jonathan had the emotionally taxing responsibility of sorting through his possessions. Even during this sad job, Colin made Jonathan laugh, as he discovered a plethora of female wigs purloined from various theatres: one was labelled with the name Elaine Paige (clearly worn for the portrayal of Eva Peron), while a pretty black bob was marked 'Catherine Zeta Jones'.

Jonathan and Margery organised Colin's funeral together. It was an incredibly moving day at St Paul's Church in Covent Garden, affectionately known as the Actors' Church. Built by Inigo Jones for the grand cost of £4,000 it has been there since 1633. Hundreds of performers have been remembered there. For Colin, it was full. His friend Sarah Hadland's rendition of Noël Coward's 'I've Been to a Marvellous Party' said it all.

The only person unable to come was Dreen Wythenshawe – but, of course, the loss of Colin meant the loss of Dreen, too. Jonathan felt this needed to be acknowledged, and wondered how Colin would have retired her from showbusiness. So, on the back of the Order of Service, a short note read: 'Dreen Wythenshawe retired, and was last seen running a cake shop in Gorleston-on-Sea, which she aptly named Crazy for Choux'.

He knew Colin would have loved that.

Above Colin's place in the dressing room at the Prince Edward Theatre, where Colin starred and Dreen had so longed to take her place on the glittering stage, there hangs a plaque bearing the words: 'She waited in the wings and now she's wearing them.'

For Dursley, Jae and me, it was another terrible loss. We were worn out with so many funerals. It was torture that no effective treatment was coming. We had known Colin for only two years, but in that time, he had given us a lifetime of laughs.


Rest in peace, sparkling Colin Bell.

# CHAPTER 21

---

*What is there
like fortitude! What sap
went through that
little thread
to make the cherry red!*

Marianne Moore

One night after a show, I was waiting at the stage door of *Les Misérables* for Dursley to come and meet me. I loved the theatrical excitement and romance of people meeting at the stage door to go out after the show. With Dursley at *Phantom* and Jae at *Crazy for You*, we would usually go to either Joe Allen or to see a late-night movie, which was one of my favourite things to do. We saw some fabulous movies together, often with our good friend Roger Bunnage – famous as Arbie the Robot – who would make a special effort to stay up late and come into the West End to meet us. We will certainly never forget *Lorenzo's Oil*, which told the story of ordinary people triumphing over a terrible disease and finding their own cure. That inspirational story and the haunting music of Barber's *Adagio* have made it a firm favourite of mine to this day.

This night, however, was very different. We had an 11.30pm table booked at a restaurant called Tall Orders for a fundraising supper and raffle. As I waited, an ambulance hurtled up Shaftesbury Avenue, cutting through the traffic. This wasn't unusual – there were always either fire engines or ambulances racing past outside. The Palace Theatre is actually right next to the fire station, and on many a night, a call-out for the fire brigade coincided with the onstage gunshots and the array of dead and wounded on the barricade. There was always a big laugh from the audience when the wailing sirens filled the London air as the war dead of Paris lay in front of them.

I carried on waiting, pacing up and down in front of the stage door. Ten minutes later, another ambulance flew by, filling me with unease. When it got to about 11.20pm, there was still no sign of Dursley, and I really began to worry. Where the hell was he? He was often a bit late, but this was too late, even for him. Jon, Anthony and Shaun all headed off to the restaurant, shouting, 'See you in a bit, Nollie!'

I didn't express my anxiety to anyone as they passed me by; I didn't want to say anything, because I didn't want to cause any gossip. I was aware that there were rumours about Dursley, and so was he, but he was not at all ready to be completely open about his status yet, and the secret was not mine to tell.

By 11.30pm, there was still no sign of him. Now I was really concerned. I decided to call Her Majesty's Theatre, and the stage doorkeeper confirmed he had left on time to meet me. This made me panic; I wasn't sure what I should do. Did he meet someone and go for a drink? Did he meet someone and go for more than a drink? Whatever it was, he would not have just left me waiting. *Something's wrong.* I walked to Tall Orders, just in case he was there, but he wasn't. Desperate, I went to a red phone box. Stepping in a pool of urine and breathing in stale cigarette smoke, I clocked the usual array of calling cards with various buxom women offering everything for a good time – I hoped it was safe sex, at least. On the black counter where they kept the telephone directories, I placed a handful of coins. I heard the Swiss Glockenspiel clock in Leicester Square chime midnight as I started calling London hospitals.

I called the Royal Free first. As I waited for someone to answer, I realised I had a problem. Who should I ask for? I didn't know what name to use: his real one, or his pseudonym. If he'd been taken somewhere while unconscious, they would look in his wallet and find his real name, but if he could speak, perhaps he would say Paul James. Or, if it wasn't the Royal Free, maybe he would just say his real name.

My mind was full of possibilities as I called the Royal Free, the Middlesex Hospital, and St Thomas'. I decided to phone each one twice, using a different voice each time to ask for the different names, so the hospital would not just say, 'I already spoke with you, madam – are you taking the piss?'

'Good evening,' I said, in my finest upper-class *Brideshead Revisited* accent. 'I wonder if you could help me. I'm trying to find out if my brother Mr Dursley McLinden has been admitted to your accident and emergency department, as he has not turned up to meet me. It's been more than two hours, and I fear there may have been an accident.'

No luck. I waited one anxious minute, then tried again, this time, trying to sound as though I was in *EastEnders:* "Ello, I'm trying to find my bruvver, he hasn't turned up to meet me and he's doin' my 'ed in. Can I check if he's had an accident or somefin'? "Is name is Paul James.'

On my fifth attempt, posh Jill found Dursley McLinden. I rushed to A & E at the Middlesex Hospital, and found him there in a cubicle, looking pale and shocked. I was horrified. I rushed to him, and a nurse told me what had happened: 'He seems to have had a fit on Shaftesbury Avenue,' she said. 'Someone called an ambulance. We don't have a bed yet, but we would like to keep him in. Lucky they called the ambulance; lots of times people just think someone's drunk and don't bother with them.'

It was horrible to hear that he had had a seizure – and just a few hundred yards from where I'd been waiting. He had been in one of the ambulances that had raced by the stage door. I knew it. Now my mind was racing with the fear of a brain infection or some sort of HIV-related brain damage. But, for Dursley's sake, I stayed calm and tried to be cheerful. It was clear he was exhausted.

He needed some clothes, so I went to his flat to get some and came back to the hospital. I waited until they had found him a bed, then headed home at about 4am to get some sleep. It had been an exhausting night, but first thing the next morning I headed back to the hospital, where the doctors said there was nothing they could see among their test results that explained the seizure. Unable to come up with an explanation, they advised him to transfer his care back to the Royal Free for further investigation and discharged him.

We went straight to the Royal Free, and, of course, once he was there, they kept him in. Tom, a lovely nurse and a man we had known since the beginning, said to me, 'Once we find him a bed, he'll need a lumbar puncture.'

'Oh, shit,' I said. 'That sounds horrible.'

Tom smiled and said, 'He'll be fine; it's a common procedure.

They put a needle into the spine to take the fluid, then check it for any infection. You need to lie flat for twelve hours afterwards; if he sits up he'll get a blinding headache.'

Common procedure or not, it sounded awful. Tom explained that they were checking for toxoplasmosis, and I wondered whether a cat had been anywhere near Dursley, or where or how he could have caught it.

I had to leave to go back to the theatre for the swing rehearsal, worrying, of course, but not saying a word to anyone. I was already planning to return to the hospital for a late-night visit after the show. I comforted myself with the thought that Dursley would probably be sleeping after the procedure, so hopefully he wouldn't be too bored or stressed. He was definitely going to be in for a few days, at the very least.

I never got used to going into the hospital and up to the ward at night. It was a disconcerting experience because, as any woman knows, anywhere dark and quiet can feel threatening. I would park on Haverstock Hill and run into the hospital, glancing around in case anyone was behind me. I always felt very nervous, because I had to enter the hospital through the lower ground floor, where the deliveries came in, not through the main doors, which were closed at night. It was always dark and empty, and I was always alone. The two lifts were never just there waiting. I quickly pressed the call button, full of unease, nervous that a lone man might get out of the lift, or that another might appear and get into the lift at the same time as me. My vivid imagination conjured up images of rapists or murderers, ready to grab me – if I heard a footstep behind me, I planned to scream or run. Once in the lift, I would sigh with relief, free to worry about Dursley again and wonder whether there would be any news.

There was a hush in the hospital at night. You could almost

call it peaceful, except for the odd bleeps and buzzes of the drips or the oxygen machines, and occasionally someone shouting for a nurse. The lighting was soft and low, and I always got a smile from the nurses' station. Most of them were familiar to me now, and I continually thought to myself how wonderful they all were.

I made a coffee in the kitchen and kept Dursley company for a while. Unusually, he was in a single room rather than on a ward. It was lonely at night, and the hours could seem long if it was difficult to sleep and you were alone with your thoughts. But, all things considered, Dursley seemed rather calm. Lying on his back, he looked up at the ceiling contemplatively, then turned his eyes to me, trying to keep his head still.

'I think there are people at *Phantom* who have guessed the truth now, so it'll probably be easier,' he said.

There was a slight pause.

I held his hand. 'I think so too,' I said. 'It would be good if people can understand why you're tired or that you need a break sometimes.'

'Robert told me he wants to do more with the cabarets,' Dursley said. 'He's been really helpful.' Robert Jon was a *Phantom* cast member, a great friend to Dursley, and a constant supporter of our shows. 'I'm going to tell him,' Dursley said decisively.

I nodded in agreement and squeezed his hand.

He then made another very confident decision: 'I want to organise a concert version of *Dreamgirls*,' he stated. 'I'm going to ask for the rights.'

Clearly, while his body had been lying still, his mind had been working overtime. He sounded absolutely sure of himself, as though this was a very simple task. I thought to myself how remarkable it was that he'd had such a grand idea when he wasn't even allowed to move his head on the pillow, but that was Dursley all over. He never stopped thinking and planning great things.

Our lovely chat about *Dreamgirls* was interrupted by a horrible screaming and shouting from one of the other rooms, which cut through the quiet of the night like a knife. We knew who it was, and we caught each other's eyes in mutual understanding. It was a man we knew was one of the waiters from Joe Allen. There had been rumours about him, but now we knew they were true.

'It's awful,' Dursley said. 'He's going mad; really demented.'

I looked towards the open door into the hallway, my eyes following the noise. It wasn't long until the screaming stopped, but the atmosphere had changed irrevocably, from calm to deeply sad and fearful. Neither of us could stop thinking about that poor man but, to keep Dursley's spirits up, I changed the subject back to something more positive.

'I'll come back tomorrow and see if they'll let you go home,' I said. 'Hopefully you can get back before I need to get to the theatre,' I added, as I got up to leave.

'Bye, Nollie,' said Dursley with a smile and a wink. He loved calling me by my new nickname. Shaun Kerrison had started it, and it had spread very quickly until everyone in *Les Mis* called me Nollie – although Anthony liked to call me Nurse Nollie instead. I smiled back as I turned to walk out the door. I knew he was serious about *Dreamgirls,* and it made me happy, because I knew Juan was just going to love the idea too.

The next day, the news was good. There was no sign of infection, and the doctors didn't seem to think there was any dementia or brain damage. They put it down to something to do with HIV that could cause epilepsy, and simply said he was going to have to live with it. They discharged him with the insight that it might happen again, but it might not. I thought I had better spend some time learning what to do if someone had an epileptic fit. I remembered kids having them back at school and finding it really frightening. There were all kinds of old wives' tales about how to help a person who is fitting, such as putting a spoon in their mouth to stop them swallowing their tongue. Really, though, you just had to let someone get through the fit and then put them in the recovery position, making sure their airways were clear. I knew it was likely they would wet themselves or possibly vomit. I said a silent prayer to the universe to please not test me with this particular trial.

As I left the ward that night and headed for the now completely empty lifts, I looked into the rooms as I passed. As usual, I saw sad and emaciated young men. In one room, though, a different sight caught my eye, and I felt compelled to pause and look in through the open door. In the low light, an extremely thin and fragile young girl was lying on a bed, looking as though she was fading away. Her skin was almost translucent in its paleness. She wasn't alone, but she certainly wasn't surrounded by love. A guard sat at her bedside, a prison warder in uniform. I felt a deep shock to see that the girl's arm – the one not attached to a drip – was attached to a handcuff, which was then attached to the warden's arm. It was this humiliating and dismal image that stuck in my head as I hurried through the dark corridors and ran to my car.

In a moving interview with the *Guardian* in June 1989, one woman with HIV, Amanda Heggs, described this horrific feeling: 'I am dying not from the virus but from being untouchable.'

That same year, it was estimated that women accounted for

a third of HIV infections worldwide. In the most recent studies from the HIV Commission, women still make up a third of people living with HIV, with an estimated 31,000 in the UK.[14] Women do not get offered routine testing, and often feel they have to borrow the language of gay men to even discuss AIDS. Many may only find out about their status during an antenatal check or other hospital treatment. I can't help but wonder whether, all these years later, we need a new fight to help improve the diagnosis and care of women with HIV.[15] As I drove home that night, I thought about the (almost exclusively female) nurses on the ward. They were all so lovely, especially gorgeous Charlotte: so caring, so positive and so full of fun.

Once again, I marvelled at how dedicated and kind they all were. *It seems odd to me*, I thought, *that they don't seem to mind people visiting at any time*.

It was at that moment that, with a sinking feeling, I realised something: there probably weren't many other wards in any hospital where every patient was expected to die, so I supposed the visitors to the Garrett Anderson ward were given a few extra privileges.

# CHAPTER 22

*Every atom of me and every atom of you . . . We'll live in birds
and flowers and dragonflies and pine trees and in clouds and
in those little specks of light you see floating in sunbeams . . .*

Philip Pullman

At the start of 1993, I attended a glamorous fundraising event
for the famous theatrical charity the Grand Order of Water Rats.
Jae (who had been advising on music for the event), was put on
the top table with all the celebrities, forgetting me completely in
the excitement, so I was given a seat on a different level. I found
myself next to a rather handsome, dark and studious-looking man
with small glasses. He was dressed in a dinner suit, but still managed to look a little untidy. As I was on my own, we chatted, and it
turned out that, of all professions, he was a doctor, specialising in,
of all things, infectious diseases. His name was Dr Mark Nelson,
and he was funny and charismatic. I didn't want to irritate him
by talking about medicine, even though I was desperate to ask all

sorts of questions. Instead, we engaged in the usual party small talk – until, all of a sudden, he casually revealed that he had been heavily involved with AIDS patients and, from what I understood, was a world-renowned expert. This was the cue I needed.

'Well,' I said, 'fate has put me next to you tonight.' He must have regretted sharing this information with me immediately, because after that I stuck to him like a limpet.

I was excited to find myself so close to a doctor who not only was involved with AIDS, but clearly in my eyes knew all there was to know. I realised this man would be aware if there were any new treatments on the horizon that might help my friends. So, for the first time, I spoke to an HIV specialist, socially, about Juan's situation. Dr Nelson nodded as I told him about Juan's diagnosis, what drugs he was taking, and even what his T-cell count was. He was lovely, giving me his number and telling me to send Juan to him so he could assess the situation and do some tests. I was thrilled – it felt great that someone in London was willing to help.

Pleased with this new development, the next day I called Juan with my news. I was really hopeful that perhaps there would be some sort of new treatment or trial on the way, and I knew that, if this was the case, it would give Juan some positive energy. I had started to believe that the mindset behind the illness made a huge difference to the outcome. I thought of Derek and how amazingly positive he always was about his cancer treatment. I was sure his spirit was part of what had cured him. Last time I'd seen him, Juan had seemed so positive and ready to fight – and now this doctor could help make that happen. Luck really had been on my side when, out of hundreds of people, I had sat next to Dr Nelson.

In the spring of 1993, I finally managed to organise Juan's appointment with Dr Nelson at the Chelsea and Westminster

Hospital. Juan's doctors in Paris suspected (but had not confirmed) that the Kaposi's sarcoma might have spread to his lungs, so Dr Nelson had booked Juan in for a bronchoscopy at the very new clinic opened by Lady Diana a few years previously called the Kobler Centre (originally part of St Stephen's Hospital). As we arrived, I noticed a boy who I knew very well from *Les Mis*. He saw me and I saw him, but such was the fear of being labelled with AIDS that he completely ignored me, averting his eyes. Of course, I said nothing. It was possible he had just come in for a check-up – people did all the time – but there was something about the look on his face that told me he was positive. From that day on, he avoided me at all costs, afraid to even catch my eye. It left me feeling awkward and sad that the fear ran so deeply.

There was new information about treatments for AIDS being bandied around on an almost daily basis, so I was feeling positive about Juan and the fact that he was about to meet one of the most forward-thinking doctors here in London. Maybe, just maybe, there would be some trial or something that he could enrol in that might help him. I had convinced myself by now that the inevitable would actually never happen: that my boys would just go on and on. I could look after them, and one day soon something would be a success. They just had to hold on long enough.

It was a Friday, and I had taken a few days' holiday to be able to spend some time with Juan. As we walked in, I said quietly, 'Don't give your own name. You never know where that could lead.'

'Who will I be, Jilly?' he giggled naughtily. 'Shall I be Pablo Streisand? Or Juan Rivera, or Minnelli?'

'They'll know you're lying if you say Minnelli, you big old queen.'

'Darling, I shall sing "Maybe This Time" for them, and they will love me!'

In the end, he opted for Rivera, laughing his big, hearty laugh as he quipped, 'I prefer Chita Armitano.' He decided to stick with Juan for his first name, and we chuckled about poor Dursley now being forever Paul.

'I think at least I would like them to call me Juan if they are telling me I have a week to live,' he said flippantly.

While we waited for his turn, we chatted about how fabulous Chita Rivera was in *Kiss of the Spider Woman*, keeping our minds occupied as the imminent procedure felt daunting. Juan began talking about his new opportunity to sing with the Opéra Comique in Paris. He was hoping his voice would be good enough.

'Of course it will,' I said encouragingly, hoping in my heart that it would be.

I had been reading about positive focus and the way that, through embracing a challenge or a life-affirming event such as a wedding, the immense power of the mind could extend life expectancy. I believed it was all possible. I thought Opéra Comique was a brilliant thing for Juan to look forward to, but as I looked at him now, I saw a man who looked far frailer and more fragile than he had before. I reflected that Juan had been HIV positive for five years now. For the most part, he had not been plagued with all the more minor opportunistic infections that tortured Dursley, but could his mental positivity keep him fit enough to work – and, beyond that, keep him alive? The Kaposi's sarcoma lesions on his skin had grown. They were dark purple, almost black against his brown skin, and hard to the touch. I don't know why, but I had always imagined the lesions would be soft, almost like blood blisters. They weren't; they were solid and aggressive.

It took all Juan's willpower to remain hopeful. He wore his heart on his sleeve and didn't hide his feelings, involving you in his emotions easily, so you were left in no doubt as to whether he was happy or sad. He had sent a fax to Dursley before he arrived in London, describing to him how he was using his willpower to allow the virus to share his body, but not to own it completely. This seemed to be his way of coping with the ongoing invasion. Dursley agreed with the idea of willpower, of course. He sent a fax back with even more positive suggestions, like that they should plan a holiday in Ibiza and just have a good time. It was their way of supporting each other. Making a plan was a way of kicking in the face the power of the virus. They developed their own parallel friendship without me as a go-between. It was future planning that helped to minimise the trauma of hospital visits.

We knew the bronchoscopy would not be a pleasant experience. Juan was given a tranquilliser, under the effects of which he talked a lot of nonsense. At one point, he announced to me: 'I am Barbra Streisand!'

At the end of the afternoon, Dr Nelson spoke to us seriously but calmly, confirming the devastating fact that there were Kaposi's sarcoma lesions on Juan's lungs. Dr Nelson advised him to discuss it with his doctors in Paris. He was pragmatic and said they would certainly be able to treat the lesions, but not cure them. He was as encouraging as he could be and he mentioned some new treatments that had been spoken about at the yearly AIDS conference. There had been talk of something called a 'protease inhibitor'.

'It works differently from AZT,' Dr Nelson said. 'So it may be good news.' He added the caveat that this treatment would not be available for a couple of years, and with those words, he could see my despondency. 'It's only in research at the moment,' he continued, 'but things are changing daily. We simply do not know; anything could happen. There is stuff around the corner.'

I knew he was trying to be optimistic, but it was difficult to feel anything other than deflated in that moment.

I drove us back to the flat, trying to be positive, but the mood was low. When we got back, Jae was home. His assistant was conducting the show that night, giving him a night off. He sensed that things were not good, and he poured us each a glass of wine.

*Here I am*, I thought, *at the age of thirty-two, with a completely different life from anything I could have imagined when I first headed to London*. I had dreamed about meeting a gorgeous man and moving into an artistic yet stylish flat in Hampstead Village. We'd make enough money to travel the world together, then return to Hampstead to our large house, where we would raise our children – who would, eventually, be responsible for saving the planet. Life had other plans, of course, and here I was: certainly with a gorgeous man, but hoping against hope that his continual flippant premonition in college about dying at the age of thirty-three was not going to come true.

Juan was deeply depressed that evening, and I could not think of a single thing to cheer him up. Everything seemed a little pointless and I sensed that he had lost heart, knowing he would now have to face more aggressive chemotherapy in Paris. It was Jae who saved our evening. He had just bought a small TASCAM Midi home recording studio, which he had set up in his bedroom.

'It's very expensive and very advanced,' he enthused. And then, sounding like he had been paid by Tascam, he announced, 'With just one cassette, you can record up to ten tracks including the voice. Let's make a demo!'

It was an absolute tonic. Juan started singing, and Jae created the backing track. I was happy just to watch, as I realised that all the stress had made me tired. It was lovely to sit and listen to music, and not to have to think about anything for a while. I coped in these moments by being stoic. There was no way I was ever going to cry in front of Juan after his news, or in front of Dursley after another hospital visit, or even in front of my mum when she'd received her cancer diagnosis. Theatre is a business where emotions are on the surface, so when I needed to cry, I cried on the barricade in *Les Mis*, or at the West End Cares cabarets. That was my release.

All in all, the recording session took three hours. Jae arranged a backing track, then, looking highly professional, Juan listened to it through his headphones and recorded the vocals over it. He sounded glorious. The result was a brilliant version of 'Love Can't Happen' from *Grand Hotel*. It's not an easy song at the best of times: it's very passionate and full of fast lyrics, and ends with a very long top A (or a Top K, as Juan once accidentally called it). Considering he was recording just four hours after a bronchoscopy, and with Kaposi's sarcoma on his lungs, it was nothing short of a mammoth achievement.

Singing was the cure that night, and I came to realise it could be a therapy for all kinds of things: cathartic and stress-relieving, uplifting and challenging, all at the same time. Not only did it bring enormous joy and purpose to Juan, but Jae enjoyed playing with his new studio, and I relaxed for the first time that week.

The following morning, I took Juan to Heathrow for his flight back to Paris. Now, feeling emotional, I cried in front of him for the first time.

He laughed kindly and said, 'I don't know why you're crying, Jilly. You should be used to saying goodbye to me at the airport by now.'

But I knew he would never come back to London, and, in that moment, I simply could not stop my tears.

\* \* \*

Back in Paris, with Frederic's support, Juan now had no choice but to tell his family the truth.

His brother Nelson lived in Cordoba in Spain. Juan knew his family were planning a visit, and that they would be there for a month. He had to see them, so he travelled to Nelson's home.

He told Nelson first. It was often the way that people's siblings would take on the responsibility of either keeping the secret or (as with Nelson), breaking the news – effectively acting as a buffer between their ill sibling and the shock and fear of their parents. Nelson took on much of the pressure himself. He had always known that Juan was gay, but he'd had no idea about AIDS. Nelson told their mother and father. The news was met with shock, denial, tears and enormous amounts of sadness. It took his father longer to come to terms with it than it did his mother, but in the end their love and strength won through. It became a huge relief and comfort to Juan to finally have his family's support.

Juan wrote a letter to my mother, thanking her for the way she had spoken to him on the opening night of *Crazy for You*. She had comforted him with the thought that, as a mother herself, she couldn't imagine that his mother would ever reject him in the way he feared.

'Dear Doreen,' he wrote. 'I shall never forget the conversation we had in London about telling my family the truth. Now it is done, and the love and support I am receiving is sometimes overwhelming. Funny how one ought to learn to receive love, too.'

Juan's mother came back to Paris with him and stayed for six weeks, as Juan now needed more and more care. As anyone would be, Juan was exhausted from his chemo. His already compromised body was struggling with the effects, and his breathing had become difficult due to fluid collecting in his lungs. As his mother would soon be returning to Caracas, I made my own arrangements to come to Paris. I booked a two-week holiday from *Les Mis*. The first week was to be spent in Ibiza with Dursley, Jae and Roger, and for the second week I would go to Paris to look after Juan during his chemotherapy, as Fred needed to be away for work. I was content with the plan and happy to help: Ibiza was important to Dursley, as he loved it there. Juan, of course, had wanted to join us, but he was not well enough.

The week in Ibiza was a somewhat uneasy waiting game. I was anxious to see Juan, and I discovered that I wasn't really in the mood for a holiday. The atmosphere was too carefree. I felt the threat of AIDS all around – a party island was sure to be a hub of unsafe sex – so I was worried most of the time. Every day at 4pm, I called the hospital in Paris and was put through directly to Juan's room. It was lovely to hear his voice. He would say he was OK, and we would chat a little.

'*Te quiero*, Jilly,' he would tell me.

'*Yo tambien*,' I would reply, in my best Spanish. It was the same each day.

On 10th September, I called the hospital as usual, but Juan didn't answer. Instead, I heard Fred's voice. He simply said: 'Jill, it is very bad here. You must come now. If you want to see him, you must come now.'

My knees collapsed, and Jae and Dursley came running over.

'I need to get to Paris,' I cried, and they immediately tried to help.

Everything about the next sixteen hours was a haze. They were among the worst hours of my life to date. I called my travel insurance company, but they could not help. The unsympathetic words that blurted out of the receiver of a very dodgy pay phone were: 'Even if it was your mother dying, we could not get you off Ibiza tonight.'

I felt completely trapped. It was a level of stress that I had never experienced. I think it was utter panic. The whole time, I was crying, but inside I was screaming, *Get me off this fucking island*. When you are so hyper and anxious inside, it feels like everything around you is moving at the speed of a narrowboat on a canal. Your mind is working so much faster than you can move your own body, so you drop things, lose things and break things. Your nerves go mad. I couldn't remember how to pack my case, nor could I even think about what I might need.

I didn't call my parents. I couldn't face saying the words. I didn't know how long Juan had left. I prayed he would wait for me to reach him, then berated myself in the same breath in case hanging on made him suffer. I have asked myself many times what it is that urgently pulls you to the deathbed of a loved one. There is a strong, fundamental need in the human heart to be with that person. Is it good for them? I don't know. They say people often slip away quietly when someone is out of the room, so perhaps it is harder to let go peacefully if people are all around you, pulling you back to the world of the living.

All I wanted to do was get to Paris, just to tell Juan I loved him one more time, even though I knew he knew. But it seemed that everything was conspiring against me to keep me on this island, a place I now hated more than anywhere else on the planet. There was no way to get off Ibiza. *Why the hell did I decide to come to an island?* I knew that Juan would never want me to agonise in this way, but I tortured myself with the idea that if I'd only called earlier, I could maybe have found a flight.

I had been by the harbour when I spoke to Fred, and I wanted to go straight to the airport. I couldn't – I needed my passport. I rushed back to the apartment, then took a taxi to the airport. There was one flight going to Paris. Although there were seats available, they refused to allow me to travel because, despite my begging and crying, there was nobody at the desk to sell me a ticket!

I looked like a mess, but I didn't care. It was horrendous. All I could do was go back to the apartment and wait for the airport to open in the morning, then get the first flight off Ibiza. I was completely defeated and spent the night pacing like a caged lion, clinging to the hope that I would get to Paris in time. During the night, Dursley decided that he was going to come with me to Paris, while Jae and Roger were going to organise getting our suitcases back to England – that way, we would just have hand luggage, and could hopefully avoid any more delays.

I called the hospital again, and they told me that Juan was holding on. I told Fred to tell him I was coming, and he told me Juan was listening to the Poulenc he should have been singing with the Opéra Comique. It was in his ears, but he was not conscious. I knew he would be able to hear it, though, and I hoped that somewhere in the spiritual world, I could send him loving thoughts and wish him peace and beauty.

At 6am, Dursley and I boarded the first flight to mainland Europe. Dursley was incredibly supportive. Over the years, he had grown to love and care for Juan. He must have been battling his own fears in this moment, but he didn't show it. I wondered if he was OK, but he seemed to want to take control. The holiday was shattered and so was my spirit. The flight was endless and, upon landing, the line through customs was moving at the pace of a tired slug. Finally out of the airport, we hailed a taxi, paid a fortune to the driver without question, and rushed into the Saint

Louis Hospital. A nurse at reception hurriedly led us to the ward. I felt such relief: after sixteen hours of desperation, as we ran along the long, stark corridor, I fully believed that, as the nurse was hurrying, we must have made it in time.

But I was wrong. He was gone. Lying on the hospital bed was the thin and tired shell of Juan Pablo Armitano, I touched his face. Still warm. His body was covered with just a blue sheet. He had slipped peacefully away just before we arrived with music in his ears. His vibrant energy was still. His journey was over, and our journey was forever altered. I was completely empty. I didn't want to be there, but I didn't want to be anywhere else.

Here at the hospital, one by one, his small 'family' arrived from around the globe, joining Frederic, who had been at Juan's bedside. All of us were too late. Juan's mother Gladys and sister Dolly arrived from Caracas; Nelson came from Cordoba; his close friend Sonya flew in from London; and Dursley and I rushed from Ibiza.

All united in grief and powerless with the inertia of loss.

We spent the next week trying to help and support each other: Juan's mother would help me, then I would try and comfort her, then we would try and look after Sonya. Nelson seemed more stoic, though we knew how much he was grieving. Frederic was devastated but seemed to be dealing with his loss in a pragmatic, organised and private way. I believed he was being strong for Juan. Apart from Frederic, we were all visitors. We stayed in Juan and Frederic's apartment: a cocoon of people united by this unspeakable grief and shock. We helped each other. And copious amounts of red wine helped us all.

Juan's funeral was powerful and uplifting. We gathered at

Église Saint-Roche on Rue Saint-Honoré, and the service was conducted in three languages: Spanish, French and English, reflecting Juan as a global citizen. The congregation did the same: from Venezuela, Britain, France, America, Germany and Norway, people travelled to Paris with their own special memories of Juan. We heard Poulenc's 'The Gloria' one last time, and the entire French cast of *Les Misérables* sang 'The People's Song' with true passion. There was a beautiful personal tribute from his friend Juan, who he had last seen on our road trip to California. He described how Juan's laugh could light up a room, and how the many facets of Juan – his extravagance, his intelligence, his naughtiness and his passion – made a whole, wonderful person. Next there was Jae, who (emotional, but keeping it together) sang 'People' by Barbra Streisand, and finally a recording of Juan himself, magnificently singing 'We Are Family' from *Dreamgirls*. I vividly remembered the first time we'd heard it, back in Dayton, Ohio, just over a decade ago, when we'd been without a care in the world. Gladys broke our hearts as she stepped forward to kiss the coffin goodbye.

It was over.

Grief is all-encompassing and inescapable. It seems to magnify the world of brightness and excitement all around you, but it grips your heart with a numbing sorrow, preventing you from fully being a part of it. All you can do is get on with life and accept that you will never again feel quite the same: that you will always carry loss, and that this grey sadness will become part of the colour of your life. This was never more intensified for me than as we passed through Montpellier to reach Juan's final resting place. The cafés were packed with beautiful people, all laughing and having fun in the glorious sunshine. I was looking at them, but inside I was seeing the shadow of the cypress trees around Juan Pablo's simple and unassuming grave.

Rest in peace, my adorable Juan Pablo Armitano.

# CHAPTER 23

*Alone, alone, all, all alone,*
*Alone on a wide wide sea!*

Samuel Taylor Coleridge

I was back in London and back to *Les Misérables*, trying to deal with Juan's death in the best way I knew how: I talked about him. I talked to friends, I talked to my parents, and I sought advice from people who had been through similar heartache (by this point, I knew a few). I put pictures of him on my mirror in my dressing room so I could remember the lovely moments we'd shared together. I missed him.

Anthony Lyn would walk into the dressing room, look at Juan on the mirror and quip, 'Nurse Nalder, don't put a photo of me on your mirror, or I probably won't make Christmas!' It made me laugh. The show and my wonderful castmates were a constant source of stimulation and fun, and going in each night gave me something positive to focus on and look forward to.

217

London was now on a par with New York in terms of how our theatre community was being attacked by the full force of the pandemic. In spite of all the warnings and messages about safe sex, it was already too late for many people. AIDS had taken over in the West End, and we heard daily about people getting sick and dying. We had to get used to attending funerals. I thought about the way elderly people often say things like, 'When you get to our age, dear, your social life is all about meeting at funerals.' It was just like that for us: there was often more than one funeral in a week, each one trying to commemorate another young life lost.

Sometimes, the families didn't want any friends to attend, and some might particularly try to prevent boyfriends and partners from coming. Boys were denied any intimacy or control over their life partners' affairs in the last weeks before they died, and often found themselves frozen out of funerals and inheritance, which could mean losing a home after years of sharing their lives together. There was no legal status for gay relationships.

After Juan's death, I seemed to worry more about everyone – particularly my mum, who was still having regular check-ups for cancer, and Jae. I was terrified that he would be next, and deep down I felt that if he also succumbed, it would be the ultimate last straw: I simply would not be able to cope any longer. Juan's death was also a terrible mental stress for Dursley, not only because he had lost a friend, but because (I believe), it made him even more conscious of his own mortality. On top of this, he was finding it increasingly difficult to perform in his show, because he was so tired and plagued with problems. Although not life-threatening, they were debilitating, like the constant need to be near a toilet. We mapped out the public conveniences across the West End, and McDonald's came to the rescue on more than one occasion. Oesophageal candidiasis (thrush) was also becoming a massive issue for Dursley – it was so thick in his mouth and oesophagus that he was finding it impossible to swallow. Even water was an effort. He took fluconazole constantly, which helped a bit, but it never seemed to cure it entirely. It was impossible for me to imagine what he was going through, but I could tell that, even though he was always stoic, it was a feat of endurance to get through each day.

Existing constantly on the edge of anxiety, I lost half a stone. That's not a complaint, just an indication of why I was always glad to get back onstage and be somebody else for a while. But one damp, cold night, I had just come offstage and was midway through changing for the finale, when I heard my name called over the Tannoy. There was a phone call for me. This was not unusual, as we would often call each other to make plans for after the show. I answered, expecting to hear either Jae or Dursley.

'Hello?' I said cheerily.

'Hello, is that Jill?' The voice was new. 'I'm calling from the Middlesex Hospital, I am a nurse here. My name is—'

Her name may well have been Judy Garland for all I knew. I didn't hear it, as my mind was already racing. *Middlesex Hospital? What on earth has happened now?* My mind rushed ahead, thinking she was going to say that Paul James (Dursley's pseudonym) was there, that he'd had another seizure, or possibly something much worse. Thankfully, my thoughts were interrupted as she explained, 'I am calling on behalf of your friend Derek Chessor. Would you be able to come to the hospital? Derek would like to see you.'

I was shocked. This was completely unexpected news. 'What's happened?' I asked, panicked. 'Has he had an accident?'

'If you are able, could you come to the Charles Bell ward for half an hour?' the nurse continued, avoiding my question.

Suddenly, my thoughts went to the night Derek and I had met, and I blurted out the next question. 'Is it cancer?' I asked, feeling my hand tremble as I held the phone.

There was a pause on the other end before the nurse responded. 'He's not well and he has asked me to call you. Can you come?'

'Of course,' I said, very confused. 'Please tell him I'm on my way.'

I put the phone down and finished changing for the finale in a daze. Why hadn't we heard that Derek was in hospital? It seemed strange. My overriding worry was that the cancer had returned. At the end of the show, I hurriedly dressed and rushed up the road. I knew from the night of Dursley's seizure that it was not far to the Middlesex Hospital from the theatre, so I was there in twenty minutes.

When I arrived, I noticed the same quiet electronic hum, soft low light and sense of watchfulness that were so familiar to me from spending days and nights at the Royal Free. But this was a much older hospital, and it carried with it the foreboding essence of its Victorian design in every brick. I had actually been born in this hospital, and I could not help wondering what sort of apprehension my mum had felt when she'd come here to give birth thirty-two years ago.

I made my way upstairs to the ward, which was closed. A fresh-faced nurse who looked about my age was there to meet me. She smiled and said, 'Ah, Derek's friend. Lovely to see you. Come through.' She took me through to the dayroom. 'Come in and sit down. Would you like a cup of tea?'

'Yes, please,' I replied. I had finished the show an hour ago, so normally I would have had a gin and tonic in my hand by now, but a cup of tea sounded lovely all the same. The nurse treated me with great care and was clearly trying to put me at ease, but I was still fearful as to how bad the news would be. Because of my mum and her cancer, I was very aware that if Derek's cancer had returned and spread, it could be very bleak news. The nurse handed me my tea and went to tell Derek that I had arrived. I was left in the dayroom, alone with my thoughts, thinking first about how lovely the nurse was, then wondering why I was here. And then it occurred to me how strange it was that Derek was being fetched. I had expected to be taken to a bedside. This felt like some kind of summoning.

Suddenly, with a rush of realisation, the penny dropped and I knew, I knew, why Derek had called me. *Oh, my God! This is an AIDS ward,* I thought. It was all so frighteningly familiar: the kind way I was being treated; the respect for me as Derek's friend; the openness of the nurses – it was just like the Royal Free. My heart was racing.

A few minutes later, the door opened. Derek came in alone. He looked tired and weak, and his familiar cotton dressing gown hung loosely on his thin body.

'Hi, darling,' I said.

'Helloo,' he replied with his lovely Scottish lilt.

Before he could speak, I said, 'You don't have to tell me. I've worked it out. I know.'

I wanted to save him the stress of actually saying it. He started to cry, and suddenly, in place of his usual bold, amazingly strong self, there stood in front of me a small boy.

'You should have told me,' I said, as I got up to give him a hug. It was overwhelming to think that the virus had yet another of my friends in its clutches.

Derek sat down a few seats away from me, and began to explain. 'I've known for some months,' he said, 'but I didn't want to worry you, because of Juan and Dursley, and all the stress you've been through.'

I fully accepted that, but I said, 'Darling, you absolutely could have told me whatever was happening. We must all stick together. I'm strong enough to cope with that.'

He looked at the floor as I continued.

'There will be a cure soon,' I said, reassuring him and myself. 'Dursley has been in hospital loads of times. They'll find out what's wrong with you and treat it. You'll be fine.'

He nodded. 'They're doing a bronchoscopy in the morning,' he told me. Before I could respond, he looked me dead in the eyes. 'Don't tell anyone.' It wasn't a request; it was a demand.

'OK,' I said. I had been in this position before.

'Really, no one.' He sounded desperate.

'I promise,' I told him. 'Really. I won't say a word. Does anyone else know?'

'Only Michael.'

Michael was Derek's friend who he often went away with, and who had helped him design his flat. I had wondered in the past about the exact nature of their friendship, and now I realised that Michael was probably a lot more important in Derek's life than any of us had previously thought.

I could only stay with Derek for half an hour, and he looked so upset as I was leaving. The whole situation absolutely shocked me. It was horrible. He had never even mentioned going for an HIV test. All I could think of was how unfair it was that he had already been through cancer, and now he had to face the horror of AIDS.

I walked out of the hospital completely devastated and still in a daze, but the cold night air brought me back to the present. The burden of yet more secrecy left me wondering how I would explain getting home so late. I was very glad Derek had told me, but I knew not telling Jae would be really hard. I would be hiding something from him that would, in the end, cause him great pain, because of how much Jae loved Derek. *This is the conundrum we get ourselves into*, I thought. *The tangled web we weave*. I had to get my positive head in gear to stop my thoughts from spiralling. I told myself that, as it was still early in his diagnosis, Derek would probably be out of hospital quite quickly. Then we could work out a plan of action.

Derek did come home for a while, and we discussed his situation, but he was adamant about secrecy. Like Juan and Dursley had been, Derek was terrified of anyone knowing at work. He was afraid of being treated differently, of being judged and talked about. At that time people were too frightened to visit the wards for fear of spreading AIDS to other loved ones in the outside world, such was the continuing misinformation. I was deeply saddened but it was not unusual, and this prospect was certainly not easy for Derek to take. Understandably, he feared abandonment. Maybe it was easier to keep a secret than live with the possibility of rejection.

Much to my dismay, Derek was back in hospital within a few short months. He had a fever, and we knew he must have an infection, but there was no firm diagnosis. This was an ongoing struggle for patients with AIDS. The scope of the disease was so wide, and the immune system was so weakened, that their symptoms could be caused by a vast number of potential illnesses. This meant that, if the infection didn't have an obvious cause, patients would only get weaker and weaker as they waited for a diagnosis and treatment. Derek was desperate for any sort of treatment, as he felt the job he loved was in jeopardy. He was currently one of a small group of booth singers working on *Starlight Express*, which was a West End sensation. Having run for about a decade, it was a great source of work for booth session singers. Derek had worked on and off in the booth there for many years. It had started as a part-time job, but he loved it – and, of course, he was the life and soul of their corner of the theatre. He was as wild as ever, playing pranks on his unsuspecting castmates and generally getting up to mischief. In the words of his friend Michael: 'He was the terror of the booth, and he had a little devil in him.' There was the time he tried to recreate in the tiny booth the Rooster MacBrewster (*Fat Pig*) character for the friends who had missed it. He got so excited by their laughter and recreated it so loudly into the microphones that the audience of *Starlight Express* got to enjoy 'Och The Noodle Noo' as well.

I longed for that carefree prankster as I sat by Derek's bedside. His face was serious, and he was visibly unwell. I knew that the issue of work would be a difficult one.

'What will you say to them at *Starlight*?' I asked him.

'Nothing. I don't need to. I'll be going in every day to do the show,' he said, defiantly.

'How on earth?' I asked, gobsmacked.

'I'll see the doctors in the morning, of course, and then I'll get the tube to Victoria and do the show,' he told me.

I didn't think he was serious, but, to my surprise, he did exactly that, for weeks on end. It's incredible to think that someone as ill as Derek was could get out of bed, go to work and come back late to the hospital. This was just a testament to his willpower, and also to the incredibly inspiring support he received from the Charles Bell ward which, under the charge of its first sister, Jacqui Elliott, allowed patients to wear their own clothes, leave and return as they fancied and even have access to a make-up artist to help disguise Kaposi's sarcoma.

Each evening, as planned, Derek left the hospital to do the show, then he headed right back to the ward and got into bed. I did my best to help him, running errands and taking care of his laundry. Thankfully, his flat was close enough to mine that I could pretend I was nipping out to the shops, or going to visit Dursley.

Derek and I continued our secret journeys for a few weeks, as there was no question of him being discharged until the doctors could get to the bottom of his illness. But the infection seemed to be unsolvable, and the doctors were baffled. It became harder for me to maintain the positive mental attitude that I believed had so helped Dursley, and, as time went on, Derek's problems grew worse. One day he had called in sick to the show, saying he had a throat infection, but the doctors told me they were testing for 'cat scratch'.

'What the bloody hell is that?' I asked. 'I've never heard of it.'

They told me that cat scratch is spread in the saliva of cats and can cause all manner of symptoms in an immunosuppressed patient. *Not cats again*, I thought.

The testing continued. The doctors tested for lymphomas, tuberculosis, viral and bacterial pneumonias, all kinds of bugs, viruses and even some tropical diseases.

'Has he been travelling?' one doctor asked me.

'Only to Sweden,' I replied. 'He played the American in a concert version of *Chess*. Do you know the song "Pity the Child"? He sang that phenomenally.'

I can only assume the doctor did not, as his face remained serious. 'It doesn't matter if he travelled somewhere years ago,' he told me. 'Infections can lie dormant until you have no immune system, and then they reactivate.'

This was a scary thought, and yet another worry to add to the already long list.

When the tests came back, there was no sign of cat scratch or lymphoma. But they did find something terrible on Derek's lungs. Only months after the tragedy of losing Juan, I was floored once more as the doctor revealed the diagnosis: Kaposi's sarcoma. It was horribly reminiscent of that awful day with Juan and Dr Nelson. I knew they needed to treat it as soon as possible, which meant that Derek would need chemotherapy immediately. It was a daunting prospect, and I felt resigned to the difficulties I knew lay ahead.

'Do they know you've had cancer treatment before?' I asked Derek, after we learned the news.

'Oh, yes. It's all on my records,' he replied, before quickly changing the subject by asking about Jae.

I was distraught for Derek. I knew that the prognosis could not possibly be good. There had been a few years between Juan being diagnosed with HIV and receiving the news about the Kaposi's sarcoma in his lungs, whereas Derek had developed it so quickly. I kept thinking how unlucky he was: he had only just been diagnosed with AIDS. He must have had low immunity for a long time without even knowing. It didn't seem fair that he'd hardly had any time to get used to his diagnosis – but then, nothing was fair about this illness.

A few days later, I headed back to the Charles Bell ward. Derek was asleep when I came in, so I sat down beside him. He was out for the count, and my eyes wandered across the room. I glanced at the pile of notes at the end of the bed. Something caught my eye, and I did a double take. 'Diagnosis: HIV Positive 1985,' it said at the top of the sheet.

*Well, that's wrong,* I thought. *Hell alive, how are they going to get anything right if they don't even know when he was diagnosed?*

I sat with him for a while, but it didn't seem like Derek would wake up any time soon, so I decided to leave. Michael arrived just as I was heading out the door. We had hardly met before, but our shared love for Derek meant that we had an instant bond.

'He's asleep. Do you want to go for a coffee?' I asked, trying to keep my voice down.

As we sipped our drinks, I told him about the mistake in Derek's file.

'No,' Michael said. 'That's right.'

It took a moment to sink in. I was gobsmacked. '1985? But that's nine years,' I said.

'Yes,' said Michael. 'Derek was diagnosed in 1985, and I was diagnosed the year after. We've been together since then.'

'Oh my God,' I said, shocked. 'He's kept it secret all that time. You and the diagnosis.'

'Derek was determined no one would ever know,' Michael said.

'But wait – what about the cancer?' I asked.

'There is no cancer, Jill. He never had cancer. Not ever.'

I felt completely dumbfounded. All our chats about cancer and my mum, all our talks about successful treatment and alternative cancer therapies . . . we should have been talking about AIDS instead. The mist cleared, and the view was crystal clear. So deep-rooted was the stigma, and so powerful was the fear surrounding AIDS, that Derek had created the perfect scenario to explain his illness to everyone he knew. He knew that one day he would become gravely ill – and when that day came, everyone would just think the cancer had come back. It was the perfect plan to ensure no one would ever know the truth.

When Derek was first diagnosed, it was not even called HIV. He was one of those young boys who had been told he was carrying HTLV-III. I learned that he was only twenty-six when Michael had persuaded Derek to join him on the first-ever trial of any AIDS treatment. The Concorde trial gave a selected number of patients either AZT or a placebo. Derek had stopped taking it, convinced it was making him more ill. A remarkable insight into the power of the mind, as Derek was only ever given the placebo.

There was so much new information to come to terms with. I wondered what sort of relationship we would have had if Derek had told me the truth from the beginning. Even the true nature of his relationship with Michael had been a secret. The relationship anxieties that Derek experienced, in tandem with the terror of HIV, meant that Derek kept Michael in a box, far away from his other friends and the rest of his life. Before I came to see Derek again the next day, I rehearsed what I was going to say to him over and over again in my head. I would tell him I had read the notes, that I knew the truth. I would say, 'Please don't try to hide things any more, because I want to help.'

My preparation was all in vain, as I soon realised we would never be able to have this conversation. Much to my distress, I arrived at the hospital to find Derek awake but not making any sense.

'Billy Connolly is in the next bed,' he told me, 'and he's driving me mad. Not only that, but the ward is disgusting. There are chickens everywhere – and no one seems to care.'

It was both funny and sad. The doctors thought he'd had some sort of allergic reaction to the medication that he'd been given. Or, they said, it could be that the virus was causing some confusion in his brain. They said he could improve.

He didn't. Derek was there, but he wasn't. I knew that we had lost him. He would never come back. Even though he had made me laugh, I was already missing him.

From our shared experience of AIDS, Michael and I knew that this was now a crisis situation. So, the four of us who now knew Derek's secret – me, Michael and two of Derek's closest girl-friends – gathered in Michael's flat in King's Cross and came to the heart-rending decision that we had to tell his parents that he was ill. It was decided that I would speak, as we believed it would be better for a girl to deliver the news. They had never been at ease with their son's sexuality, and if they thought there was a possibility of a boyfriend, it might make things worse (although I couldn't see how much worse it could possibly be). So, from a telephone in Michael's apartment, I made the call. I heard the phone ring a few times before Doreen, Derek's mum, answered in her lilting Scottish accent.

'Hi Doreen. It's Jill, Derek's friend, calling from London,' I said, shakily. 'Derek is desperately ill, Doreen. You should come to London as soon as possible.' I spoke as quickly as I could, trying to avoid any small talk as it felt wrong. 'He's had a terrible reac-tion to some medication,' I added, as calmly as I could manage.

His mum sounded so shocked and worried at first, but then so hopeful that he was going to get better. 'Derek got through all his cancer treatments before. Do you think he'll be alright?' she asked, urgently.

By this point, I could hardly stop myself from crying. 'I don't know,' I said. 'But you must come soon.'

Trying to tell the truth without being entirely truthful was exhausting. I could tell people that he was terribly ill, and probably wasn't going to get better, but I couldn't go into detail for fear of getting further into a web of lies. There was also an odd sense of relief, as I knew that I could finally tell Jae the truth. I tried to soften the blow by telling him that we did not yet know what the outcome was going to be, and that the doctors were still doing tests. Even so, Jae was devastated. Derek had been Jae's friend before he was mine, and Jae's disbelief and shock were evident: the shattering revelation that Derek had AIDS accompanied by the incredulity that I had known and he had not. When we told his friends at *Starlight* that Derek was not coming back, they were equally devastated. They immediately thought it was the cancer, of course, and we did not correct them. We let the cancer story continue. Derek's secret would still be kept.

When Derek's parents arrived, the Charles Bell ward did something incredible. They said they would say nothing to his family about his diagnosis, as they knew that Derek did not want his parents – or indeed anyone – to know he had AIDS. They removed all the literature to do with AIDS and any helpline numbers, and simply said he was having treatment for a lung tumour. It was true, but the tumour was Kaposi's sarcoma. They were only obliged to be honest if they were directly asked if he had AIDS.

Michael did tell Derek's brother, Colin, the truth, and Colin kept the secret. He remembered Derek calling their parents the previous October and informing them he had cancer, but he had told them then that he could beat it and he was doing well. They were happy to be convinced he needed no further treatment. That was all they knew until the day they received my call. Derek's parents were in shock. They were resigned and accepting of what they saw and were presented with. They sat by Derek's bedside and held his hand. They seemed overwhelmed. They loved him. They knew we did, too, and they let us organise their son's last days. They never once questioned us or the doctors.

Friends were coming in to visit now: friends who knew that he was dying, who loved him dearly. There were rumours of course; they were, after all, saying goodbye to a young gay man. But they spoke only of his fight with cancer, for that was the story he had created. There was a vigil, and people came and went – always stoic at the bedside, and always crying as they left him. His brother and parents were there, as were Michael, Jae and I.

From witnessing Derek's final journey, I learned that dying is an active process. I had not been able to reach Juan in time, and it would not have been my place to be there with Colin Bell, but now I saw that there are stages to pass through as the body shuts down. Although Derek's mind was failing him, along with most of his body, the nurses told us that his heart was young and fighting to keep him alive. He must have felt the love as friend after friend came in to sit by his side.

On 26th April 1994, Derek lost his battle with AIDS, with his unknowing parents, his secret partner Michael, his lovely brother Colin and his closest friends around his bed.

I thought back to our conversation on the balcony when we'd been on holiday in the Canaries three years before, and remembered the quote from *Peter Pan*: 'To die will be an awfully big adventure.' I said a silent prayer that Derek's mind and his soul had been ready, because now I understood the place he had been speaking from when we had that conversation.

A couple of weeks after his death, twenty of us, dressed respectfully in dark colours, boarded a plane from London to Scotland. From the airport, a small coach took us on a sombre and quiet journey to Perth Crematorium to say our final goodbye to Derek. This group of friends, all singers, formed an ad hoc choir and sang his favourite Carpenters song, 'Yesterday Once More'. It was a beautiful service, full of tears but equally full of love, joy and respect. With the sadness of the service over, we continued to Coupar Angus to toast our gorgeous friend and eventually to laugh together as we remembered his wonderful humour. And, as per the instructions that had been drilled into every mourner, no one, *no one*, mentioned AIDS.

Derek had fought an incredible battle and had saved nearly everyone any grief at all until the last few weeks of his life. He had made his whole journey almost entirely alone. From his first awareness of his sexuality to the overpowering shame of AIDS, he had lived a life full of secrets, yet he had also filled the lives of those around him with enormous fun and joy. I remain privileged to have been able to share in that fun, and to have seen and loved the real person, even for such a short time.

Rest in peace, brave and inimitable Derek Chessor.

# CHAPTER 24

*It is far more important to know what person the disease has, than what disease the person has.*

Hippocrates

A few days before Derek passed away, I found myself doing double shift as Nurse Nalder, as Dursley had once again been admitted to the Royal Free. I received a call from the company office at *Phantom of the Opera* at the end of my show. The call had, at first, filled me with fear, but I ended up laughing. Although the office did confirm my worry that something was wrong with Dursley, for once it was nothing to do with AIDS. He had been on for Raoul (his understudy role) and mistimed a jump from the stage through a trapdoor. He'd landed badly, damaging his leg, and the office were concerned it was a fracture. I was so relieved that it was something normal. Chuckling, I said, 'Oh, is that all? Thank God for that. I'll pick him up as soon as the show comes down and take him for an X-ray.'

We were sent to the private Parkside Hospital in Wimbledon, where they confirmed the ligaments were badly torn. With his leg strapped and relying on a crutch, Dursley would be off work for many weeks. He moved into our flat, as it was impossible for him to cope alone.

Jae and I switched rooms, and I was demoted to a camp bed in the same room as Dursley. His leg was improving daily, although he still needed his crutch. However, his long nightmare with thrush in his throat was not improving, and it was not responding to the usual treatment from fluconazole. The doctors at the Royal Free recommended doses of intravenous Liposomal Amphotericin B. We were told the drug could be dangerous, and could cause life-threatening damage. Many people in the medical profession call it 'shake and bake', because it can cause violent chills and fevers, but we called it 'paint-stripper'. Because of the risks associated with the treatment, Dursley needed to be in hospital and monitored while receiving it. The drug could not be exposed to sunlight, so all in all, Dursley's hospital bed was a picture of misery, with the mysterious black bag-covered drip and his leg held up in a sling.

The paint-stripper was doing its job on the thrush, but it was systematically damaging the veins in his arms, all of which had collapsed. It was decided that a subclavian line would be put in. This is an intravenous tube that goes into the chest below the clavicle, making the delivery of strong medication easier to tolerate. It reminded me that when Peg had met Duncan in the West End a few years before, he too had had a line put in his chest. It was very upsetting, and I didn't allow myself to think too deeply about the possibilities.

That night, I returned to the hospital to discover the new tube had still not been put in Dursley's chest, despite various clinicians having attempted it more than ten times that day. An on-call junior doctor was 'bleeped', and he dutifully arrived to have his go. I started to wonder if there was a prize for the winner.

Dursley, who hardly ever complained, said, 'This is bloody agony. Please get it right this time.'

But the doctor failed: his eyes were drooping and, after more than fourteen hours on call, he was falling asleep in front of our eyes, with the long needle in his hand. For once, I was angry. I marched to the nurses' station. 'This is crazy!' I said desperately. 'Surely there must be someone who can do this properly.'

It was very late, about 2am, when a new doctor walked into the room. He smiled at us both and spoke very kindly in a soft voice with a South African accent. He explained what he was going to do, and sat down on the bed. Taking Dursley's hand he said: 'I'm Dr Tyrer. I am new here on the ward. I know what has been happening. I can do it easily; don't worry.'

He did it in one go, so quickly and neatly I was astounded. He seemed lovely, and for the time he was with us, he lightened the mood. He had a big smile and sweeping shock of long hair, which he kept flicking out of his eyes. Within minutes, you could tell he had a naughty sense of humour. He chatted to us, asking Dursley a bit about how he was feeling and what he did. He read the notes and saw what Dursley was up against, and left us with the words: 'I've never liked Andrew Lloyd Webber, but I'll make an exception and come and see *Phantom of the Opera* as soon as you get out and back to the show.'

I could tell he liked us. From that point on, Dr Tyrer became a massive help, and a real beacon of light in the dark times ahead.

After his latest stint in hospital, Dursley tried to return to the show, struggling against the enormous barrage of infections that

AIDS inflicted on him: adenovirus, impetigo, herpes, diarrhoea and recurrent thrush – the list was endless, and there was the constant fear of something more serious. Nothing was scarier than the regular eye tests for CMV retinitis, and the horror of blindness should the infection be spotted. Cameron Mackintosh showed incredible understanding and allowed Dursley to do the show whenever he was fit enough. It made an enormous difference to him to know his job was secure.

In spite of all his struggles, Dursley still strove to be part of the West End community he loved – and he continued making moves towards putting on that long-awaited *Dreamgirls* concert. One of the original Broadway cast, Loretta Devine, called and left a message on his answering machine, and he was thrilled when he heard her sexy voice drawling, 'Hi Dursley. *Dreamgirls* in London is on my mind, on my mind . . . on my mind.'

As well as his continual planning for *Dreamgirls*, Dursley was still firmly involved with West End Cares. One of the activities we were involved in was the yearly Walk for Life, which started in 1990 and was organised by Crusaid. The march was held to raise money and awareness, and West End Cares became part of the institution. We walked the ten kilometres dressed in attention-grabbing regalia with all the other shows, waving banners or singing. In the past, the walk had been in Hyde Park, where the British version of the AIDS Memorial Quilt would be laid out, but this year, 1994, it was ending in Shepherd Market, with a stage and a big cabaret organised by West End Cares.

Dursley insisted on doing the walk because his leg had healed very well. I was more than a little against it, thinking it would exhaust him, but in the end it exhausted me. I was carrying his twenty-four-hour urine-collection bottle, which was needed at this point to check kidney function. By the time we got to

Shepherd Market, it weighed more than a heavy bag of shopping and I was shattered. Dursley kept saying, 'Sorry Nollie,' and then, with his best lost puppy face, adding soulfully: 'I've got adenovirus.'

That same summer, Dursley's parents came to London. The week was an act, on Dursley's part of awesome proportions, as neither of his parents knew he was gay, never mind the fact that he also had AIDS. What in the past would have been a joy was a source of great anxiety for Dursley. Not only was he concerned about his own illness, but he was now worried about his father, who had been diagnosed with chronic emphysema. This meant that Dursley was feigning energy he did not have in order to make sure his father was comfortable and well looked after. He was clearly frail and exhausted, but somehow, in spite of his severe weight loss (he would wear layers of clothes to give an impression that his body had some bulk) and the fact he appeared anything but healthy he managed to put on a convincing show.

To Dursley's great relief his parents never once commented about the way he looked. He was the apple of his mother's eye, and I think the love she had for him could not allow her to consider the truth that something was wrong. She was also at this time desperately concerned for the health of her husband, so she did what we humans are always so good at and denied to herself that there were issues to be confronted. We were sitting on a knife-edge and the expression 'the elephant in the room' never rang truer.

Dr Tyrer organised Dursley's hospital visits that week to work around the situation. Dursley would say he had to go to the theatre and we would drive to the Royal Free, where his treatment would be waiting for him. Then he would head back to the flat as if all was OK. It was a necessary conspiracy, a dark farce and there would be no happy ending.

Dursley was the fourth of five children and had always been close to two of his sisters, Tracy and Melanie. Tracy knew that Dursley was HIV positive, and for a while she was the only member of his family to know. Dursley, like a lot of gay men who had AIDS and feared causing such pain for their families, was full of guilt. On top of ill health, these boys often lived with a constant fear of what it would do to their parents when they found out. The bond between many gay men and their mothers can be deep and complicated, but when it came to the boys I was close with, they simply wanted to protect and look after their mothers, to love them and make them feel special. They wanted to be a source of pride, and AIDS left them in danger of being a source of shame. The lack of acceptance of their sexuality in the first place often meant the ground was never prepared for honesty. Many boys in the eighties and nineties were left with a bleak choice: tell and face rejection; or don't tell, and perhaps leave it too late.

Dursley, like Juan before him, didn't want to cause that sort of grief until there was no alternative. That's why he had only confided in his sister; why Juan had turned to his brother before his parents; and why Derek was never able to tell the truth. But the real truth is that years of secrecy followed by discovery at the eleventh hour causes a different kind of pain: the pain of 'if only', and the thought that you could have had the chance to do things differently. I'd had a small taste of what it was like to be on the receiving end of this secrecy when my mum had not told me about her cancer.

As Tracy had for a while been the only family member who

knew Dursley's secret, she had carried double the anxiety. She had hidden the truth from her mum, and she had borne the entire burden of the knowledge. The stress was enormous, and eventually she had begged Dursley to share the situation with one of his other sisters.

'It's too much to bear alone,' she had said to him.

Dursley agreed to tell his baby sister, Melanie who also lived in London. Tracy was very relieved, not only to be sharing the burden, but also because Melanie was nearby, and so would be able to see Dursley and provide support if he needed it. Tracy lived on the Isle of Wight, so her journey would be too long in an emergency – on top of which, she had two very young daughters.

Both sisters lived with fear that they would receive a call saying either Dursley or their father was dying, and there was the haunting question for them of which one would be first. It wasn't until September 1994 that one of these most-feared situations arose. Dursley had planned to spend some time with Tracy, and she'd travelled from the Isle of Wight to be with him. They were together when they got the dreaded phone call to say that their father was unlikely to survive the night. They both made the long journey home to the Isle of Man in time to see him take his last breath. It was heart-breaking and terrible because, on top of the loss, no one had been able to contact Melanie, who was away for a weekend in Paris. Dursley took control, trying desperately to find her, and eventually tracked down her hotel.

It was the day after their father had passed when Dursley finally spoke to her. When she received the phone call she knew instinctively it wasn't good; there were no mobiles then, nor the constant contact we have today, so such a call heralded something really serious. With trepidation, she picked up the phone, thinking, *It's either Dursley or my dad*. She heard Dursley's voice say, 'Mel?' and knew immediately it was about her father.

It was a terrible week for the whole family. A few of us went to the Isle of Man for Jim's funeral. Really, it was Dursley we were there for, although we had known his dad for many years and wanted to give him a good send-off. I knew Dursley's grief for his dad was compounded by trying to get through the funeral, trying to be a good son and care for his mum, but most of all trying to hide his illness. Dursley was ill with a fever all week. His sisters were trying to look after him, dosing him with paracetamol. On the day of the funeral, he collapsed by the grave, and they had to wrap him in blankets as he was shivering so much. I knew that, for Dursley, the day was tinged with a sad relief that at least now he would not have to face his dad with the words he would have found so hard to say: 'I am homosexual, and I have AIDS.'

# CHAPTER 25

_____

*Ev'ry time we say goodbye I die a little*
*Ev'ry time we say goodbye I wonder why a little*
*Why the gods above me who must be in the know*
*Think so little of me they allow you to go.*

Cole Porter

It was November 1994, and Dursley had been lying on the sofa for weeks. Blood test after blood test revealed nothing. He was suffering from 'profound lethargy', one of the 'symptoms' you may read on a list when you research an illness on the internet. In his case, profound lethargy meant it was only the willpower of an Olympic athlete that got him off the sofa and into the bathroom in time to avoid humiliation. He had the desire to fight, but he barely had the strength to lift a fork to force himself to eat. Sometimes, he could hardly actually lift his head to vomit. He was fading. He was skeletal, with absolutely no appetite, and I was frantic. After three weeks, there were still no answers from the blood tests.

When a hospital sends blood cultures away for analysis, it is not always easy to identify the bacteria, virus or parasite. In this case, it was failure after failure.

'He shouldn't be alone,' someone from the clinic told me over the phone. 'If he falls, he won't have the strength to get up off the floor.'

This was easier said than done, as I was rehearsing every day and had to leave the flat for long periods of time.

Back in April, during the week of Derek's death, I had auditioned for Sam Mendes. He was going to be directing Cameron Mackintosh's new production of *Oliver!* at the London Palladium. It was such an anxious time, and Derek's condition had been so fragile that I hadn't been sure if I would get to the audition at all. In fact, I'd been sitting at his bedside with my music and a feather boa (for a music hall song) in my bag. I was indecisive and anxious, and didn't know what to do. It was only when Michael insisted, 'Look, Derek would absolutely want you to go,' that I decided I would – and I got the job. All things considered, it was so exciting to be going from the Palace to the Palladium without being out of work for even a week. It was a hectic time. Emotional as it was to be leaving *Les Mis,* it was an opportunity to be part of a brand-new revival and it was thrilling to be going on to something new.

As Dursley grew weaker, I was facing busy days of technical rehearsals, the days when the stage crew and technicians spend many hours onstage checking positions, moving pieces of the set, and working on lighting, sound cues, entrances and exits. It's essential that the actors are on hand. This all leads up to dress rehearsals, followed by previews and, finally, the big opening night. I was spending practically every hour of the day at the Palladium, then staying at Dursley's at night.

I called everyone I knew Dursley felt comfortable with, and they took it in turns to come around and sit with him at his apartment. The apartment was a recent acquisition through a housing association that helped house people with illnesses or disabilities. Sister Hogg and I had helped Dursley move in. It was close to Russell Square, and had one bedroom, a large living room, a small balcony and lovely views of Shaftesbury Avenue. Among those who took shifts with Dursley were his sister Melanie (who was a stalwart), Niko, of course, Roger and Jae. Peg took an afternoon off work to come around for a few hours, and she has never forgotten the next friend on the list to arrive. The friend breezed in, looked at Dursley lying on the sofa, then peered around at the flat appraisingly. His next statement shocked the sensitive Peg, but actually made Dursley laugh out loud.

'Fabulous flat, darling,' he said. 'It's almost worth it!'

With all of us taking turns to look after Dursley, and with my busy rehearsal schedule, time began to move very quickly. Suddenly, it was just four days before the opening night of *Oliver!* Previews were underway, and I was up very early as there was quite a lot of morning medication to organise and laundry to do before my rehearsals. I was listening to the rush-hour traffic, disinfecting surfaces and getting ready to count pills when the phone rang in the living room. I managed to grab it just before the answering machine kicked in.

It was Dr Tyrer calling from the Charleson Centre at the Royal Free. He finally had the test results. Dursley had MAI: *Mycobacterium avium intracellulare*, an opportunistic infection more often seen in birds than humans. Most people carry MAI in their body, but it is not likely to cause illness if a person's T-cell count is between fifty and 200. At this point, Dursley was living with a T-cell count of two. Following on from his original idea of naming each remaining T-cell he had, when Dr Tyrer had told him there were just two left Dursley quipped back that they would now be known as 'Dick and Doris'. Laughter was how Dursley softened the blow for himself and others. Later, he took the joke further when his next T-cell count came back as zero, telling Dr Tyrer, 'It looks like Dick and Doris have gone on holiday.'

Dursley hadn't had MAI before. It was a moment of massive relief for me when Dr Tyrer seemed upbeat about the diagnosis, and it was even more wonderful to hear that there were antibiotics to treat it, and that Dursley would not have to be in hospital to receive them.

Dr Tyrer explained: 'It's a combination of four antibiotics and one of them, rifabutin, may change the colour of his skin – he should look like he has a gorgeous suntan.'

'Bloody fabulous,' I replied.

Dr Tyrer, or Mervyn, as he told us to call him, was and is a unique doctor who had the ability to connect with his patients in a way that totally surprised us. I had never imagined a doctor could be like him, and his patients and their friends and families alike loved him. He has a gift for making anyone feel that things are going to be alright, no matter how desperate the situation. He carries with him a positive force, which he can infuse into people like a holistic drip. Somehow, he gave us security and hope. It was that hope that filled my heart as I raced off to the hospital to collect the prescription before my call at the theatre. Dursley, with his usual compliance, started the regime of antibiotics to fight MAI as soon as he had them in his hands.

I often hear people in casual conversation saying, 'Oh, I don't like going to the doctor, it's not for me,' or, 'No, I never take antibiotics.' And I always think to myself, *Well that's easy to say when you don't need them.* When you do, antibiotics can literally be the gift of life. I watched a BBC TV programme called *Pain, Pus and Poison*, which stated that before antibiotics, it was not unusual to be wounded on Monday and be dead by Friday. The first man with sepsis who took a trial dose of antibiotics started to recover, but then there were simply no more available, and he died. The documentary described the incredible process of creating supplies and working out dosages using, of all things, the natural penicillin that grew on mouldy melons.

I was so relieved that Dursley was getting the proper treatment. It was as though a cloud had lifted, and I was also loving these days of our first previews. Throughout the whole rehearsal period, I had been afraid that Dursley was not going to recover, and that he would end up in hospital again – but after three more days on rifabutin, he was a completely different person! He was up – and he was hungry. He was still very thin, as he hadn't really eaten for six weeks, but he was recovering. For the second time, Dursley seemed like Lazarus.

Just like the time he had defied medical science when the lymphoma disappeared, enabling me to go to Paris for Juan's opening night, there Dursley was at my opening, along with Jae and my mum and dad. They came not just for the show, but for the party afterwards. It was a spectacular party, one of Cameron's finest. Extravagantly, he'd hired a portion of the London Underground, simply to ferry people from Oxford Circus to King's Cross – and goodness knows what lengths it took to secure the St Pancras Hotel as a venue. At that time, it was a spectacular derelict building, and for this night it had been kitted out as the back streets of London, complete with a massive oyster bar, lots of pies and fish and chips, and, to top it all, 'Nancy's Gin Palace', named after the long-suffering heroine of the show. We didn't say goodnight until 3am. Dursley happily headed home alone to his lovely apartment, while Jae and I headed to Balham with my mum and dad. I was relieved to be sleeping in my own bed again after all those weeks on Dursley's sofa. What a rollercoaster – and, once again, what a will to fight Dursley had shown.

Not only had the antibiotics saved Dursley's life, they had saved my opening night. The show was a big success and received many fabulous reviews, although there is always one; in the words of the witty *Variety* critic Matt Wolf: '*Oliver!* wants to deliver that uniquely English phenomenon, "a knees up", and accomplishes only that.'[16]

A few weeks later, the antibiotics saved Christmas, too, as Dursley was fit enough to enjoy it and look after his mum, as it was their first Christmas without his dad. That Christmas, everyone who loved Dursley gave money for an inspirational Christmas gift for him. Following that first long stay in hospital (and his miracle recovery) Dursley and Jae had taken a trip to South Africa. They'd spent ten days in the gorgeous sunshine, and it had proved a real tonic. It was to this type of convalescence Dursley's friends turned once again. Dursley had become a symbol of the fight against AIDS in the West End, and so many people admired his courage. It was decided it would be a great thing for him to spend some time in South Africa again. This was the gift from all his friends. Today you might call it crowdfunding, but back then, it was a whip-round.

We had stayed in touch with the boys we'd met on the ward when Dursley had his lymphoma scare, including Michael (the elegant South African with the textile business), who was now living permanently in Cape Town. When we called him, Michael was delighted that Dursley would be able to visit him. Michael's health problems had worsened, and he was now struggling with CMV. He was eager to see Dursley, and he said his friends would be welcome too. It was agreed that Dursley would stay there for a month.

Dursley went alone for the beginning of his trip, as I couldn't book a holiday from *Oliver!* straight away. I took him to the airport, very nervous about how he was going to cope, but determined not to let my worries show. I knew the boys would look after each other. And two weeks later, I joined Dursley in Michael's stunning townhouse in Cape Town.

It was my first time in South Africa, but I had always wanted to go there. I had imagined driving in a jeep, and going on safari to see the wild animals. I thought the earth would be baked dry and red, and there would be a few acacia trees struggling to survive by the watering holes. I had fantasised about sleeping under the stars.

Not so on this occasion. The land was green and lush, and we drove along streets lined with impressive, beautiful homes and pale purple jacarandas. I knew I would only be able to see this small and obviously privileged part of the country on this trip, but it was more about looking after Dursley's health than exploring.

Michael's town house in Cape Town was serene and infinitely tasteful in its décor, full of his beautiful fabrics and painted in soft colours that reflected the sunlight. It was possible to sit in his garden and gaze up at the magnificent drapes of cloud pouring down from the flat top of Table Mountain. It was awe-inspiring, completely spiritual, to watch the sun rise and see the colours change on the rocks and clouds, colouring the view like a Turner painting.

If his small walled garden had appeared in the Chelsea

Flower Show, it would have been called 'A vision in shades of white'. Tall agapanthus, clusters of dainty roses, scented stocks, cosmos and soft grey-green grasses enveloped you gently in a chrysalis of peace, while the view beyond enticed you to become a butterfly and fly towards the clouds. Nothing interrupted the peace.

As we sat drinking coffee early one morning, Michael said, quietly: 'It won't be long before I will be gone, Jill – and I am happy with that.' He paused for thought, then continued. 'There are many generations of my family that have lived here and looked up at the mountain, and now I am ready to join them.'

It was the first time I had ever heard someone speak in a way that seemed so gently accepting of their own death. I thought back to Derek's words about that 'something' in the brain of an older person that seemed to prepare them for the inevitability of death. *Michael must be an old soul*, I thought, and that was an amazing thing to be. In reality, he was only in his thirties.

Michael and Dursley shared a special bond, formed by the complete understanding of the road they were each travelling. I felt they were united by their shared experience, and I could only imagine the space they were inhabiting.

The three of us spent our mornings sitting around in the sun, just chatting and enjoying the tranquillity and calm. This time of day tended to be about a lot of tablets. Dursley was taking at least thirty pills a day, and the array set out in his dosette box looked like an evil sweet shop: antiretrovirals, 3TC, valacyclovir, fluconazole, domperidone, the rifabutin plus other antibiotics cocktail (to prevent the recurrence of MAI) – not to mention vitamins, immune-boosters and painkillers. Michael had his own regime too, so each morning 'ward round' took its time.

It was the only time in recent months that I had felt any sense of serenity. It was like living in a bubble of calm, but sometimes it almost left me feeling like I was on the outside looking in. I felt shallow or inappropriate discussing anything kind of frivolous or light-hearted, or talking about anything on the news that was about the future. I learned to live more and more in the moment as my world became smaller and more introspective.

This serenity didn't mean that we did nothing exciting, however. Michael was proud of his country, and was eager that we should explore some of it. Although he couldn't join us, and we couldn't travel far, there were so many beautiful things to do around Cape Town. We stuck to the simple things: the beach, a vineyard at Boschendal, and the occasional restaurant visit. We also went on the cable car that goes up to the top of Table Mountain.

The cable car had been running for sixty-five years. We took a trip in the third version, which had been refurbished in 1974. It was open from waist-high at the sides and held twenty-eight people. There were wooden struts down the sides, and although the rest of it was made of metal, it felt really precarious – but very exciting at the same time. We heard that in order to keep the cable car safe, technicians had to travel on the roof of the car, carrying out maintenance as it went up and down the wires.

We paid a few *rand* and boarded, preparing to travel 2,500 feet from the station to the top.

'Stand at the back, quick – get a good place,' said Dursley.

We moved to the back, held on to the rail – and off it went! Full of nervous anticipation, we felt the cable car rise higher and higher until, without any warning, it suddenly swung steeply up the side of the mountain, revealing breathtaking views of Cape Town and the ocean all around. As we moved upwards, the clouds wafted over the sides. I think we both shrieked and laughed at the same time. I was loving it – and loving that Dursley was thoroughly enjoying the whole experience.

The only time Michael actually came out with us was for a beautiful lunch in the shade of the trees at the Boschendal vineyard. We sat at a white table amid acres and acres of beautiful gardens in the grounds of an impressive Dutch colonial homestead, with thousands of vines stretching towards the mountains in the distance. Idyllic and tranquil, it was a beautiful day.

Dursley and I went to the beach on my last day, and I swam in the sea. It was exhilarating to be in the icy Atlantic with the white-topped, crashing waves, and delicious to run out of the sea into the hot sun. I felt so healthy and alive, and the contrast hit me like a train as I went back to Dursley, who was lying in the sun. He had not joined me in the sea. With so little body fat, he was highly sensitive to the cold.

'You go, Nollie,' he'd said. 'I'll lie in the sun.'

The sun really helped some of his skin bumps and irritations, and he loved it. I felt a bit guilty as I returned to him after my swim. I put sun cream on his back, and I could feel his ribs. There was a chill to his skin that he could never quite rid himself of. Somehow, just the way he felt to the touch told me more than any doctor's report could. I knew how frail his body was – and I knew instinctively that there would not be another holiday like this.

My visit had raced by, and I didn't want to leave. It felt like I couldn't bear to tear myself away. I had a sense that, after all the stresses of recent months, we were very close to the end. It was hard enough to say goodbye to Dursley at Cape Town, but the two hours waiting in Johannesburg for my connection to London were lonely, and I felt desolate. I contemplated just getting back on the plane to Cape Town, and I'd almost convinced myself that work didn't matter, that I would figure something out, when my flight was called. Feeling torn, I trudged reluctantly to the gate to continue my lonely journey home. It was not going to be an easy one. I had a strong feeling that this flight home was a voyage to despair.

# CHAPTER 26

*Ya luchan la paloma y el leopardo a las cinco de la tarde.*

*Now the dove and the leopard are fighting at five in the afternoon.*

Federico García Lorca,
'Lament for the Death of a Bullfighter'

At the end of May in 1995, Jae and I held a birthday party for Dursley in our new flat. He was in the last days of his twenty-ninth year and the party was his idea.

'I'd better have a party, Nollie,' he twinkled at me. 'You just never know.'

I took the hint, and it was all systems go for a party to remember. It was a really beautiful, sunny day, and the atmosphere was wonderful. Every single person he invited came, because they knew in their heart of hearts it was not just a birthday party – it was a goodbye party as well.

Most of the *Phantom* cast were there, for although Dursley

253

had only been into work a handful of times since the leg disaster, he'd made a lasting impact on everyone he'd worked with, and they had all fallen under his spell. Sharon, the company manager from *Phantom*, organised the catering, providing beautiful canapes. Robert Jon, Dursley's dear friend from *Phantom*, helped tirelessly all day, as did Jae, and Dursley gave instructions on cleaning and tidying and general staging, with clear directions for hanging balloons and ribbons – and he insisted on vases and vases of flowers.

We had chosen to hold the party in the afternoon, so that it wouldn't go on too late and Dursley could get some rest before his actual birthday, which would be the following day. It had the fresh feel of a garden party, and already the roses were blooming. A pianist played our piano, which had been moved to the central landing to give a better atmosphere to each room. The flat was full of love and care – and a lot of fun. There were beautifully thoughtful gifts, like candles and scents, which Dursley loved. It was a roaring success, and he held court all day, never faltering. I watched closely in case he needed anything, but I didn't need to worry: he was in his element. The cake was stunning, and everyone sang and cheered. There were a few secretive tears, but only in corners, and they were nothing compared with all the laughter. The party was gentle and loving, and people found it hard to leave. There were many extralong hugs as his guests left him at the end of the day.

The following morning, Dursley turned thirty. Despite my efforts to get him to rest, he insisted we go to Orso (a sister restaurant to Joe Allen) for a birthday meal, where we were joined by a few of his closest friends, including Niko, Roger, Robert Jon and Jae.

It was a supreme effort, something he really wanted to do and thoroughly enjoyed, but it was to be his last hurrah. We went back to his flat, just up the road, and sat down with a cup of tea to look through the cards and gifts he'd received. It was calm after the busyness of the last forty-eight hours, and we went to bed before midnight. But there was no sleep to be had. Soon, everything went wrong.

It was as though his body had pushed itself to the limit and was now rebelling. He had a high fever and chills, sweats and rigours, and I knew things were dire. There was an inexplicable fragility to him, as though his body was breaking and his nervous system was misfiring. I didn't know what to do. He couldn't relax or sleep, and he couldn't stop going back and forth to the loo. His hair was soaked with sweat as though he had stood under the shower, and everything hurt. As soon as the sun began to rise, we headed for the Ian Charleson Centre at the Royal Free.

Dursley was so weak by the time we got to the hospital that he couldn't walk anymore. I found a wheelchair and pushed him. At the centre, they could see how ill he was as he lay down on a treatment daybed while tests were done. After waiting what seemed like forever, it was Mervyn who gave me the devastating diagnosis.

'He is severely neutropenic,' he told me kindly, but with no flicker of real hope. 'The immune system is destroyed. He has nothing left to fight with, and he probably has multiple infections.'

'But I've been meticulous with cleaning and disinfecting and cooking everything, and we've been keeping up with the meds,' I said desperately.

'It wouldn't matter what you did,' Mervyn gently replied. 'At this point, he could even pick up an infection from his own skin. He is very sick.' His words were a terrible blow. 'We need to find him a bed on the ward.'

*   *   *

Sometimes, I would have a dream that Dursley died, and then I would wake up so relieved to know that it had just been a dream. In the same moment, I would think, *One day, when I wake up, it will be true.*

Already grieving, I called the theatre and was told to take the night off. I thought in my panic that he might die that same day, and so I phoned those I needed to and could reach, to say that he was being admitted into hospital.

The story continued. Dursley was given a bed on the Garrett Anderson ward, and given antibiotics and fluids. By the end of the day, he was sitting up, and to my amazement he looked better. The next two weeks were filled with blood tests, X-rays and lumbar punctures. I juggled my time between doing the show, briefly popping home and visiting the hospital. It was terrifying to be away from the hospital at night. Each time the phone rang, my heart sank.

Dursley's close friends visited as well. At the end of the two weeks he was taken for a CT-guided biopsy, a procedure I witnessed in order to be supportive, but regretted almost immediately. It was frightening, and reminded me of what might happen in an alien abduction. He was placed helplessly on a bed while an incredibly long needle guided by an enormous machine was inserted into his lungs. I couldn't watch.

The diagnosis was lymphoma. They were certain. Dursley would start chemotherapy almost immediately. There were no more choices left. A phone was brought to the bedside. He called his mother.

\*　　\*　　\*

Just six weeks earlier, Dursley and I had sat with his mother in his flat, and he had finally found the courage to tell her both that he was gay and that he had AIDS. It was a truly dreadful morning, and she was left in utter shock, completely devastated. She had returned to 'the Island' and in some way tried to come to terms with the life-changing information.

It was very difficult to find the right balance between the friends who had loved and cared for Dursley for four years through his illness, and the family, who were in deep shock and finding it so hard to reconcile the truth. I was terrified that I would be asked to stay away, but it was not the case. Dursley needed the support he had grown to rely on. Melanie and Tracy found the situation doubly hard. They had known, but had been coerced into protecting both Dursley and his secret in an effort to shelter their mum, who had not even had time to grieve for her husband before she was faced with the awful truth. Just ten months since Jim, his father, had died and the family were facing a second terrible loss.

June had had only a few weeks to come to terms with the revelation that her son was gay and had AIDS, and now we had to tell her the news that her beautiful boy had cancer, and that his time left would be brief and precious. It was too late for her to discover and understand so much about Dursley's life.

For me and his many friends, we were coming to the end of a road we had been travelling down for four years. For his family, it was the start of a journey of understanding that would last a lifetime. June was being asked to get to know a different person from the son she had thought she knew.

This would be hard enough for anyone, but when you consider her background in coming from the Isle of Man at that time and with the innumerable prejudices all around her, she faced her own Olympian task. She had confided in Melanie the wish that if only she could have known the truth sooner, it may have been easier, that she could have had time to care for him. The door to his sexuality was never open and that was the real tragedy for everyone. Dursley had wanted to spare her as much pain as he could. He'd wanted the family that meant so much to him to be proud of his achievements, but the shame of AIDS prevented both him and them from living with the love he so deserved.

In the end, after a great deal of stressful conversations, it was agreed that any caring Dursley might need would be shared. What came next was a production of awesome proportions. Dursley was at the centre of the 'show', while the people who loved him came and went. Old friends and lovers came to see him. They would arrive and chat and smile at his bedside, always putting on a brave face, but always, always weeping as they left, walking up the long corridor away from his private room. I remembered how we had seen this play out so many times before on the ward. Now, I realised, it was our turn and we were the ones being looked at with sympathy.

Robert Jon unflaggingly fetched and carried, bringing clean laundry for me, as I would stay overnight at the hospital after returning from *Oliver!*, sleeping on a camp bed that had been organised for me in the room.

Unbelievably, Dursley continued to hold his own. He *insisted* on having his chemo, *insisted* on having his treatments, his massage and his acupuncture. All the alternative therapists that had got to know him so well turned up at his bedside at various times, and each one did a little to ease the pain. After a massage, he would seem calmer for a while, but painkillers of the strongest kind were also high on the menu. Peripheral neuropathy meant that a brush of his skin could make him shout with agony, so he was prescribed with ketamine to numb the pain. There were all kinds of pills, drips and treatments. Procedures were made easier with the promise of a strong sedative called midazolam which we laughingly decided to call 'Razzle-dazzle 'em', and sickness was relieved with a regular supply of domperidone – or Dom Perignon, as we preferred to call it.

Dursley couldn't walk at all by this point, but he could talk and his personality was still at full force.

One day, a special new bed arrived for Dursley: a kind of 'Michelin Man' airbed with separate blown-up sections. Air was pumped into different sections at varying pressures, designed with the aim of altering the position of a body that was too weak to move itself. It was effective and comfortable, and made it easier to move him back up the bed as he slipped down. It also prevented the unnecessary pain of bed sores. Dursley could press a button and alter the bed himself if he wanted to change position.

He was showing it to Jae, who loved a gadget and started twiddling buttons. This was a bad idea. The top of the bed somehow raised itself at the same time as the bottom part, and, as Dursley was turned into the filling in a bed sandwich, another new addition to the bedside – the condom catheter – was pulled free. A shot of bloody urine went straight into Jae's face, which not only left him shrieking with the shock, but also with a niggling worry due to Dursley's laughing words: 'I don't know how the hell you've got away with it so far, but after all the safe sex you've practised, Jae, your highest risk of HIV has proved to be my air bed.'

Dursley's other use for his 'magic bed', as he called it, was when he was given the 'cocaine mouthwash'. This was supposed to be spat out after treating his gums, but he found that swallowing it 'accidentally' would give him some fun. He loved to tease Charlotte by popping it in his mouth to rinse, then tipping the bed back with his mouth still full, swallowing and then apologising profusely for his 'big mistake'.

Then there was the day when, after forty eight silent hours without a flicker of response, we watched in amazement as he was brought back to consciousness by Jae saying gently in his ear, 'Dursley, Cameron Mackintosh is on the phone.' The name Cameron Mackintosh ignited a showbiz spark and Dursley's eyes popped open. He raised the bed at full speed, and took the phone as if absolutely nothing was wrong.

'Hello Cameron, how are you?' he said chirpily. 'I don't think I can do a lot, but if you do have any small jobs that I can do from here, I am ready to try.'

It broke my heart.

Dursley was given all kinds of antibiotics to try to stem any infections, and he had yet another blood transfusion. More blood tests were ordered. There was a threshold white blood cell count under which they could not give him his chemotherapy. He was tested for CMV and MAI, although his treatments for those were still ongoing. The doctors did not want to continue the chemotherapy until they were sure he was strong enough to tolerate it, but Dursley, ever determined to recover, became anxious if things were not happening as he thought they should. He had lost his hair and was painfully thin.

His team of doctors asked me to see how he felt: was there perhaps a part of him that wanted to let go? Was he holding on and causing himself untold agony for the sake of other people?

'We don't want him to do that,' said one of the doctors, Dr Nick Price. 'The chemotherapy will probably do more harm than good at this point. Instead, we could keep him comfortable. We will respect his decision, of course.'

There are many things that are difficult to come to terms with when someone you love is dying. One of the hardest to deal with is the realisation that, even though you want to beg them to fight because that is what you want, it would be kinder to let them slip away, because that is what they deserve. It is in our DNA to want to survive, and we want those we love to do the same and stay with us.

*Get a grip*, I told myself. *Don't be selfish!*

So, I sat by Dursley's bed with Dr Tyrer and Dr Price, and tried to think carefully about what to say, and how I would say it without dissolving into tears.

'Dursley,' I whispered, 'don't have the chemo if you would prefer not to. Everyone loves you and we will all be fine. Everyone understands.'

He seemed to be listening.

'Do you think it may be a good idea to let the world slip away?' I continued. 'To not put your body through any more stress, and just perhaps pass to the next world, out of all this pain? You will be an amazing part of the universe. It might be beautiful.'

I waited. I had tried my best.

'Yes,' he kind of mumbled to me. 'That may be a good idea, Nollie.'

There was a long pause.

I thought this must be his way of saying, 'I have had enough medication. I have done enough trying.'

But then he added, 'But that will be after I've had my chemo.'

The doctors smiled. It was almost funny – Dursley was one of the strongest spirits that the hospital had ever seen, and the longest-surviving patient at the Royal Free with full-blown AIDS. It was this tenacity that, as a very young boy, had kept him for hours in the little attic room upstairs perfecting his magic tricks; later, it had given him the power he needed to get away from the suffocation of the Isle of Man, and to accept and fully enjoy his sexuality. It was this strength that had seen him working as an actor and becoming a success in one of the most difficult professions in the world. Even when he was desperately ill, he had performed brilliantly, and he had become a well-known and respected name in the business. Everyone knew and loved Dursley McLinden.

He had never stopped trying to fundraise for West End Cares, and he was always tireless in his fight for others. That same tenacity had got him and him alone to persuade the Americans to allow him the rights to put *Dreamgirls* on in London, for one night only. He had come so close to fulfilling his dream. It was the concert the whole theatre profession wanted to see.

It was this deep inner strength and belief that was keeping him alive now, while Charlotte said to me, sympathetically: 'If he decided to let go, he would probably slip away in a matter of hours. It is only willpower that is keeping him alive now.'

Over the next days and weeks, he slipped further and further from us, drifting in and out of consciousness. When he was awake, he told everyone, in turn, all the time, how much he loved them. It was beautiful. No one was left in any doubt of his feelings, and he certainly knew he was loved and adored.

At times, he surprised us. 'I'd love a whisky, Nollie,' he would suddenly say, and we would have it waiting, always trying to anticipate what he might enjoy next, which music he would like to listen to, who he would want to hold his hand, or what might give him comfort. To me, he seemed mighty in his spirituality, surrounded by a sort of serenity. Visibly, he had lost his hair, weighed less than seven stone and was attached to countless drips. Invisibly, he was a Trojan.

Our biggest surprise was the day we gathered around the bed, waiting for the worst. His breathing was almost so light, it was softer than that of a baby. We were standing there, holding hands, when he opened his eyes, looked at us all in confusion and announced: 'I would love some Marks and Spencer's chicken fajitas.'

As though we had just defused a bomb, everyone rushed into action, smiling and saying, 'Hello,' and 'How are you, Dursley?'

And of course Robert Jon immediately hurried off to M&S.


Our days with Dursley continued in this way, with his bedside surrounded by memories and tears, hugs and kisses, arguments and trauma. There was often pain, but always, and overwhelmingly, there was love.

It was late afternoon. Everyone was exhausted: June was in the large chair dozing, Melanie was by her side, Jae and I were sitting on chairs with our heads resting on the bed each side of Dursley, and Niko, Roger and Tracy were close by. I could feel the heat from Dursley's fever burning into my head as I rested next to him. Half-asleep, half-awake, I felt I was leaving my body, because I couldn't live inside my skin and feel so much love. I felt I was being lifted in spirit to the place he was heading.

Ours was the same story that played out in many hospital rooms during the eighties and nineties, each with its own unique group of family and friends, coping in different ways with the shock and the loss. At the centre of each tragedy was a hero. The word Olympian conjured in my mind images of great strength and fortitude, while the word Herculean, to me, seemed to describe a person faced with a task so great it appears that it can't be achieved, but still that person keeps trying. Dursley never gave up. Some people bow out of this earthly existence and slip away gently, all fight gone, but that was not so in our room, not with our hero.

At almost five o'clock in the afternoon on 7th August 1995, Dursley's heroic struggle finally ended.

Rest in peace, magnificent Dursley McLinden.

# CHAPTER 27

*Tardará mucho tiempo en nacer, si es que nace,*
*Un andaluz tan claro, tan rico de aventura.*
*Yo canto su elegancia con palabras que gimen*
*y recuerdo una brisa triste por los olivos.*

*t will be a long time, if ever, before there is to be born*
*An Andulusian so sure, so rich in adventure.*
*I sing of his elegance with words that grieve*
*And I remember a sad breeze through the olive trees.*

Federico García Lorca, 'Absent Soul'

One day, as we were driving to the Royal Free, Dursley noticed a horse-drawn procession leaving Leverton and Sons Funeral Directors in Camden. There were beautiful black horses with plumes and drapes.

'I'll have one like that, Nollie,' he quipped.

I said nothing, but I remembered.

★　　★　　★

265

We all worked so hard to carry out his wishes, down to the tiniest detail.

Dursley began his final journey from outside his lovely flat in Russell Square, where we'd all had so many laughs, and from there we travelled to St Paul's, the Actors' Church. Over a hundred mourners made the dignified, silent walk towards Covent Garden under blue skies and bright sunshine, led by those very beautiful black horses.

He had requested mourners should 'dress for a celebration', so with his friends and colleagues looking stylish and elegant, and his family dignified in black, we walked proudly behind the coffin, each one of us holding a single white lily.

It was overwhelming. Immense. As the procession moved through the streets, passers-by stopped, bowing their heads and taking off their hats. I was unprepared for the feeling of sad elation that came over me as complete strangers showed such respect. Niko, Jae and I walked close to Melanie, Tracy and his mum June, energised by sorrow.

A few weeks prior, Dursley, fragile but with his dazzling charm still intact, had met with the priest.

'I would like to have my funeral at the Actors' Church, but can I request no religion, please?'

Nothing could dim the McLinden charisma.

'I'll lose my job if I don't at least mention God,' the priest had said. 'Could I open the service with just a little prayer?'

Dursley had agreed. 'OK, then. Just a little one.'

The priest was not the only person to whom Dursley spoke about his funeral. Like so many gay men at the time, he wanted his life to be celebrated. These men wanted to be remembered for the joy and the love they'd shared with their partners and friends. Although hidden away with illness, they did not want their memories hidden away in shame, in the shadow of AIDS. So they made their own plans. They took back some control.

'Mervyn, darling, will you sing at my funeral?' Dursley had asked his doctor (who had become a friend) after quite a lot of morphine.

Mervyn had laughed. 'I will ask everyone to sing – I think you would prefer that!' he answered.

Dursley had also talked to Jae on one of his visits, describing some of the music he would like. 'I want a twenty-minute showbiz medley,' he'd enthused.

Jae had listened, and tactfully reined in some of his ideas. 'It can't be a full production, dear – you'll have to make some cuts. Ten minutes will be enough. Leave them wanting more!'

The horses pulled up at the Actors' Church and we paused a moment before we were led inside. With a feeling of utter amazement, I realised that our procession was not the entire congregation – only a small part of it. It was a full house! The church was already packed to the rafters, and we walked down the aisle to the pews that had been reserved for us at the front.

Dursley had asked Nickolas to give a reading, and he chose Lorca's 'A Las Cinco de la Tarde'. Lorca was a Spanish poet who was killed by the Guardia Civil for being a writer and being gay. This most famous poem is a lament on the death of his friend Ignacio Mejias, a bullfighter and the hero of Spain. Niko and Dursley had once shared a beautiful time in Granada when Niko was filming and playing the role of that poet. A poem of love, justice, stigma and grief, Niko's choice of reading was meaningful on many levels, not least because, like the bullfighter, Dursley had lost his fight as the clock showed five.

I had informed Mervyn that, in the order of service, he would be following a reading from Judi Dench. I expected him to be impressed, or even nervous, but because of the Equity ban in South Africa, he knew nothing of our national treasure and simply said, 'OK' – whereas at least half the congregation would have immediately added this fact to their CV!

Niko and I had struggled to find something appropriate for Dame Judi. We felt we would like the reading to be about magic, to reflect Dursley's talents as a professional magician and member of the Magic Circle. We settled on a reading from 'The Deptford Trilogy' by Robertson Davies as, unbelievable as it may seem today, we could not really find anything suitable about a boy magician!

Next, Mervyn stood. He spoke of Dursley's fight and courage and (without singing a note), invited the congregation to join him in the beautiful song, 'The Rose'.

This was followed by West End star Kim Criswell who sang superbly from *Dreamgirls*, the concert that never came to be. The lyrics 'How many friends have I already lost? And how many dark nights have I known?' have never been more poignant.

We were reminded of the moment as Dursley died, when the last candle in his room burned out and the candle holder cracked and fell. 'Dursley had the last word,' Melanie said.

The service concluded with the cast of *Phantom of the Opera* singing 'Make Our Garden Grow', just as they had in their first West End Cares Cabaret. It was phenomenal.

So much love, so much pain, so many tears and thousands of memories, which people shared then and still share today. As someone once said to Niko: 'Dursley was gold, silver and platinum, rolled into one.'

As Dursley left the church to be taken to his final resting place on the Isle of Man, we knew we had done him proud. He would have loved it all.

*Absence is a house so vast*
*that inside you will pass through its walls*
*and hang pictures in the air.*

Pablo Neruda

# CHAPTER 28

_Legacy. What is a legacy? It's planting seeds in a garden you never get to see._

Lin Manuel Miranda

For me, the time immediately following all the death I had experienced was bittersweet. There were times when I felt happy, but guilty at the same time: I'd take a trip or see a movie, and think, _Dursley would love this_, or, _I must tell Juan about it_, or, _Derek would have made a joke about that._ Shortly before Dursley's death, I was sitting at his bedside when a woman came into the room. She was the palliative care nurse on call that night. She carried with her an aura of tranquillity and this, combined with her gorgeous blond hair, gave her an almost angelic quality in my eyes. I have remembered the words she spoke to this day, and the way she treated death as a positive part of life.

'It is inevitable,' she said, 'but always remember that, even while someone is unconscious, they are aware of your presence.

When they pass, they can still hear you, because hearing is the last sense to go. And if you can stay with them for a while after they have gone, then do, because you will feel that something happens in the room.'

I don't know her name and never will, but for that half hour she spent with me, she gave me advice that I have carried with me ever since. I read recently that an inheritance is what you leave behind for someone, but a *legacy* is what you leave *inside* them, in their spirit. A gift of heartfelt words from an unknown person: that was her legacy to me.

The legacy of AIDS, the pandemic of forty years ago, continues to be inspiring, heart-breaking and amazing for me.

In July 1996, the Eleventh International AIDS Conference in Vancouver carried the slogan 'One World One Hope'. The conference, its speakers and their research signified the beginning of a new era – one of hope. The last day of the conference, a Friday, Dr Julio Montaner announced to the doctors, researchers, activists and health workers from all over the world that Vancouver would be the 'catalyst for change' and to go and spread the news to their colleagues and patients. The sense of excitement was palpable. Within months, mortality and progression to AIDS among people taking triple combination therapy were negligible. It was the 'Friday' that Anthony and I had waited and hoped for for so long.

It had been nearly fifteen years since I'd read that first 'gay flu' article. Now Mervyn came back from that conference in Vancouver and told me, 'For the first time, we have something. There is something that is working. Three drugs at a time. Three different ways to attack. A triple threat – and this time, the virus is not breaking through.' His words filled my heart with amazement, joy and regret all at the same time. Such wonderful news – just eleven months too late for my friends.

My relationship with Dr Mervyn Tyrer both then and now is one of the most rich and enduring personal legacies for me. Always the most creative and caring of doctors, he not only loves his work, but he also loves entertaining, cooking and, most of all, his ongoing education in musical theatre with his life-long friends. Thanks to many of the boys he cared and still cares for – and a little influence from me and West End Cares – he discovered the excitement and wonder of showbusiness.

He used this new-found passion when he was invited to speak to the Royal College of Physicians. Mervyn's talk concerned Highly Active Anti-Retroviral Therapy, or HAART for short. If there was ever a scientific discovery worth singing about, it was HAART, and in a moment of inspiration, he brought the conference to a close with a short chorus from one of his favourite shows, *Damn Yankees* (an all-American musical about the baseball player Joe DiMaggio). He belted out the words, singing: 'You gotta have HAART, miles and miles and miles of HAART.'

I heard Mervyn's words about the conference repeated over and over again by numerous doctors who had worked with AIDS since the beginning and who had seen it all. Finally, we had something. I pushed away the agonising thought, the thought that millions of people have tortured themselves with for millennia: *If only.* If only they could have hung on for a few more months, a treatment would have been just around the corner. Just like Dursley had always said. It was too late for my friends, but the drugs were an absolute miracle for so many people. Boys that were truly staring death in the face were given a second chance and real hope for a future. Lovely young Ben, the man who was so ill when Dursley made his remarkable first recovery, somehow managed to fight and survive for many years due to taking those drugs. That he died only recently is a triumph of medical science.

However, some boys have found the survival itself a huge personal struggle. That is a different kind of legacy. The enormous mental trauma of being told that there was no future for you and that you were facing certain death, to then having to rediscover your place in the world of the living – sometimes left with disabilities, health issues, gruelling drug regimens and financial problems – for some was a mental health burden. Maybe something akin to the soldier who faces the horrors of the battlefield and then has to quickly adjust to 'normal' civilian life.

As with every drug, triple combination therapy was not without its side effects. For example, lipodystrophy was common, and incredibly difficult to live with. It causes fat deposits in the body to change, move and grow. It was distressing to see a face permanently alter its shape, or to see a large lump of fat form a hump on a person's back. As the once-familiar sight of Kaposi's sarcoma subsided into the background, so the disfigurements of new treatments took its place.

Even more disturbingly, my friend Robin suffered for ten years with daytime hallucinations due to Sustiva (efavirenz). The drug itself is a NNRTI – a non-nucleoside reverse transcriptase inhibitor – aimed at preventing viral replication by blocking a necessary enzyme in the reproductive chain. On reading the list of side effects, you might notice more expected problems, like nausea or aches and pains, but you would also see that 'neuro-psychiatric' effects are common too. This friend lived with hallucinations, always in his peripheral vision, of rats running across the floor. On one occasion, he felt compelled to switch on his windscreen wipers to frighten away a mouse that was running across his car windscreen. He became so used to the hallucinations that one night, when he saw a rat in his living room, as he had so many times before, he ignored it completely. Only when he felt its paws run over his foot did he jump out of his skin and think, 'Fuck, that one's real.'

Although its side effects could be severe, triple combination therapy was quite literally a lifesaver, and a long-awaited step in the right direction. Change was coming, but not overnight, so West End Cares continued its work unabated.

Anthony Lyn, who had worked so hard for the cause, recently described it perfectly, saying: 'It was the best of times and the worst of times. The worst, as we never knew which friend would grow sick and die next, and the best, as it really did bring out the best in so many people – in selflessly caring for others and fundraising.'

It was this spirit that led the always optimistic and ceaselessly helpful Murray Lane to remember, 'We developed such a love for each other and found such a great sense of community. As sad as they were, they were joyous years too.' Murray had some extra insight into the disease as he had lodged with Dursley when he lived near the Pink Palace and for many months had personally witnessed how much he had struggled at times.

Craig Revel Horwood told me recently how he felt about West End Cares with his own inimitable slant: 'One of my very first choreographic gigs was for West End Cares, and I was thrilled to be asked to come up with an idea for the show. Not only was it a fabulous opportunity to raise money and awareness for HIV and Crusaid, but an opportunity for everyone in the West End theatres to have a good old-fashioned get-together.

'I had the idea I would choreograph a reverse strip: all the men starting naked, then putting various articles of clothing back on. The men started the dance stark-bollock naked, pretending to urinate at a urinal. They'd then "shake off" at certain times in the music. As a group, they'd bend over, flashing twelve bare backsides, then begin to pull up various pieces of fetish or humorous underwear, only to finally dress as builders and reveal who they were by turning to face the audience to finish the number. The music I selected was Rickie Lee Jones' "Easy Money". It was a crowd pleaser and brought the house down. On the strength of the number and a certain producer being in the audience, I was offered my first West End show as choreographer, *Spend Spend Spend*, for which I received my first Olivier Award nomination.

'The late eighties and early nineties was a tough time for us all in the industry due to losing so many of our talented close friends to AIDS-related illnesses. It was heart-breaking, devastating and downright scary. But just like the folk we are, the show must go on, and we all pulled together to fight. We put on cabarets, concerts, tap shows anytime we could to raise necessary funds. It became a community of travelling artists and an uplifting experience for everyone involved. We had some really good times in a world we felt was collapsing around us, making true and deep friendships that would last a lifetime.'

You could say perhaps that West End Cares changed his life.

Actor Harriet Thorpe really summed it up, too, when she said to me recently, 'All that mattered at West End Cares was treasuring our culture of acceptance, whoever you were, wherever you came from, whatever religion and whoever you loved, and that's all that matters still.'

The West End continued to come out in force throughout the nineties and into the next decade. There was so much to offer that our cabarets and late-night shows became an unstoppable avalanche of entertainment and fun. I have counted more than

200 shows in which we played a part. Our new venue, Centre Stage, saw fantastic shows from the casts of *Sunset Boulevard*, *Chicago*, *Oliver!*, *Blood Brothers*, *Company* and *Salad Days*, and a superb night organised by Anthony called Cruising for Crusaid. That evening, Centre Stage became a cabaret lounge on a cruise ship. Songs were continually interrupted by lifeboat drills and captain's announcements about the availability of huge amounts of food. There were plenty of tropical cocktails, and even more laughs.

We saw performances from West End Cares' continual supporters, including Dora Bryan, Frances Ruffelle, Rosie Ashe, Jessica Martin, Paul Burton, Myra Sands, John Barr, Stiles and Drewe, and so many more. One night I will always remember was 22nd March 1999 (the night that would have been Juan Pablo's thirty-ninth birthday). Sister Hogg showcased his music at the Talk of London, a cabaret venue located at the New London Theatre, which we were thrilled to be able to use for West End Cares. Some years prior to this cabaret, John had won the prestigious Vivian Ellis Award for his new musical *The Clip Joint*. We called our night 'Hogg in the Limelight' – see what we did there? It was a very different night for West End Cares, and it inspired us to showcase more original music from West End musicians.

It was the Talk of London that saw some of our best nights. David Pendlebury, one of the cast of *Phantom of the Opera*, had taken over as Chair of West End Cares. It had only taken one meeting with Dursley backstage to inspire him to become involved, and he stayed in that position for nearly two decades. He spent thousands of hours tirelessly inventing and organising events, and when David was subsequently cast in *The Lion King*, it meant that he remained firmly in the West End and at the helm of the charity.

One day, I came to David with an idea. I had been to a matinee of the film *The Full Monty* and loved it. It occurred to me that the concept would be a perfectly British answer to America's Broadway Bares. Our American counterparts were bold: they had invented an outrageously sexy show that involved people, both boys and girls, performing strip routines. Dressed in amazing, bespoke costumes that were eventually ripped off, they revealed gorgeously fit bodies, while the screaming audiences lapped up every second. We had known about it for a very long time, but the idea had just never caught on here. But after the success of *The Full Monty*, I thought a similar performance could sell lots of tickets. And, of course, the more tickets we sold, the more money we would raise.

David loved the idea, and so we started organising. We agreed the show would be open right across the board, with a routine from any cast that wanted to take part. I nervously approached choreographers, among them the now award-winning Stephen Mear, Nick Winston and Craig Revel Horwood (who has already described his experience) and asked if they would be involved. Once we had the choreographers, everything else fell into place.

Jae decided to take a light-hearted approach, by singing a disco version of the Shirley Bassey hit 'I Who Have Nothing', while proving he had quite the opposite in a studded thong and dog collar. He had to frantically improvise when the tape machine started playing in the wrong place, and just as he was about to fulfil his dream of becoming a sexy podium dancer, he heard (instead of his raunchy backing track), Barbra Streisand singing 'Before the Parade Passes By' from *Hello Dolly*. I really missed the boys in that moment – Derek would have loved that, and never let poor Jae forget it. 'Not bad for a shy boy from the valleys who all those years earlier was begging for a piano,' he would have joked.

We did emulate the sexy boys and girls of Broadway with the

cast of *Chicago* stripping to the Bond theme tune. The night was a huge success, and on the insistent advice of Jae, we closed the show with a real stripper, who shocked us all with his enormous *personality.*

Our celebrity contacts were so vital to the fundraising effort and to raising our profile as a charity. It was, though, the community as a whole that made it happen. Every ensemble member or leading player, every brilliant musician or inspiring musical director, all the tireless stage management, designers, choreographers, crew members, producers, theatre owners, costume designers, wardrobe departments and dressers – every single person helped to raise millions of pounds for West End Cares, and later for the Theatre MAD (Make a Difference) Trust which arose from West End Cares as a completely independent charity when Crusaid closed. We are very proud to have raised more than £10 million to support hospitals, hospices and research, and to ease the suffering of those experiencing the hardships and isolation of HIV and AIDS directly. It is a legacy of which we are all tremendously proud, but, as has been said a lot recently, there is still much to do.

There are many AIDS organisations which were developed to help sufferers in a practical way. The Food Chain, which opened on Christmas Day in 1988, still helps to deliver nutritional meals to people who struggle to maintain a good diet. Jon Osbaldeston and I witnessed their dedication and their delicious, carefully considered meal plans when, in 1993, we loaded up my new Ford Fiesta (Felicity) to deliver hot meals to various houses around north-west London, driving by the Pink Palace as we did so.

One of the main battles left to fight now is the stigma that still surrounds HIV/AIDS. There are many organisations that do just this, for example the National AIDS Trust, CHIVA (Children's HIV Association), the Elton John AIDS Foundation, Body Positive groups in regions around the UK, and, of course, the stalwarts from the very start: the Terrence Higgins Trust, who are still a major contributor to these causes, tirelessly continuing to raise awareness. The Terrence Higgins Trust is an enduring legacy from those first days. This charity has the power to influence the UK government and to ensure action, not just words. The UK government has pledged to end all new HIV transmissions by 2030, and to ensure that those living with HIV are supported through the additional mental health issues they will undoubtedly encounter, as well as the discrimination that still affects so many infected with the virus. The Terrence Higgins Trust continues to engage and push for the government to make good on these pledges, and to 'seize this once in a lifetime opportunity',[17] forty years after the epidemic started.

I have a number of friends who are HIV positive and still feel unable to speak to more than a few close, carefully chosen people about their diagnosis, whether out of shame or fear of judgement or the enduring stigma that HIV can still carry. Of course, disclosing any health issue is a matter of personal choice and should always remain so, but each of these boys bears a quarter of a century of secrecy. It can be a burden. I have now spent nearly four decades keeping the secrets of those who have gone, along with the secrets of those who remain alive today. The responsibility can sometimes feel like a great weight. But it was then – and still is now – a privilege to be trusted.

Thankfully attitudes are improving all the time and the courage of those who have been strong enough, for whatever reason, to be open about their HIV diagnosis, has helped others to understand.

The cast of *Miss Saigon* lost close colleagues to AIDS forty years ago. The story of Steve Grant from the show, perhaps more well known for his pop career in the group Tight Fit, was inspirational. On World AIDS Day 2021, he spoke openly on YouTube about his experience – the sad loss of his partner in the nineties and then his subsequent triumph over the virus is uplifting. He spoke of the support he received at the theatre. He survived through the worst of the crisis and is still strong, looking fantastic, working and achieving great things.[18]

Combination therapy has allowed many people to stay well, to work and behave as though nothing at all is wrong, and so they say nothing. It is easy to see why so many choose to keep their diagnosis a secret, especially when considering the prejudice they still face. My friend, Robin was involved in a financial dispute with his ex-partner. A witness statement was filed at court by his ex, who had legal representation, which referenced his HIV diagnosis and described his health as 'failing'. Robin complained to his ex-partner's solicitor and demanded the Witness Statement be withdrawn because the disclosure of his HIV diagnosis had no bearing on the case. This was agreed and done before any court appearances, but it left Robin feeling very upset: "I felt stigmatised, exposed and shamed." Some of the finest people I have ever known were, and are, HIV positive. Dursley, and his lasting legacy, is a testament to that fact. I am still in disbelief at how much influence he had – and continues to have – on all our lives. His influence in the West End was profound, and his continual drive to fight for himself and others made him a kind of figurehead for the cause.

Meeting Dursley just once and marvelling at his courage inspired David to run a charity for twenty years, and countless others have been moved by his story. His family now speak openly of their brother and their uncle, proud of him for his work both on and off the stage and screen. They are educating the next generation in acceptance and tolerance. Only recently Melanie was touched to find these anonymous words left, with a rainbow flag, on Dursley's grave: 'On the eve of Pride 2021 we remember you for the light you shone on a world that at times remained covered in darkness.'

The same is true for Derek's family: his nieces and nephews know about their uncle, and his brilliant life and brave battle. Juan's family, once they knew, were accepting at the time, and in subsequent years, his mother Gladys didn't shy away from the truth of how her son had died. When I spoke to Juan's brother, Nelson, in preparation for this book, he was so pleased to know that Juan's story would be told – and so proud of his brother and his legacy.

Perhaps the most well-known and powerful example of Dursley's influence came from my beautiful and superbly talented friend, Russell T. Davies, who paid tribute to Dursley in his TV drama *It's a Sin*. The tenacity of his leading character, Ritchie, and the poignant scene about filming *Doctor Who*, were direct tributes to our beloved Dursley, who once appeared in an episode of that long-running British institution. So many of our stories inspired elements of *It's a Sin*, and the show has done so much to open up important conversations about HIV and AIDS. Finally, we are shining a light on the terrible years of the AIDS pandemic, and some people, young and old, are learning about things they never even knew happened.

It is hard to believe that a tiny virus simply looking for some-where to make its home and somewhere to reproduce could shape a generation and make our world what it is today. Many people missed the AIDS pandemic completely – for some, it never even entered their lives – but those it touched are still living in its wake. And even those who weren't fully aware of it at the time are still feeling its effects today.

There is almost an entire generation of gay men (and other communities of course), missing from the world. The generations who came after have missed out on their talents and experiences. The world lost music, art, fashion, theatre, film, literature and humour, and countless business and science innovations that may have shaped our planet in a very different way. Families lost brothers, sisters, mothers, fathers, uncles, sons and daughters.

Dursley's mother left a note with her will and it contained the moving thought that part of her had died when she lost Dursley. I think that is a legacy of AIDS. Many bereaved parents would I believe feel that same loss. Although I have now been without them for more years than I knew them, I continually wonder about the men that Derek, Juan and Dursley would have become.

My experiences with HIV and AIDS have left me with a medical dictionary in my head and a fear that even a mild symptom in friends or family (including myself as I get older) might be a precursor to something far more serious. I know too much and too little at the same time. There is always a list of possibilities in my head every time anyone says they have a cough, a fever, a rash or a bad stomach – or that they've been scratched by a cat! When COVID-19 hit, viral replication, PCR (polymerase chain reaction) testing, variants, antibody testing, double-blind trials and oxygen-saturation levels were alien phrases to some, but they were already firmly etched in my brain. I can still reel off the names of medications, antibiotics and chemotherapy drugs, along with their possible side effects. I think often of alternative therapies, many of which I still like to use, especially massage, reflexology and, of course, positivity.

I do not feel that I sacrificed any part of my life in caring for those with AIDS, but rather that my life has been enriched by the love I have experienced. I ended up taking a path I had never expected to follow. I appreciate my time and health more and more, and I never, ever lose the feeling that time is short. I remain ready to take a chance – or, at least, to try to – at the drop of a hat. I feel compelled to do that after seeing so many around me lose their time and chances.

While *It's a Sin* introduced millions of people to the previously unseen world of AIDS in the 1980s, each day we learn there is still so much to discover. There is still no vaccine. It is still a battle to get treatment, education and understanding in many countries. There are new treatments being developed all the time and science is, at this moment, staying one step ahead, but HIV produces variants when it is given the freedom to replicate, so PEP, PrEP and combination therapy remain vital armour against the virus. The possibility of total eradication of this disease would be the greatest legacy of all.

As we have all learned from COVID-19, a virus does not discriminate. But the gay men who were first infected, whether they were beloved celebrities or the waiters who served them, were judged not for being ill, but for being gay. Then we saw sex workers and the drug users judged. We saw trans people judged. We saw immigrants judged. Only when 'normal' people became infected did the wider world see them as victims rather than people who had brought well-deserved horror on themselves.

So much gratitude and respect are owed to the amazing health professionals who quickly learned a new definition of family and acted upon it, and also to the LGBTQ+ community, who were giants in the face of adversity. Progress would not have been made without their solidarity and tenacity. Countless lesbian women, although not in a high-risk group themselves, worked tirelessly to support the men and boys so cruelly ostracised. The LGBTQ+ community provided – and continues to provide – help for all those struggling with an HIV/AIDS diagnosis. Amazing nurses like Charlotte and Sian are not just good friends to us today but strong allies to the community, using their experiences in the eighties and beyond to promote care and understanding. Charlotte described to Russell Davies, while he was writing, how it felt to work on an AIDS ward in the eighties when they said goodbye to every patient in their care. They are all, like health professionals today working with COVID-19, tremendous human beings.

*It's a Sin* had an amazing impact on so many people, and since it aired, I've heard so many times, 'I cannot believe that happened,' or, 'I just didn't know.' As people have learned more, I have experienced an enormous surge of love and understanding towards those who suffered at the time, and also to me personally. For all of that, I am beyond grateful, but it isn't – and never was – about me. There were Jills all around the world and I'm sure they would tell you the same; and, although maybe not as special as ours, there were probably Pink Palaces all around the world. We could never have imagined that our Pink Palace would touch so many hearts. And who could have foreseen that 'La' could become a camp greeting for so many, not just for us – not to mention also becoming a T-shirt design and raising more than half a million pounds for the Terrence Higgins Trust.

Most of all, the show was about those beautiful men, who fought bravely, set up self-help groups, put themselves forward as guinea pigs for new drugs and never ceased to try and live their lives to the full. I feel today they are all, in some way, getting the love and respect that eluded them at the time. I know that each and every one of them would be very proud and happy to have helped tell the story of the past, and to have played a role in shaping a better future.

# EPILOGUE:
## TWENTY-THREE YEARS AFTER
## THE VANCOUVER CONFERENCE

---

Excerpts from *You Couldn't Make It Up*:
A Play in Three Acts

### Act 1, Scene 1

*On board a cruise ship. Marseille. September 2019.*

*Lights go up on the top deck of a glamorous liner. It is early morning.*
  *Bright sunshine and soft blue sky. Sounds of seagulls. We see JAE and*
  *JON looking at their mobile phones and occasionally glancing over the*
  *railing to the horizon.*

JILL: Morning, boys.

JAE: Oh hello.

JON: Morning.

JILL: Looks fabulous!

JON: It does. It looks gorgeous.

JILL: My dad said the old town is amazing.

JAE: Well, if Bob said so, it must be true.

JILL: He loved France. Everywhere in France. He came to Marseille many times.

JAE: *(Showing his phone to Jon)* Good God. Look at this.

JON: *(Looking)* I know. I saw already. Can't be real.

JILL: What is it?

*JAE turns his phone towards her.*

JILL: God! Grindr! I thought you were looking up a fabulous nature reserve or an amazing restaurant up the hill for lunch.

JON: Well I wouldn't mind climbing that.

JAE: Or having it for lunch dear!

*(They laugh).*

JILL: *(taking Jae's phone)* It says he's positive and undetectable.

JON: Undetectable means untransmissible.

JAE: I didn't know that.

JON: Someone on triple combination who is undetectable and can't transmit.

JILL: Well you should know that, Jae. *(Indicates JON)* And I won't ask how you know, dear . . . happily married.

JON: Ask me no questions and I'll tell you no lies.

JAE: We're only looking for a laugh.

JON: No time for anything else!

JAE: And look at this. *(Jae scrolling through phone)*

JILL: Well hell. The Cruise Director. Looks very different in leathers.

*They all laugh*

JILL: Negative and on PrEP. Well if anyone is doing anything, be careful and get some PrEP

JAE: I've had that voice in my ear, 'be careful', for forty-odd years.

JON: Because she loves you.

JAE: I know.

JILL: And because it took a hell of a fight to get PReP available. Just ask Mervyn.

JON: Of course there's nothing to stop you Jill Nalder trawling the port for a nice sailor.

JILL: I'm waiting till Spain. You know me and the Spanish boys. *They all laugh. Exit.*

## Act 1, Scene 2

*Interior cruise ship. Outside the Fiesta Deck dining room. JAE & JON are already inside. JILL is the last to enter, followed by a smartly dressed, young, handsome waiter.*

WAITER: *(holding bottle of sanitiser)* Sanitise your hands please, madam.

JILL: Of course. It's a good idea this sanitising. I don't know why we don't do it at home.

WAITER: Yes, madam. Keeps everyone healthy. No norovirus on this ship.

*ENTER: THE CRUISE DIRECTOR: a late middle-aged man with immaculately dyed black hair, wearing a smart suit, cravat and Cuban-heeled shoes. He carries the air of a British matinee idol from the 1950s.*

CRUISE DIRECTOR: Morning, Jill. Everyone is looking forward to the WestEnders tomorrow. Lovely reports from the last two shows. Hope you can all keep it up . . . as the actress said to the bishop.

*JILL laughs out of politeness.*

CRUISE DIRECTOR: Have to dash – Quiz Time in the Lido, Acupressure Seminar with Cerise in the Jolly Spirits Bar, then a guest lecture on the drug cartels of South America from an ex-DEA agent on the Fairview Deck. It's a full life.

## Act 1, Scene 3

*Later the same day. JILL and JAE are outside the theatre after rehearsals.*
*The ship is now sailing, and there is a slight swell and movement. In*
*JILL's handbag, her mobile rings. She frantically rummages through*
*her bag to find it, then pulls it out and looks at the screen.*

JILL: Oh, it's Russell. Fab, I'll talk to him. See you later.

JAE: Give my love. I'll see you in a bit. *(JAE EXITS)*

*JILL answers her phone. In a separate spotlight stage left, RUSSELL T.*
*DAVIES is revealed.*

RUSSELL: *(singing)* And I love you so, the people ask me hooow.
How I've lived till now. (*Going up an octave*) I tell them I don't
know.

JILL: *(laughing)* You've been singing that to me every time we
speak since 1982 – and it still makes me laugh.

RUSSELL: I won't keep you. Where are you?

JILL: Just heading out of the harbour in Marseille.

RUSSELL: Of course you are, darling. I've got something exciting
for you. I'm calling to offer you a part in *Boys* – that's the
working title, anyway. There's some really nice scenes. We want
you to play Jill's mother. Well, that is, your own mother. She has
a lovely moment where she hugs Jill. Hello? Can you hear me?

JILL: Oh my God. Yes, I can hear you. Yes, I would love to. I
can't believe it. What are the dates? Hello? The signal's going.
Hello?

RUSSELL: We'll call your agent.

JILL: When's it filming?

RUSSELL: Hello?

JILL: This is incredible.

RUSSELL: It's absolutely right that you should be in it.

JILL: I'm stunned. Hello? I'll call you as soon as I get to the next
port.

RUSSELL: Bye. Love you.

JILL: Love you too. Bye. Thank you.

*The call ends. JILL stands there alone, trying to process this emotional and surprising call.*

### Act 3, Scene 5

*Media City Manchester. Outside a rehearsal room on one of the upper floors. JILL nervously enters and goes towards a door. A sign on the door reads: Red Productions. Channel 4. IT'S A SIN. She takes a deep breath and opens the door.*

*END.*

# ACKNOWLEDGEMENTS

An enormous thank you to some amazing people.

Everyone at Wildfire Books and Headline that worked on *Love from the Pink Palace*, especially Ella Gordon, Serena Arthur and the cover designer Sophie Ellis. I would also like to thank Felicity Price, Tara O'Sullivan and Kate Truman for the great work they did on the legal read, copyedit and proofread.

I would also like to think my hugely supportive agents Chris Davis and Michael Gattrell of CDM Management Ltd, my fabulous friend Linda Jarvis for the title, *Love from the Pink Palace*, and my equally fabulous friend Pinky (Philip Lewis) for being the model on the front cover.

For all the chats, memories, laughs, thoughts and details that reminded me of so much and enabled me to put things together, I have to give special thanks to David Begg (for his thoughts and advice), Paul Burton, Mary Carewe, John Hogg, Murray Lane, David Raven, Peter Stamford, Jeanette Scott, Scott St Martyn, Shaun Kerrison, Stephen Simms, Stuart Platt, Peter Stanford and Chis Neilson, Roger Bunnage, Trevor Jones, Francesca Whitburn,

Geoffrey Henning and David Pendlebury. I would like to say a big thank you also to Craig Revel Horwood and Harriet Thorpe.

A very special debt of gratitude to Nelson Armitano, Colin Chessor, Tracy Rogan and Melanie Rose née McLinden, Nickolas Grace, Michael Elles, Anthony Lyn and Jonathan D Ellis for their incredible support and for re-living both the happy and often painful memories of those brothers, friends and partners they loved so much.

Thanks to Dr Mervyn Tyrer for so much love and care and of course medical advice. Jae Alexander (a true soulmate) for a lifetime of friendship and a constant supply of food and wine while we were busy writing. Russell T. Davies for his friendship, his brilliance and of course the 'camp'.

This book could not have happened without the inspiration, patience and creativity of my close friend Jon Osbaldeston and the continual help, advice and talent of Caitlin Mellon, both of whom were involved every step of the way.

# BIBLIOGRAPHY

Abbot, George; Adler Richard, Ross Jerry; Wallop Douglass. 1955. *Damn Yankees.*

Alcott, Louisa May. 1868. *Little Women.* Boston. Roberts Brothers.

Andersen, Hans Christian. 1851 *Pictures of Travel…* (UK) *I Sverrig* (Danish) www.hcandersen.org

Angelou, Maya. 1993. *Wouldn't Take Nothing for My Journey Now.* New York. Random House.

Aristotle. 335BC (approx) *Nicomachean Ethics.* www.classics.mit.edu

Ashe, Arthur. www.kidadle.com

Ashman, Howard; Menken Alan. 1982. *Little Shop of Horrors.* www. mtishows.com

Barrie, J.M. 1906. *Peter Pan in Kensington Gardens.* London. Hodder & Stoughton.

Bart, Lionel. 1960. *Oliver!* First performance: Wimbledon Theatre 1960. www.mtishows.com

Coleridge, Samuel Taylor. 1798. 'The Rime of the Ancient Mariner' (*Lyrical Ballads*). London. Biggs & Cottle for T. N. Longman.

Curie, Marie. www.laidlawscholars.network

Dickens, Charles. 1840. *The Old Curiosity Shop*. London. Chapman & Hall.

Dickinson, Emily. 1891. 'Emily Dickinson's Letters'. (*The Atlantic*) article: Thomas Wentworth Higginson. www.theatlantic.com/magazine/archive

Fain, Sammy; Webster, Paul Francis. 1953. *Calamity Jane* (film) Los Angeles. Warner Brothers. Released 4th November 1953.

Frank, Anne. Mussatty, Susan (Ed.) *Tales from the Secret Annexe: A Collection of Her Short Stories, Fables and Lesser Known Writings*. (2003 Edition Revised). New York. Bantam.

Friedman, Peter; Joslin, Tom. 1993. *Silverlake Life: The View From Here*. www.imdb.com

Frost, Robert. 1915. 'The Road Not Taken'. First Pub: *The Atlantic Monthly*. New York.

Goggin, Dan. 1985. *Nunsense*. New York. Concord Theatricals.

Hamlisch, Marvin; Kleban, Edward; Kirkwood Jnr, James; Dante, Nicholas. 1975. *A Chorus Line*.

New York. Hal Leonard Publishing.

Henley, William Ernest. 1875. 'Invictus' (*Book of Verses*). New York. 1891. Scriber & Welford.

Herman, Jerry. Fierstein, Harvey. 1983. *La Cage Aux Folles*. First Broadway Performance 1983.

www.concordtheatricals.com

Hugo, Victor. 1862. *Les Misérablés*. Brussels: Libraire International A. Lacroix Verboeckhoven, et Cie. London: Carleton Publishing Co. Wilbour, Charles E. (Translator). Hurst & Blacket. Wraxall Lascelles (Translator).

Jarman, Derek. 1993. *Blue* (film). Basilisk Communications.

Kirby, Andy. 1986. 'Compromised Immunity' (*Gay Sweatshop Four Plays and a Company*). London. Methuen.

Kramer, Larry. *The Normal Heart*. 1985. Original production The Public Theatre. New York. 1985.

Krieger, Henry; Bramble, Mark. 1987. *Fat Pig*. Original Production: Leicester. Haymarket Theatre. 1987.

Krieger, Henry; Eyen Tom. 1981. *Dreamgirls*. New York. Imperial Theatre. 1981.

New York. Concord Theatricals.

Laurents, Arthur; Sondheim, Stephen. 1959. *Gypsy*. New York. Random House.

Lorca, Federico García. 1935. *Llante por Ignacio Sanchéz Mejias*. Madrid 'Cruz Y Raya' (magazine).

Maupin, Armistead. 1978–2014. *Tales of the City*. New York. Harper & Row. Further books in series published until 2014.

Masters, Edgar Lee. 1914-1915. 'The Hill' (*Spoon River Anthology*). St. Louis 'Reedy's Mirror' (magazine). New York. Macmillan.

Miranda, Lin Manuel; Turner, Khary Kimani; Martin, Christopher E,.; Odon Jnr, Leslie. 'The World Was Wide Enough' (*Hamilton*). New York. Warner Chappel Music. Sony/ATV Music. Kobalt Publishing Ltd.

Moore, Marianne. 1944, 'Nevertheless'. www.poetryfoundation.org

Newton, Isaac. www.citas.in

Neruda, Pablo. 1959. *Cien Sonetos De Amor*. Buenos Aires. Editorial Losada.

Niemöller, Martin. 1950s (circa). 'First They Came for the Communists'[...]

Holocaust Encyclopedia. www.encyclopedia.ushmm.org

Nyswaner, Ron. 1993. *Philadelphia*. (film) Los Angeles. Clinica Estertico/Tri Star Pictures.

O'Brien, Richard. 1973. *The Rocky Horror Show*: Original Production. Royal Court Theatre. London. 1973.

Ossler, William. 1918. *The Principles and Practice of Medicine*. New York. D. Appleton & Company.

Porter, Cole. 1944. *Ev'ry Time We Say Goodbye*. London. Chappell & Co.

Pullman, Phillip. 2000. *The Amber Spyglass*. London. Scholastic/David Fickling Books.

Russell, Bill; Hood, Janet. 1990. *Elegies for Angels, Punks and Raging Queens*. London. Samuel French. (2010). www.concordtheatricals.com

Schönberg, Claude-Michel; Boubill, Alain; Kretzmer Herbert; Natel, Jean-Marc. 1980. *Les Miserablés*. London. Cameron Mackintosh Overseas Ltd. www.cameronmackintosh.com

Sagan, Carl (attrib.). www.quoteinvestigator.com

Sanderson, Terry. 1995. *Media Watch*. London. Continuum.

Sanderson, Terry. *Media Watch*. www.gtmediawatch.org

Shilts, Randy. 1987. *And the Band Played On: Politics, People and the AIDS Epidemic*. New York. St Martin's Press.

Thomas, Dylan. 1946. 'Ceremony After a Fire Raid' (*Deaths and Entrances*). London. J. M. Dent.

Wilde, Oscar. 1891. *The Picture of Dorian Gray*. London. Ward, Lock.

Wordsworth, William. 1807. 'Composed Upon Westminster Bridge' (*Poems in Two Volumes. Vol 1*). London. Longman, Hurst, Rees and Orms.

# ENDNOTES

1  Braidwood, E. (2018) 'Gay Plague: The vile, horrific and inhumane way the media reported the AIDS crisis'. Available at: www.pinknews.co.uk/2018/11/30/world-aids-day-1980s-headlines-tabloids/

2  Clendinen, D.; Nagourney, A. (2001) *Out For Good: How to Build a Gay Rights Movement in America.* 1st Ed. New York. Simon and Shuster

3  Robertson, G. (2008) 'The Mary Whitehouse Story'. *The Times.* 24th May

4  Whitehouse, M. (1977) *Whatever Happened to Sex?* 1st Ed. London. Wayland

5  'Vivat Regina' (1987) Channel 4 / St Pancras Films & Metcalf and Mills. Available at: https://www.youtube.com/watch?v=BJxL3a4zxz4

6  Franklin, C. (2020) 'Jerry Herman, composer of *Hello Dolly* Should also be Remembered as an early HIV survivor'. *Chicago Tribune.* 2nd January

7  Garfield, S. (1993) 'The Rise and Fall of AZT . . .' *The Independent.* 2 May

8  Strub, S. (2019) 'The Denver Principles'. Available at:

https://data.unaids.org/pub/externaldocument/2007/
gipa1983denverprinciples_en.pdf

9   Russell, B. 'Elegies for Angels Punks and Raging Queens'.
    Available at: http://billrussell.net/

10  McKellen, I. (1990) 'Tribute'. Available at: www.mckellen.com/
    writings/90charleson.htm

11  MamasDoinFine. 'Jack Tinker A Life in Review' Available at:
    https://www.broadwayworld.com/westend/board/readmessage.
    php?thread=993984

12  Stanley, P. (2008) 'In Memory of Jesse Helms and The Condom
    on his House'. Available at: www.poz.com/blog/in-memory-of-je

13  NAM Aidsmap. 'Travel restrictions for people with HIV'.
    Available at: https://www.aidsmap.com/about-hiv/travel-
    restrictions-people-hiv

14  HIV Commission. 'How England Will End New Cases of HIV'
    report. Available at: www.hivcommission.org.uk/final-report-and-
    recommendations

15  Lister, K. (2021) 'The Hidden History of Women with HIV'
    Available at: https://inews.co.uk/opinion/columnists/women-hiv-
    aids-uk-1980s-activists-882211

16  Woolf, M. (1994) 'Oliver!' Review. Available at: https://variety.
    com/1994/legit/reviews/oliver-4-1200439737/

17  Terrance Higgins Trust. 'Help secure Government funding to
    end new cases of HIV by 2030'. Available at: https://www.tht.org.
    uk/our-work/our-campaigns/help-secure-government-funding-
    end-new-cases-hiv-2030

18  'Steve and Denise Talk About HIV on World AIDS Day 2021'
    Available at: https://yout.ube/K-gj3Ur7yEK